World Headquarters

Jones and Bartlett Publishers
40 Tall Pine Drive
Sudbury, MA 01776
978-443-5000
info@jbpub.com
www.jbpub.com

Jones and Bartlett Publishers
Canada
6339 Ormindale Way
Mississauga, Ontario L5V 1J2
CANADA

Jones and Bartlett Publishers
International
Barb House, Barb Mews
London W6 7PA
UK

Jones and Bartlett's books and products are available through most bookstores and online book-sellers. To contact Jones and Bartlett Publishers directly, call 800-832-0034, fax 978-443-8000, or visit our website www.jbpub.com.

Substantial discounts on bulk quantities of Jones and Bartlett's publications are available to cor-porations, professional associations, and other qualified organizations. For details and specific discount information, contact the special sales department at Jones and Bartlett via the above contact information or send an email to specialsales@jbpub.com.

The author has made every effort to ensure the accuracy of the information herein. However, appro-priate information sources should be consulted, especially for new or unfamiliar procedures. It is the responsibility of every practitioner to evaluate the appropriateness of a particular opinion in the context of actual clinical situations and with due considerations to new developments. The author(s) and publisher disclaim all responsibility for any liability, loss, injury, or damage incurred as a con-sequence, directly or indirectly, of the use and application of any of the contents of this volume.

Library of Congress Cataloging-in-Publication Data
Svara, James H.
  The ethics primer for public administrators in government and nonprofit organizations / James H. Svara.
     p. ; cm.
  Includes bibliographical references.
  ISBN-13: 978-0-7637-3626-2 (alk. paper)
  ISBN-10: 0-7637-3626-0 (alk. paper)
  1. Health services administrators--Moral and ethical aspects. I. Title.
  [DNLM: 1. Public Health Administration--ethics. 2. Codes of Ethics. 3. Ethical Theory. WA 525 S968e 2007]
  R724.S83 2007
  174.2--dc22

                          2006015558

6048

Production Credits
Executive Editor: David Cella
Editorial Assistant: Lisa Gordon
Production Director: Amy Rose
Production Editor: Tracey Chapman
Associate Marketing Manager: Laura Kavigian
Manufacturing and Inventory Coordinator: Amy Bacus
Composition: Arlene Apone
Cover Design: Timothy Dziewit
Cover Image: © Photos.com
Printing and Binding: Malloy, Inc.
Cover Printing: Malloy, Inc.

Printed in the United States of America
11 10   10 9 8 7 6 5

Dedication

This book is dedicated to my students at the University of North Carolina at Greensboro and North Carolina State University, with whom I learned a lot about ethics.

Contents

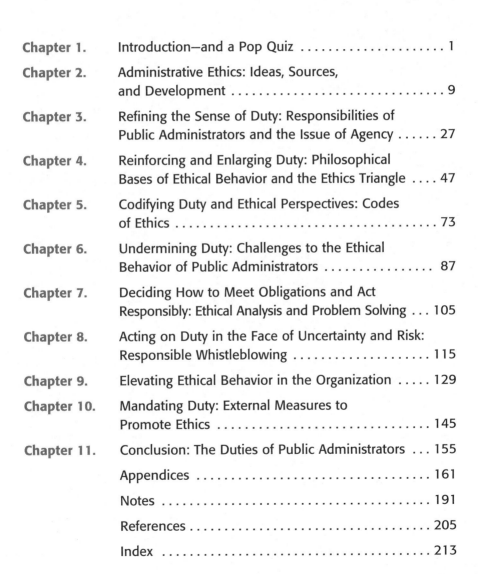

Preface

E thics is an essential aspect of public service, but it is often left out of discussions of the development of the field and its major functions. Ethics is sometimes treated as a specialized topic studied for its own sake. For ethics to guide the attitudes and behavior of public administrators, it must be integrated into the way administrators think about their practice and incorporated into their everyday behavior.

I come to the exploration of ethics from a general scholarly interest in political-administrative relations. In my research and teaching, I seek to understand how public administration contributes to the political process, how politicians and administrators interact with each other, and how administrators relate to citizens. Examining these topics naturally brings up the issue of appropriate limits, particularly regarding the behavior of public administrators. What is, and should be, the role of professional public administrators in governance? What are the characteristics of political-administrative relations? What do we expect administrators to do—and to not do? How do administrators relate to citizens? How should they balance their accountability to elected superiors and their professional standards with their responsibility to the public? The normative side of each of these questions involves "big" ethical issues, and these are the focus of this book.

John Gaus (1950) argued many years ago that a theory of public administration is also a theory of politics. I agree and hope to make the case for a further broadening of our understanding of the field: A theory of public administration in the political process is also a theory of ethics.

I believe that the same logic also applies to understanding the ethics of administrators in nonprofit organizations because of the basic similarity in the nature of administrative responsibilities in the governmental and nonprofit sectors. The city manager who works with the city council and serves the public, and the nonprofit executive director who works with a board of directors and serves clients, share many important characteristics in their work, in the ethical challenges that they face, and in their duty to serve. The book is also concerned with administrators who have little direct interaction with the public, whether in national or state government or in nonprofit organizations.

The book is a primer that introduces the reader to the fundamentals of administrative responsibility and ethics. It links these ideas to the nature of the administrative process and the work of professional administrators. It seeks to help the reader understand why ethics is important to persons who choose to be administrators in governmental and nonprofit organizations and how to relate their own personal values with the norms of the public sector. Furthermore, the book offers assistance in working through the complexity and controversy surrounding ethical problems in public administration. It avoids prescription—thou shalt, thou shalt not—as much as possible and seeks instead to enable the reader to form his or her own judgments about ethical choices. It is an introduction to fundamental issues that equips readers to make informed choices about their own behavior. It also provides a foundation for exploring the topic in more depth in other courses or training opportunities.

I approach this book with 10 years of teaching ethics and professional practice—a core course in the master of public administration (MPA) degree—and more years teaching related topics. I hope to create in these words-on-pages some of the dynamic exchange that occurs in the classroom as students grapple with the important issues in administrative ethics. From this experience, I know quite well that this book does *not* "teach" ethics in the sense of trying to fill in a blank slate. The reader already has a basic understanding of what it means to be an ethical person. Like my students, the reader comes to this book with a reservoir of ethical and moral values upon which he/she can draw.

In addition to my teaching, I bring perspectives from the experience of being an administrator as a program director and department head. Some important generic issues in supervision, interpersonal relations, resource use, reporting, and planning are encountered even in the rather disorganized sphere of academic administration. I also benefited greatly from a year on leave working in Washington, D.C., in 1976–1977 at the Department of Housing and Urban Development as a National Association of School of Public Affairs and Administration (NASPAA) Fellow. Furthermore, a lot of my research and training involves interacting with politicians and administrators, both in the United States and other countries. I think that I have come to appreciate the kinds of challenges that administrators face and how often there is an important ethical dimension to these challenges.

My research reflects a blending of my early focus on urban politics and political leadership and my deepening interest in administrative leadership and values. I explore professional administration in a political context.

Although much of my writing has focused on local government, my teaching addresses issues at all levels of government and in nonprofits. I conduct empirical research on topics that have a normative dimension and examine the normative implications of my quantitative research. I have merged empirical research findings with analysis of the development of public administration to suggest a new (but I believe historically grounded) way to conceptualize political-administrative relations. This approach stresses the complementarity of politics and administration rather than a dichotomy or strict separation as the conceptual foundation of the field. This model informs my approach to administrative ethics.

The Ethics Primer for Public Administrators in Government and Nonprofit Organizations presents a simple theme that, of course, gets complicated in the telling. Persons enter the field of public administration, just as the reader enters this book, with an interest in public service and a set of values shaped in part by that interest. These values reflect most of the essential elements of ethical thinking, but they are not developed in a very sophisticated way. Like most adults, persons who have not formally studied administrative ethics tend to have values that are grounded in respect for conventional norms. Also, they tend to have fairly substantial respect for persons in positions of "authority." This condition creates tension between the sense of duty to serve and act responsibly, on the one hand, and the deference to the superiors and established rules, on the other. Most persons who have not expanded their knowledge or thought systematically about ethics and the nature of public service are dependent on external sources of direction.

I hope this book will help the reader broaden and deepen his or her understanding of the nature of the public service duty and major approaches to thinking about ethics. I hope the reader will internalize this knowledge so he or she is able to form independent judgments about ethical options based on universal values. The reader will not necessarily reject the external influences he or she receives, but he or she will be better able to weigh his or her own reasoned sense of what is right against what others tell him or her is right. Finally, I hope the reader will be able to use this knowledge to take actions that are ethically sound based on a careful consideration of all the relevant options. Because the reader is already or is preparing to be an administrator who is responsible for directing other persons and shaping his or her organization, I hope this book will also help the reader see ways that he or she can raise ethical awareness in others.

I am now a member of the faculty in the School of Public Affairs at Arizona State University, but I want to express my gratitude to a number of colleagues and students at North Carolina State University who helped directly and indirectly with this book. Debra Stewart helped me understand the importance of the development of ethical reasoning and how it changes over time. Jim Brunet offered comments, suggested sources, and made a test drive in a class he taught with an earlier version of the manuscript. Former and current doctoral students Dr. Jack Kem and Dr. Julie Raines wrote dissertations on ethics topics and added to my knowledge of the issues and the literature in administrative ethics. Dr. Irvin Vann investigated the content of the Whistleblower Protection Act and how it would be applied in a complex case. His results are reflected in the discussion in Chapter 8. Mr. Van Kloempken helped me examine issues in research ethics. Finally, MPA student Jennifer Moore provided research assistance with thoughtfulness and care.

The Political Science Department (Institut for Statskundskab) at Southern Denmark University in Odense hosted me for a research sabbatical during the time that I finished this book. I appreciate Niels Ejersbo and his colleagues for the intellectual stimulation and gracious hospitality they provided.

My wife Claudia has been both patient and supportive over the extended period of this writing project. She is also a model of the ethical professional who exemplifies the duty to service at the highest level in her practice of medicine.

This book is dedicated to my former students in North Carolina. I have learned a lot in the interchange with them over the years. I hope I do credit to them in the way I have conveyed our shared learning in this book.

Chapter 1

Introduction–
and a Pop Quiz

This book is a primer on *administrative ethics*, a term that refers to the ethics of persons who occupy career leadership and staff positions in government and nonprofit organizations. It brings to mind oxymorons, which are a form of satiric humor. "Military intelligence," "jumbo shrimp," and "airline food" are popular examples. To be honest, "administrative ethics" is probably pretty high on the list of commonly used oxymorons, but more to the point at the start of this book is the possibility that "ethics primer" itself connects two elements that are incompatible. To cover a complex topic such as ethics in the public service in a small, introductory book may seem to be an impossible task. Is it sufficient to briefly introduce and provide initial instruction—the dictionary meaning of a primer—for a subject as weighty as administrative ethics?

Based on my experience in teaching administrative ethics in a short-course format for many years, there is an important precondition. What makes it possible to introduce in a meaningful way this vast topic is the fact that the reader already knows a great deal about the topic. I am assuming that the reader is an adult—young or otherwise—who is either interested in entering the public service or already works for a government or nonprofit organization. As we shall see, both the characteristics of relative maturity and self-selection for a public service position are important to having a substantial amount of knowledge and fairly extensive attitudes about administrative ethics.

The tone of this book is personal, the style is a dialogue, and the purpose is exhortatory. The first and second person will be used extensively. "I" will direct comments to "you." It is not possible to create the interaction of the classroom, but an effort will be made to encourage an exchange in which your response in the form of answers to questions that I pose will help to carry forward the dialogue. Finally, I believe that knowledge provides the basis for understanding and action, and the discussion in this book will provide extensive information. The underlying intent, however, is not pedagogical; that is to say, to teach you the subject of administrative ethics. The purpose is to exhort you to engage yourself in ethics; to be more aware of the ethical dimension of public service, to be ethical in a more thoughtful and thoroughgoing way than before, and to do more to encourage others to be ethical. The purpose of the book is to promote ethical behavior by public administrators on the individual and organizational levels. Specifically, the book enables the reader to:

1. Appreciate that ethics is integral to the nature of democratic public administration
2. Understand the responsibilities of public administrators and the bases of administrative ethics
3. Understand the tenets of the codes of ethics for various professional organizations in the public sector and how they are applied
4. Be aware of the pressures and forces in public administration that can contribute to unethical behavior
5. Develop the knowledge and skills needed to deal with ethical problems that arise in public service
6. Strengthen the ethical climate in organizations

All of these serve to support ethical action.

It is obvious that this book will cover a great deal of intellectual territory. The discussion of topics is limited to the presentation of the material that is relevant to the line of argument that I am developing. Necessarily, this approach leaves the reader without the full exposition of a topic that it would receive if it were being considered on its own. Readers may pursue topics in more depth by following the guide to the literature provided in footnotes. I seek to offer a serious but accessible conversation about ethics in the text, and a more scholarly examination of ethics in the endnotes.

Pop Quiz: Do You Have a Code of Ethics?

I do not expect that you will have a well-formed, explicit code of ethics that you follow in your administrative work. Before examining the subject matter of this book in more depth, however, it is useful to establish a baseline. Here are some questions you can answer for yourself before proceeding further in the book.

What is or should be your code of ethics for work in government or nonprofit organizations?

What are the standards of right and wrong that should guide your work; the "do's and don'ts" of public service?

If you will take the time now to record your thoughts, we will refer back to what you have written and compare your responses to other professional students in public administration.

Understanding the Setting for Administrative Ethics

The discussion of "administrative" ethics applies both to those who work in government and in nonprofit organizations. Why is ethics a special concern in these particular organizations? It is important that administrators operate within legal and/or organizational controls. They serve the public but not as private professionals who operate on a fee-for-service basis. Although there are important differences between the two sectors, the similarities are even greater and staff members in each can benefit from knowing more about the ethical challenges of the other.

To simplify the discussion throughout the book, four terms will be used generically to describe both the governmental and nonprofit setting: organizations, administrators, political superiors, and citizens or clients.

Organizations refer to governmental entities such as a city government as well as to nonprofit organizations. Depending on the context and the nature of the organization, the term will encompass the specific unit to which one is assigned; for instance, a section, the whole department, or the entire organization. For example, a municipal police officer will deal with some ethical issues in his or her area of assignment such as the patrol division, with some in the department as a whole, and with others as an employee of city government. For a staff member in a small nonprofit agency, the distinctions may not be useful or necessary, but larger nonprofits will have similar divisions.

Administrators refer to the civil service or career staff in government and the professional staff in nonprofit organizations. These positions range from the top executives (city managers in municipal government or executive directors in nonprofit organizations) to the staff members who handle a variety of specialized tasks. Some will have supervisory responsibilities and, therefore, are the administrative superiors of the staff they supervise. Others work without subordinates; for example, analysts and many front-line service providers including teachers, counselors, eligibility specialists, or police officers.

Political superiors, on the other hand, refer to persons who set the official goals and policy for the organization and oversee the administrators. In government organizations, this category includes both elected executives and members of legislative bodies as well as the politically appointed and politically oriented top layer of officials chosen by political executives such as the president, governor, or "strong" mayor. In local governments and special purpose agencies such as school districts, the political superiors hold positions such as council member, board member, or commissioner. In nonprofit organizations, these persons sit on the board of directors.

Finally, the words *citizens* or *clients* refer to persons served by governmental and nonprofit organizations. In some respects, this is the least satisfactory of the generic terms. When stressing the recipients of a service, the word *client* is generally a suitable term for both government and nonprofit organizations, but it works less well for persons who are audited by an IRS agent or given a speeding ticket by a police officer. Those who do not choose their treatment may not feel that they are a "client" or are being "served," but we will still include them in this category. *Citizen* implies not just the person who is impacted by organizational action, but also the person who provides the support and legitimacy for government. This term does not have the same meaning for the nonprofit organizations whose leaders are not chosen by or directly accountable to the public. Still, nonprofit organizations also have broad responsibilities to persons beyond those who receive services or provide contributions. If a nonprofit organization is perceived by the public to be wasteful and ineffective, it will probably not be able to survive just because it keeps a small group of clients happy. Furthermore, nonprofits operate within a legal framework that is sanctioned by government and the people. Thus, the basic idea of a service and fiduciary relationship between the organization and the people or some segment of it is common to the public and the nonprofit sectors.

These terms suggest the four responsibilities that are shared by government and nonprofit administrators. These responsibilities are the foundation for identifying the nature of the duty of public administrators: their responsibility to serve individuals, their responsibility to be accountable to the "people" and promote the public interest, their responsibility to their organization, and their responsibility to political superiors and to uphold the law and established policy. Some administrators in governmental and certain nonprofit organizations have the authority to exercise coercive power to support the discharge of their assigned responsibilities.[1]* Others in government and nonprofit organizations invite persons in need to accept services or assistance; they don't coerce them to do anything. Frequently, it is citizens who initiate the contact to request or demand actions, remedies, or attention. In any of these circumstances, public administrators relate with citizens in a

---

*Please see the Notes section for further information on footnoted resources throughout this book.

distinctive way. This is not a market-exchange relationship in which a service or commodity is offered, and customers can decide whether the price and quality are acceptable. In some interactions between citizens and officials, citizens are dependent and vulnerable and have no other source for the service. In other interactions, citizens are the "bosses" of officials. The citizens or clients who interact with public administrators have reason to expect that they will be treated fairly and with respect, that they will be informed and listened to, and that they will receive the service or benefit that they deserve.

The responsibility to the "people"—to serve the public interest—means that administrators should also go beyond one-on-one encounters with individuals to consider general concerns of groups of people or society as a whole (Frederickson 1997). Their awareness of social needs and changing conditions provides the basis for identifying possible changes in procedure or policy that they may initiate or propose to administrative or political superiors. They also have a broad responsibility to make good use of the resources that have been entrusted to them whether they come from taxes or contributions.

Public administrators should also be responsible to the organization of which they are a part. As we shall consider in the next chapter, this does not mean that the administrator is bound by the organization or loses his or her own voice in discussions of ends and means. Still, public administrators are not sole practitioners who set up their own practice. They operate within an authority structure, they work with others to advance organizational mission, and they have a responsibility to make the organization as strong, effective, and ethical as possible.

Administrators also have a responsibility to their political superiors. This relationship involves a complex mixture of control and freedom, accountability and independence. Examining how political-administrative relations relate to the duty of the public servant is the focus in Chapter 2.

The Setting Continued: Differences Between Government and Nonprofit Organizations

Significant differences exist between public and nonprofit organizations.[2] Nonprofits have freedom and flexibility not available to governmental organizations. This freedom applies to generating resources, but nonprofits lack the relatively certain revenues of government and the coercive power to enforce the collection of taxes. Nonprofits have a basic mission that is central to the work of the organization, and it is usually much narrower in scope than the typical general-purpose government. Nonprofits are sometimes referred to as *mission-driven organizations.* In a sense, the mission has an overriding impact on all those who work for a nonprofit, and this condition differentiates it from government. Consider this comparison. City council members are elected to determine the mission and goals of their city government; the choices the members make may be hotly debated within the council and in the larger community, and the specific goals may change dramatically over time. On the other hand, the persons who work in a nonprofit as board members or as staff members typically begin with a commitment to the organization's mission. They are expected to allow the mission to "drive" them, although they make the detailed decisions about how to translate the mission into reality at a given time. If some persons want to pursue the mission differently or pursue a different version of the mission, they may choose to leave and even to start their own organization.

This option points to another basic characteristic that makes nonprofits distinctive: Nonprofit organizations are competitive service organizations. They do not have a monopoly on the provision of a service, as is sometimes the case of government agencies. In addition, they do not provide a product through the market, as is the case of businesses. Still, they offer a purpose, a service, or a product that benefits society (like government) in a competitive setting (like business). To succeed, they must attract clients, volunteers, supporters, and contributors in the face of other organizations that are trying to have the same success. Thus, the staff members in nonprofit organizations are public servants who operate in a more open, flexible, and competitive environment. The underlying presumption of this book is that the shared commitment to serve (as well as the absence of profit motive) makes the staff in nonprofit and governmental organizations more alike than different.

Overview

What can this book do—and not do? It most certainly cannot "teach ethics" by specifying what is the "correct" way to behave. Furthermore, it does not "teach ethics" in the sense of introducing the reader to a previously unknown subject or by treating the reader as an ethical blank slate. You come to this book and a course in administrative ethics with a reservoir of ethical and moral values on which you can draw. Hopefully you recorded some of those values earlier when you completed the pop quiz about your code of ethics. Rather, I write this book with the intention of helping you to understand the integral role of ethics in public administration, organize your thinking about ethics, understand the sources of ethical thinking and linkages between your personal values and the ethical values of public service, and heighten your awareness of the ethical content of work in the public sector.

If the grasp of fundamental ethical concepts and standards is widespread, sophisticated and reflective ethical reasoning is not. The book seeks to encourage you to attain this level of ethical reasoning and to enable you to do so. The effort starts in the next chapter where we consider the nature of ethical ideas and from where they come. We also examine more fully the various levels of ethical reasoning and help you understand where you are compared with a range of possibilities. Throughout the book, a touchstone of administrative ethics is public duty. In Chapter 3, we seek to refine the sense of duty and make it more active rather than reactive. One view of duty defines serving the public in terms of observing the law and obeying superiors. A refined sense of duty is based on careful reflection about the nature of responsibilities to the public, political superiors, and the organization. It also requires that you develop a reasoned view about your obligations and the constraints under which you operate as an individual engaged in public service. This refined sense of obligation supports postconventional ethical reasoning. Chapter 4 will broaden the discussion to examine the philosophical perspectives on virtues, principles, and consequences that contribute to universal standards of ethical behavior. Having examined the basic elements of a model of administrative ethics in Chapter 2, a complete model that incorporates the expanded sense of duty and philosophical perspectives will be presented in Chapter 4. The "ethics triangle" provides guidance based on the ethical ideals of public interest, justice, character, and the greatest good. The model will be used as a framework for examining codes of ethics for professionals in government and nonprofits in Chapter 5.

The next four chapters will consider ethical challenges and actions. Chapter 6 identifies the extensive factors that can undermine ethics. Chapter 7 explores complex ethical problems and presents a guide to problem solving in these situations. The special considerations and complexities of a particular kind of ethical problem—whistleblowing—are presented in Chapter 8. The distinction between internal complaints and going outside is examined along with the choice between public and anonymous whistleblowing. Chapters 9 and 10 explore ways to promote ethics through the actions of managers and supervisors within organizations and through external mandates, particularly ethics laws. The final chapter summarizes the obligations and responsibilities of public administrators who are committed to a principled, virtuous, and utilitarian sense of public duty.

Chapter 2

Administrative Ethics:

Ideas, Sources, and Development

Filling in the content of administrative ethics will proceed in two stages. In this chapter, we will define ethics in general and administrative ethics in particular and examine the prevailing or conventional model of ethical thinking among public administrators. This is called the *basic ethics model*. In the next two chapters, the major approaches to ethics will be examined in more depth, and an advanced ethical model will be developed.

The first questions pursued in this chapter are big ones: What is ethics, and where do ethical ideas come from? An important source to these answers is philosophy and its major theories of ethics. Our discussion, however, of the sources of ideas for administrative ethics will focus initially on the ethics derived from the nature of the administrative position itself; in other words, the standards and expectations that are based on a duty to serve the public. It will then be possible to consider how this duty-based ethics is linked to other approaches that draw on philosophical approaches. Having identified major approaches, two more questions arise: How does ethical thinking develop and what are the levels of ethical reasoning? The responses from other students who completed the pop quiz about their code of ethics are linked to the sources and levels. There is some direct evidence from the student responses as well as results from other research to justify the characteristics of the basic ethics model. If you have not completed the pop quiz, backtrack to Chapter 1 before going further. The chapter concludes with an examination of other key concepts and considers what ethics shares with morality and legality, and how it is different from these concepts.

Definition and the Sources of Ethical Ideas

A general definition of ethics follows:

> Ethics refers to well-based standards of right and wrong that prescribe what humans ought to do, usually in terms of duties, principles, specific virtues, or benefits to society.[3]

This definition identifies four dimensions or sources of ethics; one based on the nature of public service and three based on the philosophical perspectives to ethics. They are:

1. Duties: the behaviors expected of persons who occupy certain roles; i.e., the obligations taken on when assuming a role or profession
2. Virtues: qualities that define what a good person is; moral excellence
3. Principles: fundamental truths that form the basis for behavior; "kinds of action that are right or obligatory" (Frankena 1963, 49)
4. Benefits to society: actions that produce the greatest good for the greatest number[4]

For persons who work in government and nonprofit organizations, duty has a special importance. They must serve the public, fulfill the expectations of public office, and be trustees of public resources. These are the actions required by their occupation or role independent of—but reinforced by—other ethical considerations.

The ethics of public administrators begins with and is grounded in duty. Duty is an old-fashioned term that at first glance may seem too narrow to be more than the starting point as the basis for administrative ethics. In a narrow view, duty implies the restricted range of actions one is required to take without question, as in the phrase: "It is my duty to . . ." *Ethics* implies a broader range of expected behaviors and reflection about what should be done, and definitions of duty can encompass such views. *Duty* means the "action required by one's business, occupation, or function" but also "the action or behavior due by moral or legal obligation."[5] Thus, duty implies obligations, responsibilities, and meeting expectations. It entails acting in terms of "norms of appropriateness"; the standards that are fostered by institutions (March and Olsen 1995). However, it also entails choice on the part of the official who accepts the duty. Cooper (1982, 112) notes the following observation of Fritz Marx:

> Judicial redress, official liability, and the whole gamut of disciplinary measures are poor substitutes for a sense of duty. No formal device for accountability can give us a clue as to the components of answerable conduct. One cannot commandeer responsibility.

One can only cultivate it, safeguard its roots, stimulate its growth, and provide it with favorable climatic conditions.

Thus, duty as an internalized set of values is the foundation for accountability.

Others have also recognized the centrality of duty and seen it as an orientation that draws out a broad range of responsibilities. For example, Mark Moore (1981, 5) distinguishes the narrow requirements from the broader possibilities in this statement:

> The duties of public officials are not simply to be passive instruments in policy-making but to work actively in establishing goals for public policy in their area, and in advocating those goals among the people who share their responsibility. In short, they have the opportunity and duty to conceive of and pursue the public interest.

Public administration ethics is rooted in duty in the sense that persons who seek positions in government or nonprofit organizations (or who pursue educational programs to prepare themselves for such positions) are commonly motivated by a sense of duty to serve, sometimes called the *public service ethic* (Perry and Wise 1990). They wish to help others, to benefit society, or to serve the public interest.

With a bit more thought, one could identify ways that administrators should handle key relationships guided by duty. The relationships are the interactions with the public, with the organization of which one is a part, and with political superiors—either elected officials (or their appointees) in government or boards of nonprofit organizations. Public administrators should not lie, withhold information, or put their own interests above serving the public. They should be accountable to their superiors and to the public. These duties will be examined in more depth in Chapter 3. The point of these examples is simple: Without even considering ethical theories or philosophy, it is possible to elaborate an extensive list of standards of right and wrong that prescribe what humans ought to do based on a sense of duty as a public servant. Thus, it is useful to start with duty-based ethics because it is obviously related to many important aspects of public service work. Furthermore, this is the kind of ethical reasoning that students in public administration and persons entering public service start with.

It is possible to expand duty-based ethics by thinking about the qualities that a person should manifest and the actions that he or she should take because that person occupies a position as a public servant. Public administrators should be honest, independent, competent, and committed to doing their best and they should demonstrate integrity. These are *virtues*. They should treat all persons fairly and equally, observe the law, and follow the direction set by their leaders and their organizations. These are *principles*.

The Ethics Primer for Public Administrators in Government and Nonprofit Organizations

James H. Svara, PhD

Professor, School of Public Affairs
Arizona State University
Tempe, Arizona

JONES AND BARTLETT PUBLISHERS
Sudbury, Massachusetts
BOSTON   TORONTO   LONDON   SINGAPORE

Public administrators should try to achieve the greatest good for the most people. This is a *beneficial consequence*. Thus, the other dimensions of administrative ethics based on the philosophical traditions of virtue, principle, and consequences are integrally linked to conceptions of duty. These reflect common patterns of ethical thinking. In the following section, we will examine how well-established these types of thinking are in adults, particularly those attracted to public service.

Each of these dimensions can be expressed in a basic question:

- What are the expectations of persons holding public offices? (duty)
- What are the qualities of a good person? (virtue)
- What is the right thing to do? (principle)
- What is the most beneficial action to take? (consequences)

The framework for ethics developed in this primer is not a contest between perspectives but rather a blend of perspectives. One approach is not superior or first in the sense that it is the beginning of ethical thinking from which the rest follow. As we shall see, young adults have developed most of these aspects of ethical thinking to some extent and can use them without difficulty. Still, duty has a special salience and relevance for persons who are attracted to public service positions. The service orientation seems the proximate reason for pursuing the position or career whereas the other approaches help to shape how one serves others and handles the challenges that are encountered in a public service position and career. Thus, duty is central to administrative ethics.

Your Code Compared to Others

For many years in my course on ethics and professional practice in public administration, I have been asking students in the first class session to answer the question included in Chapter 1 about their code of ethics.[6] As a method of examining ethical attitudes, there are some important disadvantages to using this exercise. It is done without warning and opportunity for preparation or much reflection. There is no way of knowing the level of commitment to the items that are listed, much less whether students' actions will match their ethical intentions. Still, I feel that the exercise can be illuminating for several reasons. First, the lack of preparation contributes to spontaneity. There is no time to develop an elaborate set of statements that may not reflect the values students actually hold. Second, the responses give some indication about the nature of ethical reasoning that public administration students use. Once written, the ethical statements (or tenets) become explicit but before the exercise, they have been implicit. These ethical standards are present without being consciously organized. Students often comment that they have never considered their code of ethics before doing the exercise, but they clearly have ethical ideas in their minds.

Students provide varying but usually extensive responses. Each distinct idea with clear ethical content is counted as a tenet. There are several features of the codes that are worth noting. Less than one in five students list only three or fewer tenets, and two in five provide four to six tenets. The remaining students—over 40 percent—list seven or more tenets and 14 percent list 10 or more. For those who could list only three or fewer distinct tenets, one would have to feel some concern about the limited scope of their ethical commitment (or how seriously they took the exercise). Still, a short code can be thoughtful and encompass several important concerns even though the code is not comprehensive. In the following example, Student 5 of my Spring 2002 class identifies the ethical reasoning associated with each statement.

1. The first tenet of a code of ethics would be honesty. [virtue]
2. The second tenet would be to follow the law. [principle]
3. The third tenet would be to be a just public employee; Meaning: a public employee should always evaluate how his or her behavior affects the public, and the employee should always remember that he or she was hired to work for the public. [duty]

Most students are not at a loss for words or tenets. Long statements sometimes approximate a comprehensive professional code of ethics, as in this example done by Student 7 in my Summer 1999 class:

1. Maintain integrity of policies and ordinances. [principle]
2. Avoid personal favors. [duty]
3. Base actions on public good. [duty]
4. Faithfully execute wishes of elected body. [duty]
5. Maintain high standards of morality and honesty. [virtue]
6. Avoid conflicts of interest. [duty]
7. No lying, stealing, or cheating. [principle]
8. Treat everyone fairly. [principle]
9. Avoid any actions that advance personal interests (financial). [duty]
10. Full and honest disclosure of public information. [duty]
11. Have a strong work ethic. [virtue]
12. Maintain objectivity. [principle]
13. Provide sound professional advice to elected officials. [duty]
14. Avoid even the appearance of impropriety. [virtue]
15. Keep everyone informed. [duty]
16. Avoid deception and misleading statements. [principle]

The impression one has from examining these statements is that most students carry around in their heads something approximating a code of ethics *before they have taken a course on professional ethics*. Still, the scope of values and expectations incorporated in that code varies considerably. How does your code compare in terms of its length and scope?

Each statement was examined to determine what approach to ethical thinking is reflected: duty/public service, virtue, principle, consequences, or some other source. Obviously, this is a subjective judgment. The following guidelines, which were used in making the classification, are based on the characteristics of each approach to ethics. Tenets that stressed public service or behaviors that are expected because one is a public employee were classified as duty based. Tenets that included general statements about what one should do were classified as principle based. For example, saying "an official should not deceive the public" was considered a duty, whereas the statement "a person should never lie" was considered a principle. Tenets that stressed qualities (how a person should *be* as opposed to what he or she should *do*) were considered virtue based. For example, in contrast to the principle about not lying, "one should be honest" is considered virtue based. A tenet that stressed doing what helped the most people or produced good outcomes was considered consequentialist, whereas a general statement about promoting the public interest was considered duty based. To give examples, the classification for the tenets in the short and long examples just given was indicated in brackets at the end of each tenet. The summary classification of the reasoning contained in the student statements suggests the characteristics of a basic model of ethics. It is presented in **Table 2.1**.

Table 2–1 *Type of Ethical Reasoning Reflected in Statements*

	Percent (in %)	Number
Based on duty/public service	37.5	297
Virtue	21.4	170
Principle	28.4	225
Consequences	0.6	5
Professional standards	10.8	86
Other	1.3	10
	100.0	793

Note: A total of 123 students listed 793 separate tenets.

Based on this analysis of all statements, duty-based reasoning is the most common, representing over one third of all tenets that could be classified. Principle-based and virtue-based reasoning are also very common. The following is a list of examples of each type of statement ordered from most to least common within each category:

Statements based on duty or public service:
- Serve the public.
- Avoid conflict of interest or personal gain.
- Promote the public interest.
- Act as a steward of public resources.
- Take responsibility for actions; be accountable.
- Share or disclose information to the public.
- Blow the whistle (report) on wrongdoing.

Statements based on virtue:
- Display honesty.
- Show integrity.
- Be respectful.
- Be consistent.
- Avoid impropriety.

Statements based on principle:
- Follow the laws, policies, or regulations.
- Act with fairness.
- Treat all equally.
- Protect confidential information.
- Follow the Golden Rule.
- Do not lie.

In addition, a modest number of statements are based on standards of professional practice rather than other forms of ethical reasoning. Examples are maintaining a professional demeanor, sharing credit with coworkers, or promoting professional development of staff.

It is interesting to note that students do not use consequences as the basis for ethical tenets. It seems likely that making choices to produce good outcomes is common behavior, but it appears that students do not necessarily see such behaviors as ethical in nature. In fact, the argument that the "ends justifies the means" is likely to be seen as a rationalization for a questionable action rather than an ethical justification. One may choose to take the action justified in this way, but it is not considered to be ethical. This issue is examined further in

Chapter 4, but it appears that consequentialist thinking is not an important aspect of the basic components of administrative ethics.

It is also possible to focus on the overall code of each student (as opposed to analyzing the breakdown of the separate tenets). Almost every student in this exercise includes in their code at least one tenet that is based on duty or commitment to public service. Almost as many—approximately three out of four—use principle and virtue as the basis for tenets. As noted, very few use consequentialist reasoning.

Thus, all the approaches except consequentialism are present in the thinking of most public administration students. Still, from the samples that are offered, it is apparent that none of these ways of thinking about ethics in public administration is fully developed. This suggests that the underlying concepts are not fully understood before students have undertaken formal study of administrative ethics. With study and reflection, it is possible to deepen ethical thinking by more fully understanding the ethical approaches that are being used informally and by more clearly linking these approaches to the issues and challenges of public service.

What about the code that you wrote? How many tenets did you include, recognizing that you may have combined more than one in a single statement? What kinds of reasoning were reflected in your tenets?

In the further discussion of the four approaches to ethics in public administration, the duty-based approach will be developed first. In Chapter 3, the nature of the public service position and the handling of critical relationships will be analyzed as the source of fundamental standards for behavior. In other words, what are my duties as a public servant and what kind of behavior is expected of me as I interact with political superiors, the public, and my organization? In Chapter 4, the other ethical perspectives will be examined to show how they broaden and deepen duty-based ethics: What kind of person should I be, what is the right thing to do, and how much emphasis should be placed on achieving good results as I do my duty? By organizing and integrating these approaches, I hope that the reader will have a stronger and richer sense of what it means to do one's duty in public service and will be better equipped to accomplish it.

In short, duty—the core of the public service ethic—is reinforced and expanded by balancing attention to virtue, principle, and good consequences. Thus, we may revise the earlier definition to create this definition of administrative ethics:

> Administrative ethics refers to well-based standards of right and wrong that prescribe what public administrators ought to do, in terms of duty to public service, principles, virtues, and benefits to society.

Students in public administration programs and persons in public service very likely have a working version of this definition in their heads and carry around tenets that are based on duty, virtue, and principle. The challenge is to bring this definition forward in the consciousness of public administrators and to deepen and broaden the understanding of what it means. In other words, you are challenged to further develop your ethical judgment. Before thinking about doing that, however, it is important to consider in general how ethical reasoning develops and better understand the levels of ethical reasoning.

Ethical Development

How people acquire attitudes about ethics and morality is a large topic, but it is important to examine the question briefly here as part of the introduction to the subject of administrative ethics. As noted, adults, obviously including those who work or wish to work in government or nonprofits, are likely to have a reservoir of ethical ideas and moral commitments. In the process of growing up, getting an education, and absorbing values from people around them, they are undergoing moral development that takes them through different stages of reasoning about why they should act in a moral or ethical way and what it means to be a moral person. Family interactions influence development. Membership in a church or an organization such as the Boy Scouts, Girl Scouts, or Boys and Girls Club expose children to experiences that are intentionally designed to promote social and moral development.

Lawrence Kohlberg (1981) offers a model of moral judgment that helps to understand how the capacity for ethical reasoning develops and explains the motives for acting at different stages of development. Kohlberg is concerned with morality broadly, but we can assume that the level of moral reasoning will be transferred to the way that individuals make ethical judgments about their role and behavior in an organization or profession. Stated differently, we expect that individuals will work through choices about behavior at the same level whether they are making a moral choice in their personal life or an ethical choice in their work as a public administrator.

Kohlberg identified six stages that children go through in the maturation process as they are influenced by a variety of socializing forces. The levels are preconventional where the child is starting to respond to rules but has values that are self-centered; conventional where the older child and adult internalizes the values of doing the right thing in order to meet the expectations of others or to comply with prevailing standards; and postconventional or principled levels where moral values are grounded in universal principles

(Stewart and Sprinthall 1994; Kohlberg, 1981).[7] The levels and Kohlberg's (1981, 17–19) Stages of Moral Development are the following:

Level	Stage	Social Orientation
Preconventional	1	Punishment and obedience
	2	Instrumental relativist
Conventional	3	"Good boy; nice girl"
	4	Society maintaining/law and order
Postconventional	5	Social contract
	6	Universal ethical principle

Kohlberg believes that the stages always occur in this order and that one always incorporates the values of one stage before moving to the next. Although others argue that reasoning may draw from more than one stage, it is presumed that each stage reflects a dominant mode of thinking about moral choices at any given time. Most adults have moved to Stage 4, but most do not move beyond that stage. Stage 4 reflects reasoning that emphasizes what is legal and supports social institutions. Sophisticated moral or ethical reasoning reflects postconventional thinking, but it appears that this level of reasoning is somewhat uncommon. Thus, an important implication of this work is that all persons go through a progression of thinking about morality in which they broaden their views to think about what is good for the society, not just for themselves. At Stage 4, they have developed "a conception of the social system as a consistent set of codes and procedures that apply impartially to all members" based on law or religious canon, and "the pursuit of individual interests is considered legitimate only when it is consistent with maintenance of the socio-moral system as a whole" (Colby and Kohlberg 1987, 28–29).

Kohlberg's model is also useful for identifying why people behave the way they do at each of the differing levels of morality. Each stage is associated with a different motive for following rules or taking moral action. Kohlberg (1981, 19; 411–412) offers these "word pictures" of the reasons for behavior in each stage:

1. Punishment and obedience: Stimulus/response

   Obey rules to avoid punishment

2. Instrumental relativist: Self-serving good behavior

   Conform to obtain rewards, have favors returned, and generate other's goodwill

3. "Good boy; nice girl": Meeting the expectations of others with whom one interacts

   Conform to avoid disapproval and dislike by others

4. Society maintaining/law and order: Meeting standards imposed by society through law and convention

   Conform to avoid censure by legitimate authorities and resulting guilt

5. Social contract: Seeking to promote rights of all as agreed to by society

   Conform to maintain respect of the impartial observer judging in terms of community welfare

6. Universal ethical principle: Seeking to act in ethically principled way

   Conform to avoid self-condemnation for failing to live up to the values to which one is committed

These motives are ones to which we can easily relate in our everyday or organizational lives. At Stage 1, a person does whatever he or she can get away with and avoid getting caught and punished. Some cynics portray this orientation as common among self-serving public administrators. It would represent a base level of moral reasoning and is likely to be rare, although instances of such behavior certainly occur in government and nonprofit organizations. Stage 2 reflects a narrow cost-benefit calculation: "I will follow the rules because I benefit more from doing so than from breaking the rules." There is no respect for the value of the rules themselves. Stages 3 and 4 differ in the breadth and source of expectations. When we act at Stage 3, we do the right thing because it is expected by those with whom we interact. We do not want to disappoint them or let them down, and we do not want to incur their displeasure. It is a highly personalized approach to deciding what is right and wrong.

Persons acting at the Stage 4 level accept the legitimacy of laws and other rules of behavior, including codes of ethics. They feel obligated to act in terms of these laws, policies, and rules, based on the narrow or reactive sense of duty described earlier. In the view of Rest and his collaborators (1999, 38), conventional morality "is duty oriented and authoritarian (in the sense of affording unchallenged powers to authorities and in deferring to authorities)." Persons at this stage may not understand the reasons for the rules or feel a sense of commitment to the principles or purposes on which they are based, but they feel an obligation to follow the rules. They feel a sense of guilt when they do not.

The postconventional stages are somewhat difficult to distinguish and now are usually combined by scholars. For example, Stewart and Sprinthall (1994) refer to the "*P*" or *principled stage.*[8] The P stage reflects a deeper understanding and broader commitment than Stage 4. At this level, there would be much more likelihood of critically examining the reasons for acting and seeking to alter unfair laws, policies, and rules than at the lower levels. For example, Kohlberg had great respect for Martin Luther King, Jr., who for principled reasons resisted and acted to change unjust laws. Rest and his collaborators provide this description of postconventional ethical reasoning:

> The positive and constructive aspect of postconventional thinking is to provide some idealized way that humans can interrelate, some ideals for organizing society. Examples of ideals for society that have been proposed include creating the greatest good for all, guaranteeing minimal rights and protection for everyone, engendering caring and intimacy among people, mandating fair treatment, providing for the needy, furthering the common good, actualizing personhood, and so on.

In their view, the ideals of postconventional thinking are "sharable"—not supported by dogma and the preferences of a selected group—and thus open to rational critique and subject to the test of logical consistency (Rest et al. 1999, 42).

Why do you act the way you do when you decide what is right and wrong in your professional work? Presumably your reasons go beyond Stage 1 (simply avoiding punishment for doing something that violates policy or rules), but there are widely supported explanations of motivation that approximate Stage 2. One may be good for self-serving reasons. Public-choice theory in general and principal-agent models in particular assume that pursuit of self-interest is the key factor that drives behavior (Peters 1999). One may do what is right and expected in order to obtain rewards or cooperate with others to reduce *transaction costs* (being trustworthy so that favors will be returned), but the underlying concern is self-interest. Unfortunately, this motivation is a limited and narrow foundation for ethical action.

Reasons for acting ethically that extend farther beyond one's self are found at the conventional stage. The good-boy; nice-girl orientation involves meeting the expectations of others, especially coworkers. Presumably, the expectations of the "organization" also have weight in defining behavior, although the expectations may be shaped more by the response of immediate superiors and coworkers than by the broad purposes and values of the organization. At this stage, you conform to avoid disapproval and dislike by others or the sense that you are out-of-step with prevailing values in the work group. In contrast, at Stage 4, one's behavior is guided by standards that are embedded in law and convention. In other words, the standards have been codified, and you are motivated to follow the standards to maintain order in society. An important aspect of these types of ethical reasoning is that there is limited internal control—or internalized reasons, if you prefer—for ethical action. One is guided by the reaction of others or external standards that are accepted with little reflection.

At the postconventional stages, one has socially beneficial reasons for acting ethically. There may be concern for expanding shared benefits or promoting the public interest. There may be a commitment to act in an ethically principled way, which entails having a grasp of guiding principles and the ability to apply them appropriately to a given situation. One does not operate "above the law" in the sense that one is free to decide whether to follow the law. Still one is "beyond the law" in the sense that one understands the reason for the law, is able to relate it to broader reasons for ethical action, and is capable of questioning whether change in the law—or in policy or program goals—should be considered.

It is not clear from research on moral development what proportion of adults attains this level of moral reasoning. Kohlberg found that most middle-class Americans were at Stage 4 and that Stages 5 and 6 reasoning was relatively uncommon. Most college students operate at Stages 3 and 4 (Gardiner 1988). Stewart, Sprinthall, and Kem (2002) in their inventory of ethical reasoning in resolving hypothetical dilemmas in government found that public administrators in the United States and Poland are most likely to use Stage 4 reasoning, somewhat less likely to use principled stage reasoning, and least likely to uses Stages 1–3. Using the Defining Issues Test (DIT), Rest and his collaborators found that the reliance on the P stage thinking advances with higher education and can be the dominant mode of reasoning for a specialized group such as graduate students in political theory and moral philosophy (Rest et al. 1999, 67–68). Furthermore, educational intervention to broaden ethical thinking can increase the use of stage P reasoning (Rest et al. 1999, 74–75). Most useful in raising the level of moral reasoning are techniques that include the active involvement of students in learning Gardiner (1998, 73). Considering cases that present moral dilemmas and relating the levels of moral development to resolving these dilemmas help students recognize how one reasons at a higher level. We will use these strategies throughout the book. As you explore a topic or examine a case study, it is useful to consider why you think about alternatives in the way you do when confronted with an ethical choice and whether there are alternative ways you might use to think about the situation.

Basic Components of Administrative Ethics

We have examined the meaning of administrative ethics and briefly introduced philosophical approaches to ethics, the content of ethical thinking typically expressed by persons interested in public service but without formal education in ethics, and the major stages in the development of ethical reasoning. Together they represent the basic elements—a basic model—of administrative ethics. We introduce the components at this point in the discussion for two reasons. First, it closely reflects the attitudes that are commonly held by those who enter public service or have been working for government and nonprofit organizations. Second, the elements will be developed further at a later point in the discussion. Some time ago, I suggested that a person can think of ethics as a triangle with the points defined by the three philosophical approaches: virtue, principle, and consequences (Svara 1997). It has been a useful approach in the classroom and in training activities with practitioners, and it is the advanced model to which we shall return—but how do we get to this model of ethics, both conceptually and developmentally? The foundation on which we build is the simpler and not-quite-complete version composed of the basic components presented here. The basic components reflect Stage 4 ethical reasoning, whereas the advanced model to be developed later will reflect a principled level of ethical reasoning.

In the basic components, there is a strong emphasis on basic duties, principles of fairness and legality, and the virtues of honesty and integrity. It seems appropriate to place duty at the center, in particular the commitment to serve the public and the obligation to put the interest of the public above one's personal self-interest. It is striking that many students in their implicit codes of ethics mentioned some aspect of selflessness: not seeking inappropriate personal gain from holding office and steering clear of situations that create a conflict of interest. Despite the importance of consequentialism as a major conceptual approach to thinking about ethics, it does not seem to be an important part of the basic way that public servants think about their ethical standards. The basic components that involve the interplay of duty, virtue, and principle are presented in **Figure 2.1**.

An important example of the emphasis on duty as the core element in a basic approach to administrative ethics is the U.S. government's Standards of Ethical Conduct for Employees of the Executive Branch, contained in **Appendix 1**. The basic obligation of public service consists of 14 princi-

Principle	⇔	Duty	⇔	Virtue
Fairness/ Legality		Serve the public/ Public interest over self-interest		Honesty/ Integrity

Figure 2–1 *Basic Components of Administrative Ethics with Stage 4 Reasoning*

ples. Eleven elaborate on the basic theme that public service is a public trust, especially the emphasis on serving the public and not allowing private gain, self-interest, or conflict of interest to interfere with the responsibilities of office. The other points deal with fairness and legality: Point 1 stresses legality and loyalty to the Constitution, Point 8 deals with impartiality, and Point 13 stresses equal opportunity. This statement does not include any reference to the personal qualities of honesty and integrity that are commonly mentioned in the implicit codes of ethics by persons in or preparing to occupy positions in public administration. Still, the statement illustrates how a set of ethical standards can be developed that reflects the basic components of administrative ethics grounded in a narrow definition of duty.

The basic components correspond to conventional or Stage 4 ethical thinking. This is not surprising given the prevalence of Stage 4 reasoning among adults along with the special characteristics and expectations of public service. The importance of law and an authoritative system of governance, fair process, personal virtues, and putting the public interest above self-interest are all consistent with a style of ethical reasoning that stresses maintaining law, order, and social norms. Stage 4 and the basic components meet the minimum standards for administrative ethics in a democratic society, but they do not meet the highest standards. At the end of Chapter 4, we will revisit and develop the full model—the ethics triangle—after further examination of each of the basic components along with the addition of a consequentialist component.

Other Definitional Issues: Distinctions Between Ethics, Morality, and Law

When discussing ethics, it is common to use the terms *morality* and *law* that also convey standards of behavior. It is important to distinguish what it means to be moral, ethical, and legal and to establish the basic meaning for these terms that will be used throughout the remainder of the discussion. The main elements, including standard definitions of the terms, are the following:

> Moral: "of or pertaining to human character or behaviour considered as good or bad; of or pertaining to the distinction between right and wrong, or good and evil" (Brown 1993, 1827)

The basis for making these moral distinctions may reflect the values of a society, religion, ethnic or social group, or an individual's conscience.

> Ethical: "in accordance with the accepted principles of right and wrong governing the conduct of a group/organization, or the rules or standards governing the conduct of the members of a profession" (Brown 1993, 856)

These standards are accepted by persons who seek entry into the group/organization or profession and apply to all persons encompassed by the organization.

> Legal: "falling within the province of law; . . . founded on or deriving authority from law; permitted or not forbidden by law" (Brown 1993, 1561)

One can see in the definition the basis for the defense sometimes given by public officials that their actions are acceptable because they are not prohibited by law. This definition links legal to the law or "the body of rules . . . which a particular state or community recognizes as governing the actions of its subjects or members" (Brown 1993, 1544). There is no reference to right and wrong as in the definitions of moral and ethical.

In this book, the term *morality* will be used to refer to the sense of right and wrong that an individual has based on personal upbringing and commitment to the values of a variety of groups. *Ethics* refers to the standards of right and wrong behavior that is voluntarily accepted by persons who choose to be part of a professional group, including the profession of public administration. When one accepts membership in a profession or accepts a public service position, the ethical standards become binding. The distinction between ethics and morality can be illustrated by the potential conflict between my sense of morality—what I personally believe is right and wrong—and the standards I am expected to follow as a professional or a public official. One may personally find it morally offensive to harm another person, but it is not unethical to use deadly force as a police officer or soldier engaged in authoritatively sanctioned activities. Indeed, it would be unethical not to carry out one's duty.

The relationship between morality, ethics, and law are somewhat problematic. Phillip Cooper (1998, 76–79) points out that they can be at odds with each other. He offers these points:

- What is immoral is not necessarily illegal; e.g., dishonesty is not illegal except in particular instances.
- Some laws regulate behaviors that are not inherently immoral; e.g., driving 5 mph above the speed limit.
- Some laws violate ethical principles; e.g., legislating special benefits for particular groups can violate the principle of fairness.

- Finding ways in veterans administration hospitals to treat veterans for Agent Orange disorders as service-connected disabilities was not immoral although for an extended period it violated regulations.
- Relying on law to promote ethics does not necessarily promote ethical behavior. Not breaking the rules does not mean that one is necessarily ethical.

Public administration ethics apply to those who enter public service. The ethical obligation to uphold the law requires that one subjugate one's personal beliefs (i.e., one's sense of morality) to discharge the duties of the office. Furthermore, it is a violation of administrative ethics to substitute one's own view of morality for law and policy. The administrator can seek to change the policy through appropriate channels and methods within his or her organization (an issue examined in the next chapter), but if these efforts are not successful he or she must accept the established policy. If one cannot subjugate their personal morals to the law, however, he or she should change positions or leave administrative office to seek to change the policy as a citizen through the political process. He or she should not ignore the law nor try to covertly undermine it.

Ethics and legality are not synonymous but public administrators have an ethical obligation to observe and uphold the law as well as to seek to improve on the law through the governmental process; for example, by conducting research on needs and by policy recommendations. Thus, legality has a special importance to public administrators but what is legal is not necessarily moral or ethical. In the next chapter, we seek to refine the sense of duty and identify aspects of duty that are active rather than reactive.

The distinction between legality and morality is related to the stages of moral reasoning. Stage 4 law-and-order thinking reflects a limited view of duty; one that defines serving the public in terms of observing the law and obeying superiors. A refined sense of duty is based on careful reflection about the nature of responsibilities to the public, political superiors, and the organization. It also requires that one develop a reasoned view about his or her obligations and constraints when acting as an individual engaged in public service. This refined sense of obligation supports postconventional ethical reasoning. In addition, philosophical perspectives on virtue, principle, and consequences contribute to universal standards of ethical behavior.

In conclusion, it is a plausible assumption that you and most public servants at a minimum have a grasp of the basic components of administrative ethics. It is likely that you consider the ethical choices you must make and that you are guided by a sense of duty to serve and by basic virtues and principles. These standards reflect a reliance on ethical judgment that stresses maintaining law and norms that promote order in society. In the next two chapters, we will examine how these components can be broadened to reflect postconventional ethical reasoning based on universal values.

Chapter 3

Refining the Sense of Duty:

Responsibilities of Public Administrators and the Issue of Agency

T he duty-based approach to ethics derives the responsibilities of public administrators from the nature of the position they occupy. In accepting office, officials make a "promise to live up to the obligations of office . . . and to frame their judgments by standards embedded in the office's responsibilities" (Dobel 1999, xi). Admittedly, it is somewhat artificial to separate the duty-based approach from other approaches to ethics. When public administrators think about the obligations of a public servant, they are also likely to be thinking about the qualities, i.e., virtues they should have and the principles they should uphold. For example, in York Willbern's (1984) six types of public morality, the first three types conform exactly to elements in the basic components of administrative ethics. According to Willbern, public administrators should manifest the key virtue of honesty, should act on the duty to serve the public and avoid conflicts of interest, and observe the principles of legality and procedural fairness. Dobel (1999) sees official responsibilities and the virtue of integrity as essentially linked.

Still, it is useful to focus initially on the expectations of persons occupying a public service position and to explore the full scope of their duties. Public administrators are expected to serve individual citizens and to be accountable to the "people." These responsibilities can be extended to include promotion of the democratic process itself (Burke 1986; Cooper 1991). They are responsible to their organization and to political superiors, but they also have responsibilities to themselves as professionals. When considering their professional identity, their role, and their relationships, administrators must grapple intellectually and in practice with a complex issue: What does it mean to be an "agent" of the various parties that administrators serve—the public, political superiors, and the organization? An *agent* is one who acts for another, but how much of his or her own independence is given up when assuming this role? In this chapter, we start with the expectations linked to the public service role and then turn to the issue of agency. The chapter concludes with suggestions about balancing the potentially conflicting norms and pressures that administrators encounter. From this discussion, we will refine the sense of duty and elaborate what duty entails for public administrators.

The Responsibilities of Democratic Public Administrators

Many of the basic responsibilities of administrators in a democratic society are part of the orientation that administrators bring to public office. These responsibilities can be summarized as follows, each of which later is discussed further and illustrated with cases:

1. Put the public interest over personal interest.
2. Display a service orientation and a commitment to serve.
3. Have a commitment to procedural fairness.
4. Exercise fiduciary responsibility.
5. Be bound by and uphold the law.
6. Support the democratic process.
7. Be responsive to the policy goals of political superiors while fairly examining all policy options and exercising leadership appropriate to position.

Why are these points important to establishing an ethical foundation based on duty? If administrators are to serve the public, it must be clear that they are *putting the public interest over self-interest.* This is the core of the Standards of Ethical Conduct for Employees of the Executive Branch in Appendix 1 (discussed in the previous chapter.) Furthermore, to ensure that they are making a full and balanced assessment of a problem that fairly assesses all those potentially impacted by a decision, administrators should seek to be certain that any potential personal factors that impact them will not limit and impair their judgment. This is the fundamental requirement to avoid conflict of interest.

The standard for public administrators is often expressed in even more demanding terms: There should not even be an appearance of conflict of interest. This may seem like an unnecessary and unfair expectation. It gives rise to the complaint that administrators are held to a higher standard than persons who work in the private sector. The importance of the standard, however, is that it helps to protect the integrity of the organizational process. In view of the high level of cynicism that the public feels about government and the high level of trust that is required for nonprofits to secure support from contributors and volunteers, public administrators should feel a special obligation to act in such a way as to strengthen the integrity of the process. They should disclose any interests that may affect or be perceived to affect objectivity in making decisions. Furthermore, promoting the integrity of the process requires that public administrators not use public office for personal gain or to advance personal or private interests.

Consider **Case 3.1**[9].

Case 3.1   *Weekend Outing*

The board of directors of the chamber of commerce has an annual weekend outing at a resort some miles from your city. During the weekend, there is golf, tennis, swimming, card games, dinner dances with entertainment, and numerous cocktail parties. During the day, there are sessions at which the chamber board reviews progress for the past year and discusses plans for the upcoming year. For several years, the city has contributed $100,000 annually for the support of the chamber. You, the city manager, are invited to the chamber's weekend outing with all expenses paid by the chamber. Do you accept the invitation and go for the weekend?

At first glance, it may seem to be completely appropriate to attend with expenses paid by the chamber. The chamber is an important actor in the affairs of the community, and the top administrator in city government should have active communication with it. The free ticket is a small part of the money paid by the city to the chamber each year. From the perspective of responsibilities of the office, however, this situation creates the possibility of inappropriate personal gain and potential conflict of interest. Attendance at the outing is appropriate, and it is useful for the city manager to be present and interact with other participants. The cost, however, should be covered by the city if the trip is considered to be worthwhile city business. The city manager should not accept the weekend as a gift from the chamber. At the very least, there is an appearance of conflict of interest. Beyond that, the manager should be conscientious about maintaining detachment from the chamber in order to objectively assess what the city is getting for its large annual payment. Typically, this kind of funding is intended to support economic development activities for the city. In some cases, the accomplishments of chambers are limited and the value of the allocation is questionable. The manager must be in a position to assess the program without being influenced by social ties to the organization or its leaders, and favors he has received from the chamber.

Public administrators are *dedicated to service*; they should not behave in ways that are convenient for themselves or their agencies with little regard for the citizens or clients with whom they interact. The service orientation also implies a commitment to serve, i.e., to persist and persevere in order to carry out all of the tasks one is supposed to complete. A sentiment such as that contained in caption on a New York post office "neither rain nor snow nor heat nor gloom of night stays these couriers from the swift completion of their appointed rounds"[10] captures the essence of what it means to do one's duty in meeting the responsibilities of office and epitomizes the service orientation.

Consider **Case 3.2**.

Case 3.2   *Cutting Hours of Service*

You are the county library director. Due to budget reductions, you must cut 2 hours per day from the schedule of all the branch libraries—either 8:00 to 10:00 A.M. or 7:00 to 9:00 P.M. Staff members strongly prefer to work the morning hours. Do you cut the evening hours from the schedule?

The reality of budget limitations makes it necessary at times to reduce the level of services. In this situation, the user patterns and preferences of clients should be a major consideration and do not appear to have been taken into account. If the greater use of library is in the evening hours, the closing time should remain at 9:00 P.M. even though the staff members prefer to work during the day.

A consideration of service naturally leads into matters of principle. Service is to be provided with diligence and also with attention to how people are treated. *Procedural fairness* is a basic value of responsible administrators. As an aspect of the principle of justice and a bedrock of social equity, it ensures that all persons are treated in the same way or treated consistently in reference to some qualifying characteristic. It guarantees *due process*, the full set of prescribed steps that are to be taken before providing or denying a benefit, considering guilt or innocence, or being reviewed in a competitive selection process. Finally, it assures that all receive equal protection. The commitment to procedural fairness helps to ensure that citizens and clients are not treated arbitrarily, discriminated against, or ignored when others are receiving a service. Using race or ethnicity alone as the basis for identifying suspects or determining who should be subjected to more intensive methods of investigation violates this principle as does giving preference to friends in deciding who will receive services from a nonprofit organization.

What kinds of issues are present in the situation presented in **Case 3.3**?

Case 3.3   *Free Donut*

For some time, police officers on three adjacent beats have met each day for a coffee break at a restaurant near a point where the three beats intersect. They usually have coffee and a donut and occasionally a piece of pie. You are newly assigned to one of the beats. When you go for the coffee break the first day and you walk up to pay the check, the proprietor says, "No charge. I am glad to have you officers around." The others leave without paying. Do you pay your check?

This classic case involves each of the elements of public service duty considered so far. First, there is personal gain because police officers are personally benefiting from the "generosity" of the restaurant owner. The value of the gratuity is less important than the sense of entitlement that it seems to be engendering. The fact that the same location is chosen each day suggests that the officers come to receive free food and expect it. Some times sincere expressions of gratitude cannot be graciously refused, but when one goes back for more, it seems clear that the officers are seeking a special benefit. On a larger scale, such behavior reinforces the idea that the police are different and that the normal rules do not apply to them. Second, the officers provide a valuable service when they are present on the premises of a business, as the owner acknowledges, but the officers are providing that benefit to just the one business which offers favors in return. Other restaurants that do not provide free food are being deprived. Third, the officers might be inclined to give special treatment to the restaurant owner in his business or elsewhere in exchange for the favors they have received.

As part of the responsibility to serve the public, public administrators have long recognized the need to make the best possible use of the resources entrusted to them; in other words, their *fiduciary responsibility*. Two interrelated management values convey this responsibility. According to the value of economy, public administrators should spend frugally. They should use resources efficiently seeking to produce the most units of services at the least cost.

In **Case 3.4**, is the director being a trustee of scarce resources in this situation?

Case 3.4   *Insider Bidding*

Your nonprofit organization is getting ready to award a major contract to provide services to your organization. A member of the board of directors is the owner of a business that provides these services. You know that because of the inside information the board member has about the contract, the board member will be able to substantially underbid all her competitors. Therefore, awarding the contract to the low-bidding board member will result in substantial cost savings to your organization. As executive director, do you allow the board member to bid on the contract?

This offer represents a false savings, and one that may not be sustained over the long term. The director would be violating normal procedures by allowing the use of insider information. When the board member expressed interest in the bid, she shifted from being a board member to being a potential service provider which alters the relationship with the director. What if she receives the contract and the services are not provided in a timely or satisfactory way? Will the director be able to hold the board member to account in the same way that a true contractor would be? Nonprofit board members commonly provide contributions to support the organization, and there are many projects that depend on the in-kind contributions in the form of materials and services from many sources including board members. To mix contractual relationships with board-administrator relationships, however, is not a good practice.

As a final aspect of public administrators' fiduciary responsibility, they should seek to be effective and to achieve the greatest accomplishments with best use of resources available. As an extension of these values, administrators should be willing periodically to question the methods they use and consider whether some other source would be better able to achieve the appropriate balance of economy, efficiency and effectiveness (while maintaining a commitment to equity and assuring accountability) than the staff members of the organization itself. Outsourcing may be disruptive to internal staff, but under certain circumstances, it is warranted. Even more difficult is recognizing that a program should be discontinued, but public administrators need to be able to make this tough recommendation if a program has outlived its usefulness.

For administrators to be accountable and responsible, they must be *bound by and uphold the law*. A central feature of democratic governments is that they are based on laws, not the personal preferences of the men and women who work for government. If government employees believe that they cannot enforce the law, they should leave government and seek change through the political process. According to Henry David Thoreau (1849), even private citizens who commit acts of civil disobedience to protest laws believed to be unjust must be willing to pay the consequences. Indeed, their legal punishment adds moral weight to their protest. No person is above the law. Staff members in nonprofit organizations do not enforce the law in the same way that government agencies do, but they should uphold the law as it pertains to their organization and observe the legal requirements that govern how an organization operates as a nonprofit with exemption from taxes.

Consider **Case 3.5**.

Case 3.5 *Relocation*

As a staff member in the community development department, you are instructed to initiate procedures to relocate residents from two blocks in a low-income neighborhood. The city council has approved clearance of these blocks for a redevelopment project. Full relocation benefits are provided to cover the costs of moving, and your office will help the residents find alternative housing. Some of the residents are elderly and have lived in the neighborhood for a long time. They object to leaving their old neighborhood. Do you proceed with relocating the elderly residents?

The lives of some vulnerable citizens are being disrupted by this program. It is, however, a policy that has been authoritatively determined by the city council. Fairness issues have been addressed by providing assistance and relocation costs. It is natural and appropriate to feel compassion for the elderly residents who do not want to move, although their living conditions may be improved as a result. Administrators must enforce the law consistently and fairly. They may be able to exercise discretion and display initiative by arranging for the elderly residents to move back into rehabilitated units in their old neighborhood or even move directly from their current residences to ones already renovated without the need for temporary housing.

Administrators also have an obligation to *support the democratic process*, what Willbern (1984) calls the "ethic of democratic responsibility." Administrators have responsibilities to both political superiors and to citizens and clients in supporting democracy. Administrators differ in how they balance the two. A survey of top city government administrators in 14 countries in the late 1990s revealed that just over half believed that administrators should be primarily responsible to the political leadership and only secondarily responsible to the public. In six of the countries including the United States, however, a majority of administrators gave as much emphasis or more to citizens as they did to elected officials in defining their responsibilities (Mouritzen and Svara 2002, 87). Maintaining this dual responsibility is one of the challenges that administrators in government must face. Nonprofit administrators may encounter a similar situation in balancing the interests of clients, on the one hand, and donors and board members, on the other. Neither, however, can choose to ignore either key referent group.

In order to meet the expectation to support the democratic process, public administrators have the responsibility to share information with the public and ensure transparency. They should also support citizen participation. To promote social equity, it is particularly important to encourage the participation of individuals from groups that are typically less involved, even if these groups are more likely to put pressure for change on the administrator's political superiors. Such groups could include low-income citizens with low voting rates in elections or clients of a nonprofit who passively receive the services provided.

Democratic responsibility requires that administrators be *responsive to the goals of political superiors* and faithfully implement their policies. Administrators, however, also make policy recommendations. They have the obligation to identify all options for achieving goals and provide complete and unbiased information about them. They should identify trends and needs even if public and political superiors may be ignoring them. In addition, administrators should provide the information needed by political superiors to assess the quality and effectiveness of administrative performance. Administrators have responsibilities to both political superiors and the public and at the same time should uphold professional standards and communicate honestly, even when the information provided is not what the audience wants to hear. Consider **Case 3.6**.

Case 3.6   *Renewing Funding*

As research analyst for the city council, you feel it is your obligation to make the strongest case possible for the continuation of funding for a low-income neighborhood improvement program. The city grant is the organization's major source of funds for rehabilitating deteriorated housing, and there would be serious unmet problems if its funding were reduced. Critics on the city council are looking for an excuse to cut the problem. You are aware of some minor problems that have been detected in performance reports on the project. Do you omit reference to these problems in order to not give the critics ammunition to use against the program?

Is there any difference in the circumstances in **Case 3.7**?

Case 3.7　Budget Recommendation

In the county in which you are the manager, a majority of the voters in a recent county election supported a slate of candidates pledged to a substantial reduction in local taxes. Based on recommendations from department heads and your own assessment, you feel that a tax increase is needed to meet pressing needs in the community. Do you recommend a budget with a modest tax increase?

In the first situation, you as a staff member are tampering with the democratic process by withholding information from council members. You are imposing your judgment about the seriousness of the problems and preventing the elected officials from fully reviewing the new request. The continuation of funding should be determined after a full airing of the facts. In the second situation, the county manager is identifying needs and bringing them to the attention of elected officials. The manager has an obligation to the public to make clear what the needs in the county are and the consequences of choosing to fund or not fund programs to meet those needs. The decision is still in the hands of the elected officials, and they may choose to turn down the recommendation. Making recommendations to the board is compatible with their policy-making authority and supports it. Withholding information from the board undermines or weakens that authority.

Administrators should look for ways to improve performance from the perspective of their position. They might suggest changes in old policies or propose new policies, or they might make innovations in implementation or management procedure to make a program work more effectively, efficiently, or equitably or with a higher level of service to clients. Administrators must be careful not to exceed their authority or violate agency norms and standards in making changes (Terry 1998; deLeon and Denhardt 2000), but evidence from studies of innovators indicates that they typically achieve beneficial results and act with integrity (Borins 2000).

Responsibilities to Elected Officials and to the Organization: The Question of Moral Agency

As noted, public administrators have a responsibility to serve the public, be responsive to it, and help ensure that citizens are informed and actively involved. They are not, however, directly accountable to the public, but rather to political superiors and to their organization. The top administrator reports to political superiors, and the other staff members are answerable to their administrative superiors in the organization. Furthermore, all administrators are broadly responsible to advance the mission of the organization. In seeking to discern how public administrators should meet their duties to directly serve political superiors and their organization, it is necessary to examine in more depth what it means to be an agent. Public administrators must balance two characteristics that are in conflict: being controlled and being independent. Independence does not mean being a free agent who can do anything he or she wants to do, but it does mean having the capacity to act individually and without coercion in deciding what to say or do. The foundation of administrative ethics offers a clear understanding of the nature of administrators' roles as agents. Although public administrators commonly recognize their obligation to follow directives from superiors and provide accurate information to them, it is not clear that administrators have a clear sense about other aspects of the relationship that entail more initiative on their part.

Two contrasting questions have dominated the discussion of agency in the literature on public administration. First, can public administrators be considered to be responsible for the actions they take? In other words, are they independent moral agents? We shall devote most of the discussion to this question, but there is a second: Can public administrators be counted on to do what they are supposed to do—are they accountable agents? Some see the two characteristics as mutually exclusive. Administrators are "servants" or "masters," "agents" or "independent tools" (Barker and Wilson 1997). Administrators whose behavior is controlled are not responsible for their actions. This view is based on pervasive arguments that administrators are simply the instruments of political superiors—elected officials or nonprofit board members—and/or are subsumed in complex organizations that strip them of the capacity to make individual decisions. On the other hand, some argue that administrators who have sufficient independence to be considered responsible for the choices they make may operate beyond the reach of accountability. They may defy or undercut the instructions of the "principal" for whom they work.

Restating these counterarguments, ethical problems for public administrators may arise if they are too passive due to the nature of the administrative role in large organizations or if they are too active. Are they merely passive instruments or are they usurpers of the authority of political superiors (Heady 1984, 408)? *Neither of these alternatives is ethically acceptable.* In the discussion that follows, being responsible for actions and being accountable for actions are both viewed as necessary for ethical administrators. There is tension between the two characteristics, but they do not undermine each other.

Do Role and Structure Allow Administrators to Be Responsible for Their Actions?

There are legitimate concerns about ensuring that administrators do not operate outside a set of controls. They do not own their organization nor should they unilaterally determine its policies. This concern leads some to the extreme conclusion that administrators cannot be moral agents because of the role they fill. In this view, the public administrator is a narrowly neutral agent whose only options are to obey orders or resign from the organization. Administrators are seen to be so completely neutral that they are not supposed to make any value judgments, because such judgments are to be made by political superiors alone. This condition would mean that administrators cannot be moral agents within a public organization because their actions are controlled by others.

This approach is conceptually grounded in the politics-administration dichotomy model (Svara 1998). In the strictest statement of this model:

- Elected officials do not get involved in administration.
- Administrators have no involvement in shaping policies.
- Administrators occupy the role of a neutral expert whose responsibility is restricted to efficiently and effectively carrying out the policies of elected officials.
- Presumably, administrators do not exercise discretion. To do so opens the door to interpreting policy and choosing how and to what extent it will be applied.

In this view of the dichotomy, according to an influential article by Wallace Sayre (1958, 102–03), administration was to be in a "self-contained world of its own, with its own separate values, rules, and methods" and "concerned exclusively with the execution of assignments handed down from the realm of politics."

A second argument for the lack of moral agency is that the organization is so large and complex that individuals have no control over what happens. According to the ethic of structure, it is the organization, not the individual, who should be held responsible. Similarly, systems theory contends that organizations do not behave rationally. There is a gap between individual intention and collective outcome, and individuals do not control the consequences of their behavior. Individuals are simply "cogs in the wheel." So many hands contribute to an action that it is not possible to assign responsibility to any one individual. If responsibility can be assigned to any one person, it is only to officials at the top of the organization. Officials at the middle and lower levels have no control.

It is certain that many administrators have felt pressured by their superiors or the organization to do things that they believe unwise or even improper.

Some accept the control of superiors and release themselves from responsibility with the rationalization "I was just following orders." A more modest version of this orientation—consistent with the dichotomy model—is the attitude that "political superiors make policy, and I just carry it out." Once again, responsibility has been shifted from the administrator to the political superior along with the claim that this is how functions are supposed to be divided.

There are a number of counterarguments to this simplistic position.[11] First, roles are not defined so precisely that room for individual choice is eliminated. Unless coerced, administrators are not relieved of moral responsibility for their actions. The strict dichotomy view underestimates the extensive discretion and influence that administrators often have. They are not helpless instruments of elected officials and, indeed, we shall see that there are concerns that administrators have too much influence. Furthermore, people bring ethical values and professional norms and expertise to their positions, and it is appropriate to draw on these sources in making recommendations and deciding whether to carry out instructions. Administrators should be neutral, but administrative neutrality means not taking sides and supporting some political superiors over others. Neutrality between parties, groups, or contenders for office does not preclude expressing value preferences, nor does it remove the obligation to display honesty and independence; "to speak truth to power." Public administration entails an obligation to *serve* political superiors *and* the public, not simply an obligation to obey political superiors. In Dobel's (1999, 214) words, administrators "defer to, but not surrender to, authority."[12]

All staff members make a contribution to the overall work of the organization. Even in large organizations,[13] individuals should not hide behind the system. By viewing themselves as "cogs," they are putting on ethical blinders to not see the results to which their actions contribute. In many instances, individual actions can affect outcomes. Complicity and "going along" are often required for organizations to act the way they do, but individuals can refuse to go along. Various methods of dissent are available to administrators to raise concerns about organizational problems. High-ranking officials obviously have considerable clout, but responsibility for outcomes is needed throughout the organization, not just at the top.

In contrast to the dichotomy model, there is extensive evidence of political-administrative interaction and administrative influence in government (Svara 2006). In nonprofit organizations, the relationship between the board and director is typically even more fluid than in government. The director and staff have substantial potential not only to influence board members but to determine who the board members will be. At the end of this chapter, an alternative to the dichotomy model—a model of complementarity—will be offered.

There is also clear ethical and legal support for administrative independence in the face of official pressures. The Nuremberg Charter used as the basis at the trials of Nazi war criminals provides a sweeping statement of the scope of individual moral responsibility:

> Article 7. The official position of defendants, whether as head of state or responsible officials in government departments, shall not be considered as freeing them from responsibility or mitigating punishment.

> Article 8. The fact that the Defendant acted pursuant to order of his Government or of a superior shall not free him from responsibility, but may be considered in mitigation of punishment if the Tribunal determines that justice so requires.[14]

In the British civil service, there are explicit requirements of noncompliance in the face of improper orders. The top administrator in a department or the accounting officer is "required by law to question any ministerial scheme for unlawful, improper or ineffective use of public fund . . . with a formal warning to the minister" (Barker and Wilson 1997, 227–228). This step is rarely taken since the minister—the top politician—usually backs off when encountering resistance from the top civil servants. However, occasionally, senior officials will ask that the orders be put in writing which also provides a warning that the action is questionable.[15] In interviews by Barker and Wilson (1997, 230), only 6 percent of top officials in Britain indicate that they would comply with an inappropriate task, although another 15 percent would comply but complain about the order. The others would refuse, and over half would report the order to top civil service staff (Barker and Wilson 1997, 230). These counterarguments are not meant to deny the pressure that can be exerted on staff members in organizations, but they are not powerless to act nor without legal grounds for refusing to obey.

The issues surrounding moral agency can be examined in **Case 3.8**.

Case 3.8 *Discharge from Rehab Program*

You are an assistant director in a local rehabilitation program for teenage drug abusers. The goal of the program is to return a client to the community when the professional teams are convinced that the individual can remain drug free. Recently a treatment team's decision to discharge a young woman from the program was strongly objected to by her parents. Adamant about continuing program treatment for the young woman, the parents used influence with a legislator on the appropriations committee to bring pressure on the agency head. You are the intermediary between the agency head and the treatment teams. The agency head has asked you to intervene and halt discharge plans. What would you do?

Source: Richter, Burke, and Doig 1990, 146.

In this situation, the first issue is whether it is appropriate to question the decision of the treatment team. Does asking them to reconsider constitute questioning their judgment? Obviously, administrators prefer that clients and their relatives deal with them directly, but the parents' request conveyed through the legislator potentially indicates that there is new information that the treatment team did not have at its disposal to consider. The parents may know something about the home or community situation that makes discharge unwise. On the other hand, the parents may simply find it inconvenient that their daughter is being returned to their home at this time. It is the agency's obligation to release clients when they are ready, and there is a backlog of others who need to receive the care. Based on the new information, the treatment team should decide the case on its merits and, if they reconfirm their original decision, you should support them.

One should not presume that a legislative inquiry is connected to a specific outcome. Often inquiries referred on behalf of constituents are simple requests for information or explanation. The agency can use the request as an opportunity to educate the elected official about what the agency does, how it makes decisions, and what its needs are. The agency director may discover that the legislator actually does want to force the organization to bend or break its rules, but you and the director should not do the bending because you suspect that this is the intent of the request. If this is the case, the director will have to decide if this is the battle he or she wants to fight to uphold the independence of the agency. There could be serious consequences for the clients and staff if the demand is refused that cannot be ignored. Still, in instances of this kind, you should avoid a pseudomoral agent argument: Just because someone tells you or tries to pressure you to do something, it does not absolve you of moral agency. You are still responsible for your actions. If you accept the action that is being forced on you, you share in the responsibility for the outcome.

Are Public Administrators Accountable Agents?

It is important to consider briefly the other side of the moral agency issue. If public administrators have sufficient independence to be responsible for their actions, are they possibly out of control? There is a need for accountability in government and nonprofit organizations. It is a critical part of the oversight of administration provided by political superiors. A number of factors raise doubts about the adequacy of accountability. Many of the counterarguments that support the position that officials are responsible for their actions suggest a degree of autonomy that could interfere with accountability and reliable implementation. There are a number of ways that agents may defy the directions of their principal. Indeed, the relationship is commonly discussed under the heading the *principal-agent problem*.

There is an extensive body of writing in political science and public administration about the supposed autonomy of administrators and the self-directed nature of bureaucracies. The autonomous administrator is distant from politicians and is self-directing to the point that political control is questionable (Jones 1995). Public-choice theorists argue that administrators act in terms of their own interests or their own perception of the public interest rather than the public interest as translated by elected officials.[16] Often it is suspected that administrative agencies are "bureaucratic fiefdoms . . . that cannot be held accountable through the normal mechanisms of representative democracy" (Stein 1991, 1). The standard popular perception of administrators—and one held by many scholars as well—is that bureaucracies are lumbering, unresponsive, self-interested, and out of control (Wood and Waterman 1994, 141). Nonprofits have not been free of criticism, and public trust has been weakened by the perception that some nonprofits put their own organizational interests above serving those in need.

The counterarguments regarding the willingness of administrators to be accountable are substantial. Observing the law and promoting agency mission are important to administrators. There are fallacies in principal-agent model that assumes that agents only pursue narrow self-interest and can be expected to shirk their duties and defy control. Many administrators are "principled agents" who take on thankless tasks and go above and beyond the call of duty (Dilulio 1994). There is evidence that administrators support oversight by elected officials and board members. Nonprofits have developed new mechanisms for accountability (Independent Sector 2002). There is a need for a new model for conceptualizing the relationship of politicians and nonprofit board members and administrators that accommodates the possibility that administrators are neither subservient (and thus not responsible agents) nor autonomous (and thus not accountable agents).

In conclusion, there are several questions to use for self-examination. What is your own responsibility for the actions you take when you are carrying out instructions? To what extent should you take the initiative to raise issues with or make recommendations to your superiors? Do you tell political and administrative superiors what they want to hear or provide honest and complete analysis? Do you do what is expected and provide a full account of your actions? Responsibility and accountability go hand in hand.

Complementarity as Conceptual Foundation for Administrative Responsibilities

Although it has been common to think that political superiors and administrators were once strictly separated, especially in government, considerable evidence states that they interact extensively in a complementary relationship with each providing important contributions to the other. In nonprofit organizations, although one can hear the statement "The board makes policy and the staff implements it", the interaction and shared involvement is widely recognized. A case can be made that this *model of complementarity*, as I have called it, is more valid historically than the dichotomy model discussed earlier in the chapter (Svara 1999; 2001), and it certainly matches current realities in government and nonprofits. The model acknowledges both distinction and separation between politicians and administrators and also overlap and shared functions. It provides a basis for identifying the obligations and duties of public administrators in the political-administrative relationship.

Substantial evidence supports complementarity. The interactions of elected officials and administrators have the following characteristics that have been observed in various studies (adapted from Svara and Brunet 2003):

1. Political superiors and administrators maintain distinct perspectives based on their unique values and the differences in their formal position.

2. Officials have partially overlapping functions as political superiors provide political oversight of administration and administrators are involved in policy making.

3. There is interdependency and reciprocal influence between political superiors and administrators; each impacts the other.

The balance between the two sets of officials depends on administrators meeting certain obligations in their relationship to political superiors. These obligations blend independence and deference on the part of administrators. They recognize the need for external control and the importance of an "inner check" of internalized standards of behavior.[17] The obligations include the following:

1. Administrators should support the law, respect political supremacy, and acknowledge the need for accountability. They should be loyal to the mission of their organization.

2. Administrators are responsible for serving the public, promoting the broadest conception of the public interest, and supporting the democratic process. Serving the public interest may bring administrators into conflict with political superiors and with segments of the public.

3. Administrators should take responsibility for their actions.
4. Administrators should be independent with a commitment to professional values and competence.
5. Administrators should be honest in their dealings with elected officials and act in an ethically grounded way.
6. Administrators should encourage political superiors to fulfill their responsibilities.

The final requirement of complementarity is especially tricky for administrators because it involves efforts to shape the behavior of their bosses. Still, for there to be a constructive relationship between political superiors and administrators, it is necessary for political superiors to meet their expectations as well as to respect the contribution of professional administrators and the integrity of the administrative process (Burke 1986). Political superiors have the ultimate responsibility to set policy and establish the goals for the organization, and they must carry out this responsibility. Otherwise, administrators may either be uncertain about what they are trying to accomplish or may quietly fill in the void with their own preferences. Political superiors should expect complete and accurate information about how programs are carried out and how services are delivered, but they should take seriously the difficult task of oversight—it is time-consuming and not very exciting—and provide a clear assessment of how policies and programs are working.

Negative behaviors result from going too far in either direction regarding respect for administrators or in controlling them. If the respect is excessive, political superiors may simply rubber stamp the recommendations from administrators; if it is deficient, they may ignore recommendations and take actions that are politically expedient but unsound. If the effort to control administrators is excessive, political superiors may interfere with the performance of administrators and undermine important administrative values such as fairness, impartiality, legality, or efficiency. On the other hand, if the control of administrators is deficient, political superiors may fail to hold administrators fully accountable.

Our focus in this discussion is the responsibilities of administrators, not political superiors. How can those in a subordinate position affect the behavior of their superiors? They should seek to encourage appropriate behavior and resist behavior that is inappropriate. The former is clearly easier to accomplish than the latter, but both can be challenging. Administrators may fail to encourage political superiors to more actively review recommendations or scrutinize performance because it is more convenient to operate with a free hand. How to resist negative behavior takes us back to the points already discussed in this chapter about why and how administrators can assume responsibility for their actions. Administrators have resources to support their position in disagreements with political superiors, and political superiors are to some extent dependent on administrators.

The recommendations of the complementarity model reflect the duty-based approach to defining responsibilities. Thinking about the basic responsibilities of public administrators, it is straightforward to identify complying with organizational directives, avoiding conflicts of interest, and service orientation. As stewards of scarce resources, administrators should be committed to efficiency, economy, effectiveness, and innovation. There are also additional reciprocal commitments that involve action, not just reaction on the part of the public administrator. The administrator should maintain the integrity of organizational process and support the democratic process. In dealing with organizational superiors and elected officials, administrators have responsibilities to push back and help shape decisions as well as to follow and comply.

The complementarity model recognizes the extensive interaction between administrators and political superiors and entails a high level of responsibility for administrators. Rather than operating with the incomplete assumption that they are simply doing what political superiors tell them to do, administrators need to hold in balance contradictory expectations. Their responsibilities to political superiors, the public, their organization, and professional standards may sometimes pull them in different directions. Although it is challenging to balance these perspectives, it is the inescapable reality of administrative life. Administrators should be guided by the duty to uphold democratic *and* professional values.

Building a Model of Administrative Ethics with Duty at the Core

In Chapter 2, we noted Moore's contention that administrators "have the opportunity and duty to conceive of and pursue the public interest" (1981). This statement indicates the ultimate goal of public service duty—to advance the public interest. The commitments discussed in this chapter all contribute to pursuing this ideal: the obligation of public officials to meet the expectations of their position, to respond to the public and to political superiors and support them in discharging their roles, and to address the long-term needs of society. The phrase public interest is an illusive but important standard. In the view of Rosenbloom and Kravchuk (2004, 8–9) "even though it is often difficult to say precisely what is in the public interest, there can be no dispute about the obligation of public administrators to consider it as a general guide for their actions." To Bailey (1962, 106), it is nothing less than "the central concept of a civilized polity."

The public interest is a demanding ideal with both substantive and procedural dimensions (Wamsley et al. 1990, 140). It entails meeting the aspirations and needs of citizens by offering sound programs, finding better solutions to problems, and creating new ways to use scarce resources effectively. It requires a long-term perspective and sustainable approaches, putting the shared interests of the majority—the public good—over special interests but at the same time protecting the rights of minorities. Advancing the public interest also entails protecting and improving the process of public governance—promoting participation by all citizens and supporting political superiors. Concern for the public interest encourages "public administrators and others to be logical, to be rational, and above all, to give reasons" for their actions (Wamsley et al. 1990, 143). The public interest requires that public administrators maintain the delicate balance of accountability and independence, responsiveness and neutrality, and deference and assertiveness in their relationship to political superiors. They are like an acrobat keeping his or her footing on top of a moving ball, to use Radin's (2002) analogy of an artful and "accountable juggler." The "genius" of the public interest concept, according to Bailey (1962, 106) "lies not in its clarity but in its perverse and persistent moral intrusion upon the internal and external discourse of rulers and ruled alike." The intrusive question is: What action should I take to advance the public interest?

In fulfilling their duty as officials for the public, public administrators should meet the basic expectations of serving the public and controlling their own self-interest. They should also seek to promote the public interest in whatever ways are available to them. In the model of administrative ethics that will be completed at the end of Chapter 4, duty is the core and the ideal that is pursued is the public interest.

In dealing with complex situations, administrators can usefully draw upon their understanding of philosophic perspectives of ethics as well as their sense of duty. These perspectives are examined in the next chapter, and they will contribute the other elements and ideals to the complete model of administrative ethics.

Chapter 4

Reinforcing and Enlarging Duty:

Philosophical Bases of Ethical Behavior and the Ethics Triangle[17a]

Three major alternative approaches to grounding and organizing ethical thinking are drawn from philosophic traditions: These approaches are based on virtue, principle, and consequences. Each has important advantages and amplifies the understanding of duty, but each has shortcomings as well, especially if used alone and in a limited or distorted way. As noted in the previous chapter, it is possible to develop a robust and highly relevant set of ethical expectations based on examination of the requirements of public duty.

Extending the discussion to consider philosophical approaches, however, is important for three reasons. First, it is not possible to describe the basic responsibilities of public administrators without reference to these traditions, particularly virtue and principle. For example, we have already considered the service orientation, which reflects the virtue of benevolence and the principle of procedural fairness. The values that support the complementary relationship of administrators and political superiors presume that administrators are ethically grounded. Having greater understanding of the perspectives helps to deepen the understanding of ethical choices based on a sense of duty-based responsibility. Second, the duty-based responsibilities are useful as far as they go, but these responsibilities do not attempt to probe the nature of goodness, the meaning of justice, or the weighing of benefits. Understanding the philosophic perspectives helps to broaden the range of ethical choices beyond those that might be identified considering duty alone. Third, using all the perspectives can help to assure that all possible options have been considered in examining a complex ethical decision. The perspectives help to identify and sort out ethical choices.

The major contenders for the selection as the philosophical base of administrative ethics are virtue, principle, and consequences. These approaches have been summarized well by Richter, Burke, and Doig (1990, 2–3) in their essay for the American Society for Public Administration collection of readings, *Combating Corruption/Encouraging Ethics.*[18] The first, which looks to the qualities of the good person for the standards of ethical conduct, has been advanced by Cooper (1987) and the Josephson Institute (1988) among others. The second, the principle-based approach, applies universal principles to determine ethical choices, as advocated by Ralph Chandler (1994) and by David Hart (1974) drawing on Rawls' theory of justice. Although Kathryn Denhardt (1988, 53) is reluctant to make a clear-cut choice between deontological (principle) and teleological (consequences) approaches to ethics, she acknowledges that she considers the former approach to be "more defensible." The consequentialist approach, a third perspective, looks at the results of actions and seeks to promote some end, such as the greatest good, drawing on utilitarian ethics. It has few proponents but many practitioners. Reviewing the three ethical approaches supports the conclusion that use of all of them helps to avoid the shortcomings and potential misuse of any of the models used singly as well as the shortcomings of using duty alone. One is best grounded when operating within an ethics triangle formed by the three approaches with duty at the center.

Each of the elements has a different kind of "claim" for its validity. As noted, duty has obvious validity because it is derived from the nature of the public service position itself. The virtue-based approach looks inward at the qualities that characterize an exemplary person and claims that these should guide ethical thinking. The principle-based approach looks to external standards of behavior and claims that these standards should always be observed. The consequentialist approach looks at the results of actions and claims that the best outcome should justify ethical action.

In the next three sections, we will examine each approach and consider their advantages and disadvantages as guides to ethical analysis and behavior. For each approach, the central idea will be identified. It represents the "ideal" quality, behavior, or condition associated with each approach, just as public interest is the central idea of the duty-based approach. In the concluding section, we will combine the three approaches, along with the duty-based approach, in a model of administrative ethics. Using the model, we will present ways to use the perspectives together.

Virtue and Intuition

Two distinct but related elements are included in this approach. First, the basis of ethics is a set of qualities that defines what a good person is. The virtuous person manifests and acts on the characteristics that mark one as a person of character and integrity. Second, the nature of ethical decision making is intuitive. One grasps in a holistic way what a good person would do in a given situation. The sense that "I know what I have to do" comes from one's being, instead of coming from reflection or from an analysis of the situation (which are necessary in the next two approaches). Charles Garofalo and Dean Geuras (1999) present these two as separate approaches, but they are so closely linked that separation seems artificial.[19] Intuition may provide the spark of recognition that an ethical issue is being encountered, and it may provide the initial impulse for action. In so far as there is critical examination, it is guided by the question "What would a good person do?" This in turn may lead to considering how different aspects of one's nature might impel one to choose alternative courses of action. The guiding impulse, however, is the feeling that one should act based on one's character. Dobel (1999, 217) acknowledges that ethics based on character does not address the larger issue of "the right" (the principle), but he believes that "focusing on integrity does illuminate many powerful obligations of officials." Thus, in his view, one can rely on a virtue-based approach alone to achieve ethics, and it will lead one to consider other approaches to ethical action as well.

For administrators to be virtuous, they must develop their personal traits and put them into practice. To Aristotle, the ultimate good is an active life in accord with excellence, and virtue is required to achieve excellence.[20] Virtues are within us, but their utilization is not automatic. "Virtues exist innately, as potentialities, within each individual," David Hart (1994, 113–114) argues, "and they push for actualization in the life of the individual." The expansion of virtue is based on practice and the development of habits of goodness (Wilson 1991). Speaking about the virtue of courage, James Toner (2005, 111) offers this explanation of how practice contributes to virtue:

> Aristotle believed that we become brave by doing brave acts. At the time of an act, *we are*; we do the act and *we become*. We become, we are. The next time we encounter a challenge, we are better than we were before. This is a virtuous circle in much the same way that a vicious circle means failure leading to failure, resulting over time in a character of failure.

The result is not simple mechanical habits, but "habitus" or a disposition to lead a moral life (Toner 2005, 120).

Some debate exists about which virtues are most important or are essential to other virtues (the cardinal virtues) and Hart (1994, 118) acknowledges that the cardinal virtues must be "intentionally cultivated." Some argue for the minimal number of virtues with others being derived from these cardinal virtues. Frankena (1963, 50) takes this approach and uses benevolence and justice as the essential virtues. Toner (2005), who focuses on the ethics of military officers, stresses prudence, justice, courage, and temperance. The Josephson Institute (2002), on the other hand, has identified six pillars of character (ethical values to guide choices), each of which is associated with additional virtues:

1. *Trustworthiness*
   Honesty
   Integrity
   Reliability (promise keeping)
   Loyalty

2. *Respect*
   Civility, courtesy, and decency
   Dignity and autonomy
   Tolerance and acceptance

3. *Responsibility*
   Accountability
   Pursuit of excellence
   Self-restraint

4. *Fairness*
   Process
   Impartiality
   Equity

5. *Caring*

6. *Citizenship*

Beyond these, Cooper (1987, 324) adds rationality, prudence, respect for law, self-discipline, civility, and independence.

Advantages of the Virtuous Approach

As just noted, one of the advantages of ethics based on virtue is that ethical choice is intuitive. Essentially, one asks the question: "Who shall I be?" This gives what Bernard Mayo (in Sommers 1985, 175) calls a "unity to our answer." It is not the logical unity that a set of principles would purport to provide, but rather "the unity of character. A person's character is not merely a list of dispositions; it has the organic unity of something that is more than the sum of its parts" (175). Thus, whether one's list of virtues is short or long, it should have coherence if one has developed the habits and dispositions that help one achieve an active life in accord with excellence.

From one perspective, it is hard to fault this approach because of its emphasis on goodness. Wouldn't it be desirable to direct an agency full of virtuous employees? Posing the question in this way may, in fact, produce some reservations. For this approach and the others, there are advantages and disadvantages in using the approach in "pure" form as well as some problems that might come from using the model too much—overutilization—and using it too little—underutilization.

The chief advantage is easy accessibility to ethical standards. Virtues commonly draw on the core societal values that are inculcated from childhood. Thus, the administrator does not have to learn how to be virtuous, although his or her virtue must be practiced and honed. Hart (1994, 114) reminds us that one pursues virtue rather than ever achieving it. An additional advantage is that acting virtuously reflects an intention by the individual to be good. Unlike the other approaches that stress reflection and analysis, the virtuous approach is based on positive motives. It is also clearly an individual choice to be virtuous; there is less inclination to rely on or defer to external authority or sources of guidance in resolving ethical issues. In the best sense of the term, virtue can become one's "second nature."

Disadvantages of the Virtuous Approach

Disadvantages of the virtuous approach are several. An administrator may want to *be* good, but does he or she know how to *do* good? In other words, he or she may not know what actions are appropriate for each of the virtues. Definitions of virtues may be circular. For example, Mayo (in Sommers 1985, 172) defines the virtue of justice as "a quality of character, and a just action is one such as a just man would do." To decide what a just person would do without consulting a principle of justice is difficult. In addition, how does one choose among alternative virtues that may lead one to act in different ways (choosing between competing "goods")? The very simplicity of virtues and their proximity to values of everyday living make them poor guides if used exclusively in dealing with complex situations in which the special conditions of the public sector must be taken into account. For example, is it right to participate in an urban renewal project which harms some in the short run—those displaced and relocated even if "fairly" compensated—and destroys some features of the built and natural environment in order to produce change that brings greater benefits to more people in the long run (assuming for the sake of argument that the project actually does accomplish these ends)?

Related to this problem is the question of where the ethical private person ends and the ethical administrator begins. Hart (1994, 116) asserts that "virtue requires that followers *always* question the ends to which their actions are to be directed, and never allow their virtue to be used to advance morally wrong causes." From what perspective, however, does one question the end pursued if one's own ideological preferences or personal (nonmoral) values differ from the values that have been authoritatively and legitimately established through the political process? How does the administrator balance appropriate accountability and respect for political supremacy with being virtuous?

In sum, the truly virtuous administrator may be good but not know how to do good, not know which way to be good among alternative virtues, and not know how to distinguish being good as a private person and as an administrator. It is hard to resolve these issues without reference to other sources of moral guidance that could come from other ethical approaches; by referring to principles or consequences.

Problems with Over- and Underutilization

Other problems occur when an administrator over- or underuses virtue. We cannot dismiss the possibility that an administrator will think that he or she is "too" good. Self-righteousness can lead the administrator to believe that only he or she knows what is right. A sense of moral superiority can follow. Another potential pitfall is confusing being and doing. If an administrator is convinced that he or she is good, then it is not hard to believe that what he or she does is good and right as well: "My goodness makes my actions good" or "my pure motives make my actions pure." The "Robin HUD" case during the Reagan administration that involved a person who misused government funds out of a misplaced definition of goodness is an example (Lewis 1991, 42–43). An independent test of whether one's good-intentioned actions are right based on principles or consequences may be an important corrective.

If the habits of virtue are not firmly established or well-honed, then the problem of drawing guidance from virtue in the choice of action is exacerbated. Relying on virtue potentially permits wide variation in interpretation and action. In addition, one might choose a virtue that works even though it is not the best for a situation, for example, being benevolent when one ought to be just or being loyal when one should be courageous. When virtue is weakly developed, the intuitive approach to decision making can be simplified to the point that ethical content has been lost. The newspaper or mirror tests rely on questions such as "would I want my mother or my children to know I did this?" These tests promote "virtue" only to avoid punishment or embarrassment. If an administrator could convince him- or herself that no one would ever know about an action, then there is no reason not to do it. The gut reaction that can become very sensitive to wrongdoing by developing the habits of virtue can also be desensitized as well by weakly developed virtues and poor habits.

In conclusion, administrators should be virtuous but not only virtuous. They should be intuitive, but also reflective and analytical. The central idea that can be taken from this approach is character.[21] It goes beyond separate virtues that guide facets of behavior (being honest in communication with citizens or being loyal in dealings with the organization) and unifies them into a coherent and comprehensive commitment. Character also links values to action. Character is the "predisposition to behave consistently with one's espoused values and principles" (Cooper 2004, 398). The Josephson Institute (1988) views values as the "pillars" of character. To Edwin DeLattre (1994), the hallmark of ethical police officers is excellence of character. To Toner (2005, 144), "character is about habitus, settled dispositions toward the good."

Deontology and the Principle-Based Approach

If administrators are principled rather than virtuous, they base their ethical decision making on the application of principles. Deontologists use agreed-upon or settled values to determine one's moral obligation to act. Virtue and principles are not in conflict and may reinforce each other. According to the Josephson Institute (1988), "we translate values into principles so they can guide and motivate ethical conduct. Ethical principles are the rules of conduct that derive from ethical values."[22] Still, the principle-based approach would refer to and rely on the rules rather than the virtues. To use this approach, administrators need to have knowledge of a set of principles and the deductive capacity to appropriately apply those principles to actual situations.

Principles identify "kinds of action that are right or obligatory" (Frankena 1963, 49). Rule-deontologists seek to establish principles that will apply to a variety of situations.[23] This approach is closely related to the duty-based approach to ethics.[24] The distinction made is between what is right and obligatory. The principle-based approach emphasizes what is right in a universal or objectively verifiable sense, whereas the duty-based approach emphasizes obligations derived from the nature of the public service role (as presented in Chapter 3). To state the distinction differently, obligations in the duty-based approach may be—but are not always—based on principles. In the principle-based or deontological approach, obligations are based on principles.

A critical issue in this approach is from where the principles come. At a basic level, we look to law as the source of direction for how to act. For administrators to be accountable and responsible, they must be bound by law. A central feature of democratic governments is that they are based on laws, not the personal preferences of the men and women who work for government. If government employees believe that they cannot enforce the law, they should leave government and seek change through the political process.[25] No person is above the law. Staff members in nonprofit organizations do not enforce the law in the same way that government administrators do, but they should uphold the law and observe the legal requirements that govern how an organization operates as a nonprofit with exemption from taxes. To act according to the law, however, does not necessarily mean that one understands the principled basis for the law nor the principles that might raise questions about whether the law is sound. To look only to the law as a source of principle is to remain at Kohlberg's Stage 4 of moral development.

One way to identify universal principles is to identify overarching guidelines from which the principles can be derived. There are two important systematic approaches to identifying principles that are commonly cited in the literature on public administration ethics. One is Kantianism. In Immanuel Kant's approach (adapted from Chandler 1994, 149), consequences or the ends attained by actions are not what determines moral obligation. The moral worth of an action is determined by the principle from which the action is performed. As a guide to developing principles, Kant provided the categorical imperative:

> one should act only as if one were legislating a universal law for everyone to follow in a preferred world.

There are two principles that Kant derived from the categorical imperative that stand out. First, people are never to be treated in an instrumental way as a means to an end, but only as ends in themselves. Second, one should never lie. The Kantian position is that principles are universally and invariably applicable.[26] Thus, one should never deviate from principle regardless of the consequences. This injunction points to the likelihood of tension between the principle-based and the consequentialist approach that we will examine later.

A second major contender for a systematic framework for deriving principles is John Rawls' *Theory of Justice* (1971, 302). Rawls' starting point is to create a hypothetical situation.

> It assumes that the "original position" of persons is behind a "veil of ignorance" which prevents them from knowing their age, sex,

religious beliefs, social standing, etc. In this situation, when they make rational calculations about principles of justice, they will choose two principles:

- First principle: Each person is to have an equal right to the most extensive total system of equal basic liberty compatible with a similar system of liberty for all.

- Second principle: Social and economic inequalities are to be arranged so that they are to the greatest benefit of the least advantaged.

These principles provide a philosophical justification for definitions of equity that target benefits to individuals in need or redistribute resources to reduce social and economic inequalities.

Denhardt (1988, 45) argues that certain principles are widely accepted in western society. These are:

- truth telling
- promise keeping
- the sanctity of the individual
- the sanctity of life
- justice

Additional sources of principles for American public administrators include basic cultural, social, and political values that define a society and its system of governance (called regime values) such as democracy, freedom, property, and the like (Rohr 1989).

David Rosenbloom (1992) has identified the Constitution's protection of substantive rights (freedom of speech, due process, and equal protection) as ethical guides. He also points out, however, that the Constitution that once supported slavery and still permits capital punishment and has limited protection for women's rights cannot be relied on exclusively as a source of ethical principles. Still, there are important principles imbedded in Constitutional amendments. These include[27]:

- All persons have the right of free exercise of religion, freedom of speech and the press, and the right to assemble.
- Every person should be accorded "equal protection of the laws."
- No one will be "deprived of life, liberty, or property without the due process of law."
- Private property can be taken only for public use and with just compensation.
- Persons should not be subjected to unreasonable searches and seizures.
- No person shall be subject to cruel and unusual punishments.

In your view, what are the most important principles that should guide the work of public administrators? To some extent, the answer will vary with the nature of one's work and responsibilities and with work in government and nonprofit organizations. Other principles will apply to all those who serve the public. How would you answer this question?

Issues in the Principle-Based Approach

Several issues need to be resolved regarding the deontological approach before proceeding to an assessment. One is the source of principles, which we have already considered. In addition, conflict among principles and exceptions to principles are additional issues.

A commonly cited problem with the deontological approach is conflict among principles. Not only may these instructions that counter each other immobilize the administrator as he or she ponders which principle to follow, but the conflict casts doubt on the universality of principles. If one does not always follow a principle, how can it be universally applicable? Frankena (1963, 23) explains that a distinction can be made between actual duty and *prima facie* duty, "between what is *actually* right and what is *prima facie* right." The latter refers to a principle that is a "duty other things being equal, that is, it would be an actual duty if other moral considerations did not intervene" (24). One should always try to act in terms of a *prima facie* duty but on occasion it may be outweighed by another. According to the Josephson Institute (1988), it is ethically proper to violate an ethical principle when it is clearly necessary to advance another true ethical principle. The National Association of Social Work (NASW) (1999), which builds its code of ethics around a set of principles, does not specify an ordering of principles or which ought to take precedence over others when they conflict. The association leaves it to the "informed judgment of the individual to make a decision, taking into account how the issues would be judged in the peer review process" (NASW 1999). To some, the deontological approach requires a set of principles that constitute "a system and not merely an aggregate," as Mayo (in Sommers 1985, 175) argues, and "the attempt to construct a deductive moral system is notoriously difficult." Public administrators can draw on a number of sources of principles, as we have seen, but is there coherence and internal logic among these principles?

A related issue is how to handle exceptions. If one allows for exceptions to be made, does this not also call into question universality? Once again, Frankena offers a straightforward solution. If an exception is built into the principle, it is not an exception but part of the principle. Sissela Bok (1989, 30) essentially does this when she identifies carefully limited exceptions to the principle that public officials must tell the truth to the public. Dealing with exceptions complicates the deontological approach but does not invalidate it.

These issues all raise questions about the extent to which one must be universally directed by a coherent system of principles in order to behave ethically. Although this is a perplexing intellectual question, in practice, we will not rely only on the principle-based approach to provide such complete guidance. The logic of the three perspective approach is that principles alone do not determine ethical choices.

A pragmatic approach can be taken to determine which principles to follow. Like Denhardt, it seems likely that administrators will commonly look first for a principle-based answer to an ethical problem, although this reliance should not mean that one is trapped in a Stage 4 dependence on following the rules. The logic of using virtue and consequences as well as principles negates the idea that principles are universally applicable. For public administrators, one may suggest the following approach to sorting out principles.

Determine what other principles are relevant to the situation.

If there is a constitutional principle involved, it should take precedence over other principles.

Apply the *prima facie* versus actual duty test to the other principles.

If the appropriate choice is still not obvious, turn to the other ethical perspectives for guidance, as we shall see later in this chapter.

Advantages of the Principle-Based Approach

The advantages of this approach are fourfold. First, it provides an external source of ethical guidance. The principles are greater than oneself, one's organization, and one's society. Rather than relying on what any of these sources might say about how one should behave, there is the guidance of universal ethical principles to apply to specific situations. Second, the principles are by their nature, good reasons to act—not because of the consequences—but because they are independently valid. Third, the deontological approach reinforces the sense of duty to be ethical. If administrators are public servants, they have an obligation to adhere to basic principles whether it is convenient or advantageous or because it accords with one's sense of virtue. Finally, the principles on which this approach is based offer guidance about how to act or what to do. They are stated in terms of required actions rather than traits one should manifest. They compel action without the distraction, uncertainty, and pitfalls of considering the consequences.

Disadvantages of the Principle-Based Approach

There are, however, problems with the approach. The source issue cannot be ignored. Even though one assembles a comprehensive compendium of Constitutional and universal principles, is it certain they are valid and complete? If a situation arises for which there is no principle, administrators must either adopt a new principle or inappropriately fit the situation to an existing one. Second, the principle-based approach requires knowledge of the principles; they are not intuitive. Third, although a *prima facie* principle may have to give precedence to another, there is still no guidance about the ordering of principles. Which is *prima facie* and which actual? The more the principles are a collection of discrete instructions as opposed to a coherent set, the less clear it will be which should give way to another. Fourth, the deontological approach has been criticized as lacking in positive motives or a spirit of ethical commitment. Stewart and Sprinthall (1994, 344) note the objection that principled reasoning could represent "an extremely 'thin self,' much disembodied from feelings and operating as a cold, calculating version of Immanuel Kant." It can be an essentially analytical approach to ethics unless humanized by virtue. Finally, principles, although they instruct, are not so precise as to preclude disagreements over interpretation and application. Observing a principle could frequently be accomplished by alternative possible actions. How is an administrator to be guided? Choosing among alternatives might need to be guided by virtue and/or identification of stakeholders and consideration of the consequences. In sum, even if administrators seek diligently to base their actions on principle, they may be poorly guided or even misguided by using this approach alone.

Problems of Over- and Underutilization

The possible flaws of underutilization of this approach are mistaking rules and laws for principles. The administrator may rigidly adhere to rules without recognizing that they do not incorporate universal principles. Similarly, the administrator may focus on the letter rather than the spirit of the principle. Overutilization can also produce rigidity if the administrator uses a principle as the basis for unfairly sitting in judgment of the behaviors of others.

In conclusion, the deontological approach offers the ethical anchor that public administrators need. It is more challenging to choose a single central idea that can be taken from this approach, but the most appropriate choice seems to be justice. Not all principles that should be followed by ethical public administrators are directly linked to justice, but many are. A commitment to acting with justice embodies fairness in the treatment of individuals and social equity across groups.

Using this approach to the exclusion of others, however, may fail to provide clear guidance and may produce differing degrees of aloofness and inflexibility. Public administrators should act in a principled way but also be virtuous and consider consequences (without allowing consequences to trump principles). They should be analytical but also be intuitive. The issues of source of principles, universality, ordering, and exceptions do not invalidate the use of principles in making ethical decisions, but these issues remind us that principles must be used with care taking into account the other ethical perspectives.

Consequences-Based Ethics: The Utilitarian Approach

Teleology contrasts with deontology because of its emphasis on ends, purposes, and goals that result from actions rather than principles that precede actions. Consequentialism—one form of the teleological approach—generally and utilitarianism specifically holds that there are no moral principles that provide justification for an action *a priori*. An action is right or wrong depending on its consequences.

Mill (quoted in Richter et al. 1990, 23) rejects the other two approaches when he criticizes applying a "sense of instinct, informing us of right and wrong," or a general principle to a specific case. An action is good insofar as it contributes to good ends. Although there are various ways of calculating benefits depending on whether the individual or society as a whole is the referent, it is generally "ethical universalism," as Frankena (1963, 14) has called it, or utilitarianism that is incorporated into thinking about administrative ethics. When examining utilities for society as a whole, the preferred choice is that which produces the greatest good for the greatest number. One can either assess the consequences of each separate act or assess the consequences of rules that will persist as long as they produce the greatest net good. The problem with the first of these approaches—act utilitarianism—is that one cannot learn from experience in order to formulate general rules (Frankena 1963, 51). Still, it is presumably this form that is typically the focus in discussions of administrative ethics, and I will use act utilitarianism in assessing the consequences-based approach.

The approach appears to be a practical, even savvy, way to prepare our administrator to make tough ethical choices. Its values are pervasive and it is widely practiced. Gerald Pops (1994, 159) observes that the public-choice model is largely derived from utilitarianism: "maximizing individual preferences is the major teleological value." What is sought is "a maximum amount of individual choice (presumably leading to a maximization of satisfactions that citizens can enjoy) in a society" (Pops 1994, 159). H. George Frederickson (1993, 250) notes that in university studies of public administration and public policy, "the teleological perspective holds the high ground." Because of the emphasis on efficiency, cost-benefit analysis, the market model and theories of games, and public choice, Frederickson argues, "what is right or wrong, what is moral or ethical is to be judged in terms of utility of consequences." It is certain that this rationale is used to determine what is more or less preferable; for example, in choosing among policy alternatives, but the use of consequentialist ethical analysis may be more limited. For example, we noted earlier that students rarely include tenets based on consequentialist thinking in their implicit codes of ethics. Is there a distinction between using consequences as the basis for making a decision, on the one hand, and for explicitly making an ethical decision, on the other hand? We shall return to this issue after considering advantages and disadvantages.

Advantages of the Utilitarian Approach

Public administrators like their political superiors are committed to producing positive outcomes. Improving the welfare of society and increasing the happiness of citizens are worthy goals. The utilitarian approach is based on the premise that the action that produces the best outcome is ethically acceptable. Instead of being oblivious to results as could be the case with a virtue-based approach or bound by principles that lead to bad consequences, the approach has the advantage that it looks beyond the act to the consequences of the act in determining whether it is right or wrong. It also permits flexibility. One might argue that it is not right to treat all people who differ in individual characteristics in the same way. Rules are rigid, and flexibility is needed to respond to changing situations. It is what one accomplishes that is important—the results—rather than how it is done, taking into account the interests of all concerned.

Administrators often encounter situations in which action seems to be stymied by constraints that appear to be consistent with ethical requirements. "It wouldn't be right to . . . ," "you are not permitted to . . . ," or "you don't have the authority to . . ." are examples of such arguments. The utilitarian approach offers the possibility of an alternate ethical basis to justify action. For example, does one break a promise that turns out to have unacceptable consequences? Does one lie to a criminal suspect in order to get a confession? Does one break rules to get good results; for example, spend money in the current budget year for work that will be done in another year, or authorize that work commenced to keep a crucial project on schedule even though all reviews of the project have not been completed? The question is whether these rationales can be used in an ethically responsible way.

Disadvantages of the Utilitarian Approach

The problems with the approach are numerous. Rosemary Tong (1986, 82) notes that the approach seems appealing until one starts asking questions such as

- What is happiness?
- Why should it be pursued?
- How is it measured, now and in the future?
- How does one weigh the utility of the many with the harm to the few?
- Are some things intrinsically wrong?

The difficulty in calculating utilities stems in part from the obvious fact that it is not possible to foretell the future nor be aware of all the ramifications of an action. The more complex the act, the more difficult it is to produce convincing comparisons of their consequences (Bok 1989, 51). Applying the reasonable-man test about the future, as Pops (1994, 158) suggests, is acceptable in judging the policy choices made by administrators on nonethical grounds (administrators should be accountable for only those consequences that could "reasonably have been predicted"). Can one justify as *ethically acceptable*, however, an action that would not otherwise have been chosen on the basis of a necessarily imprecise and incomplete calculation of costs and benefits?

A second major flaw is the absence of any intrinsic worth of actions. Bok (1989, 51) objects to the idea of considering a lie and telling the truth to be equivalent as if the rightness or wrongness of each depended entirely on the consequences. As Richter, Burke, and Doig (1990, 2) put it: It is "absurd to imagine that a malevolent act which turns out to have beneficial effects might be considered more ethical than a benevolent one which fails to do so." If an administrator is amoral with regard to means, considering only the ends of his or her actions, there is great potential for abuse. On the other hand, if one says that some means will not be acceptable because they are ethically objectionable, then one presumes that there are some ethically superior ways to behave based on virtue or higher ethical standards derived from principles that override or precede the calculation of utilities. This concession and the other concerns raised preclude a complete reliance on the utilitarian approach.

Third, the information costs of the utilitarian method are high and the analytical capability required is considerable. Knowledge of the impact of decisions declines as one moves to more distant stakeholders. Even without intending to be biased, it is difficult not to give undue weight to the personal or agency impact of a decision. There is a likely "self-bias" that results from knowing best how a decision impacts one's self and one's agency. One also cannot rule out other forms of intentional and unintentional bias. Certain stakeholders may be excluded because of prejudice or their values and preferences may not be adequately understood. A hidden bias that is shared by cost-benefit analysis generally is giving greater weight to costs and benefits that can easily be given a monetary value. For example, the costs of acquiring property and relocating residents in an upper-income neighborhood will be greater than in a low-income neighborhood but the psychological impacts are the same. Indeed, the impact of disrupting the social networks of the poor may be greater than for the wealthy who have more social connections.

Fourth, Bok (1989, 51) argues that some actions are wrong and engaging in them does harm to the perpetrator. Therefore, the impact of committing the act itself must be considered, not just the consequences of the act.

A final fundamental problem is balancing the good of the few and the many. The utilitarian approach could be used to justify benefiting the majority at the expense of the minority. It also could justify a decision because the benefits for the few are so great that they outweigh the costs to the many. As Frankena (1963, 33) put it, "the operation of a rule may be beneficent, that is, it may maximize the sum of good in the world, and yet be unjust in the way in which it distributes this sum."

Problems of Over- and Underutilization

Overutilization of the consequentialist approach does not raise additional concerns. The problems already identified all reflect an excessive reliance on a calculation of net utilities to the exclusion of other tempering or offsetting factors. A number of difficulties, however, are magnified by underutilization. One form of slippage from the ideal would be failing to consider the good for the greatest number. A fallible administrator might give precedence to some stakeholders over others or fail to identify all stakeholders in considering consequences. Now the likelihood of giving too much weight to one's own interest is much greater. It is easy to fall into a Machiavellian perspective which equates the good of the agency with the good of society without calculating all of the consequences of an action. It would not take long moving down a slippery slope to justify expediency and self-serving behavior in the name of utilitarianism. Clearly, such a justification is a perversion of utilitarianism, but there is an inherent risk that an administrator might resort to such thinking if he or she relies exclusively on the utilitarian approach.

The shortcomings of each ethical approach can be offset by using multiple approaches. Public administrators should consider consequences, but not reject the considerations of virtue, which can guide and constrain utilitarian thinking. As Dobel (1999, xii) reminds us, "integrity helps to ensure clarity of reflection and to resist temptation to self-deception." Furthermore, promoting good consequences cannot be allowed to override the clear dictates of principle; some would say ever and others would argue only with clear-minded and intensive scrutiny and overwhelming benefits on the side of the utilitarian alternative. A model to guide this kind of scrutiny in decision making is provided in Chapter 7.

In view of the disadvantages of utilitarianism and the risks associated with using it, should the consequences-based approach be part of an ethical model for public administrators? We can return to the puzzle of reconciling the widespread utilization of consequentialist thinking in decision analysis with its less common use in ethical analysis. One possible explanation is that consequentialism is viewed as *counter* ethical thinking. There are the good reasons for an action based on duty, virtue, or principle, and then there are the realistic considerations (the need to get results and/or the attractiveness of the benefits that can be obtained). This view put simply is that one should not confuse ethics and results. Based on the response of students in my classes, I would contend that most people do not accept the argument that the ends justify the mean as an *ethical* argument. Consequently, it is not subjected to rigorous scrutiny as ethical arguments would be. Given the problems with using utilitarianism, perhaps it is best to let this sentiment prevail without challenge and abandon the use of consequentialism as an ethical approach. It is important, however, to bring utilitarianism into an ethics model in order to identify the requirements that must be met to support an action on utilitarian grounds. That is done here. In the concluding section, we examine how to constrain it by also using the other ethical approaches.

The ideal standard promoted by the utilitarian approach is the greatest good for the greatest number. This is a very demanding test and ground rules should be followed to ensure that self-serving and expedient perversions of the greatest good test do not occur.[28] First, as noted earlier, the assessment of benefits should be "universal" and insofar as possible take into account the consequences for all persons, not a select group. Second, equal consideration should be given so that *all who count, count equally*. Finally, the assessment should be done as if one were a *neutral* observer—consequences for one stakeholder in a decision should not be given higher value than consequences for others. The ideal of achieving the greatest good may require self-sacrifice.

Thinking about all three approaches with their respective advantages and disadvantages, it is evident that the most difficult ethical dilemmas occur when the perspectives are in conflict, in particular the choices derived from principle versus those based on consequences. For example, should one bend the rules to help an individual who is truly in need but does not meet normal eligibility requirements for an assistance program? The same issue presents itself at the level of national and international policy: Should the president set aside international law and treaties in order to advance national security? Considering the nature of professional independence and the need for accountability discussed in Chapter 3, is an administrator ethically bound to resist the use of extreme tactics in interrogation of suspected terrorists—tactics that FBI agents viewed as improper at the detention facility in Guantanamo?

Using the Approaches Together

In common practice, we use more than one perspective to clarify and justify our ethical judgments. For example, in the Guantanamo situation, an FBI agent objected that the practices he observed violated principles that ban torture but were also questionable "in terms of effectiveness" (Zernike 2005). Many proponents of using multiple perspectives among scholars conclude that public administrators should actively utilize the key ideas of each of the three major approaches. Denhardt (1988, 53) concluded that, if philosophers cannot agree on a choice between the competing ethical models, why should public administrators try to do so? She suggests that using various approaches can be helpful.[29] Bok (1989, 55) sorts out her position on the practice of lying by starting with the "principle of veracity." Telling the truth is preferred, and one is expected to not lie. The ethical weight is on the side of truthfulness because telling the truth normally requires no justification whereas lying does require justification. For a lie to ever be justified, it needs to produce clear balance of benefit over harm. Thus, a consequentialist ground for making an exception is offered. Stewart and Sprinthall (1994, 344–345) advocate "principled" ethical reasoning consistent with the highest stages of moral development, but they recognize the importance of both principle and virtue to ethical reasoning. Such a balance is reflected in Kohlberg's definition of Stage 5 of moral development that seeks to promote benefits for all (consequentialist) and Stage 6 that refers to an "orientation to conscience [i.e., virtue] or principles, not only to ordained social rules but to principles of choice appealing to logical universality and consistency; conscience is a directing agent, together with mutual respect and trust" (in Stewart and Sprinthall 1994, 327). Rest et al. (1999, 42) also refer to the "principled" postconventional stage based on "ideals for society" that are the following: creating the greatest good for all (consequence), mandating fair treatment and guaranteeing minimal rights and protection for everyone (principle), engendering caring and intimacy among people (virtue), and furthering the common good (duty).

The merging of philosophical perspectives in describing the postconventional level creates some confusion over the use of the term *principled* to label the P stage, as Rest and associates and Stewart and Sprinthall do. Thinking at this level may be based on principle, but it may also be based on virtue or utilitarian thinking as they make clear. To avoid confusion between one of the ethical approaches and all of the possible bases for the highest stage of ethical reasoning, we shall refer to the postconventional level as the *universal-values stage* because it may draw on any one or a combination of the approaches.

Logic of Combining Approaches

Garofalo and Geuras (1999, Chapter 4) propose a "unified ethical theory" that combines teleological, virtue-based, deontological, and intuitive approaches to ethical thinking. They argue that deontology and teleology are two different ways of seeing the same thing; or in the case of ethics, of explaining or justifying the same action. For example, advocating a program to promote social equity across racial groups may reflect both a commitment to the principle of justice and also the intent to improve the living conditions of a minority group. To Garofalo and Geuras, a correct teleological act is also correct deontologically and vice versa, even though the actor may not be aware of the other aspect of his or her decision. Furthermore, virtue and intuitively "good" actions contribute to social happiness. Garofalo and Geuras (1999, 125) offer this summary argument:

> Human reasoning, love of happiness, benevolence, respect for moral character, and intuitive reactions are almost certainly parts of a unified, evolved human nature. If so, deontology, teleology, character theory, and intuitionism must be in a unified harmony.

In later work, they suggest using questions associated with each approach to help determine how to resolve ethical problems (Geuras and Garofalo 2002, 60–67). The approaches sometimes lead to different conclusions, but they each help to illuminate the problem. We will suggest using a similar approach as part of a problem solving model presented in Chapter 7.

With three major parts to his argument, Frankena provides a convincing argument for the complementarity of all three approaches. First, utilitarianism is not acceptable without a deontological mooring. If we would agree that "a less beneficent rule which is more just" is preferable to one that produces greater net utility but is less just, then the criterion for determining the rules of morality combines justice and utility (1963, 33). Second, he argues that the deontological approach, though superior to others, depends as well on utilitarianism. Deontologists are not sufficiently concerned about the "promotion of good" (29). He prefers a "mixed deontological theory, since it recognizes the principle of utility as a valid one, but insists that another principle is required as well." In other words, one should not act on the basis of consequences alone. Third, Frankena sees principle and virtue as interdependent. It is not necessary to choose one or the other.

> It is hard to see how a morality of principles can get off the ground
> except through the development of dispositions to act in accor-
> dance with its principles, else all motivation to act on them must
> be of an *ad hoc* kind, either prudential or impulsively altruistic.
> Moreover, morality can hardly be content with a mere conformity
> to rules, . . . unless it has no interest in the spirit of the law but
> only in its letter. On the other hand, one cannot conceive of traits
> of character except as dispositions and tendencies to act in cer-
> tain ways in certain circumstances (53).

It would be hard to know what virtues to develop "if we did not subscribe to
principles" (Frankena 1963). Thus, he views these two approaches not as
competitors but as "complementary aspects of the same morality." For every
principle there is a supporting virtue.[30] Thus, the commitment to utility and
the principles of benevolence and justice are supported by the cardinal
virtues of benevolence and justice.[31]

Examples from Ethics Guidelines

Guidelines offered by organizations that work with practitioners also illustrate how the different approaches can be blended. A major examination of
ethics in nonprofit organizations culminated in the publication of the *Statement of Values and Code of Ethics* by the Independent Sector in 2004.[32] The
key values identified in the study are presented here grouped into the categories of duty and the three philosophical approaches:

1. Obligations/duty: Behavior expected of public servants as trustees
   or stewards.
   - Commitment beyond self
   - Obedience of the laws
   - Accountable to the public
   - Commitment to public good; service orientation
   - Responsible stewardship of resources
2. Virtue
   - Openness and honesty
   - Benevolence
3. Principles *making decisions based on the law*
   - Respect the worth and dignity of individuals
   - Tolerance, diversity, and social justice
4. Benefits to society
   - Commitment to the public good

Thus, all four elements provide a comprehensive and mutually reinforcing
set of expectations.

Similarly, the decision-making model of the Josephson Institute contains three guidelines that draw on all the approaches. First, all decisions must take into account and reflect a concern for the interest and well-being of all stakeholders (duty and consequentialism). Second, ethical values and principles always take precedence over nonethical ones (virtue and principle). Third, it is ethically proper to violate an ethical principle only when it is clearly necessary to advance another true ethical principle (principle). This guideline addresses the problem of establishing an ordering among principles. The criterion, used to make the choice is as follows: The principle to be followed is the one, which, according to the decision-maker's conscience (virtue), will produce the greatest balance of good in the long run (consequentialism). Rather than being caught up in the differences among the approaches, the Josephson Institute uses them to support each other.

The Ethics Triangle

Following the lead of scholars and professional associations who have supported the combined use of all ethical approaches, it can be argued that each of the three depends on and is supported by the others. Furthermore, the responsibilities derived from duty give a focus and direction to the ethical commitments of public administrators. Drawing on the philosophical perspectives, what virtues, principles, and consequences are in the public interest? The elements can be combined to form a triangle with duty at the center. Using this graphic representation of the model suggests that the four elements are interconnected and contained within a common space. The central ideal is the public interest, and the ideals at each point of the triangle are character, justice, and the greatest good. The model of administrative ethics is presented in **Figure 4.1**. The ethics triangle conveys the idea that administrators should act on their duty to promote the public interest by seeking a balance of virtue, principle, and good consequences.

Using the ethics triangle helps to prevent the problems associated with using any of the models alone. The examples of overutilization discussed earlier illustrate the problem of stressing one approach excessively to the exclusion of other ethical considerations. For example, the possibility that the principle-based approach will lead to rigidity is offset by considering how to achieve the greatest good and thinking about what it means to be virtuous in a given situation. The misguided pursuit of virtue can be informed by principle and refocused by assessing consequences. The pursuit of a beneficial end without considering the ethical implications of means that are being used can be checked by principle and humanized by virtue.

When used separately and underutilized, the approaches can even appear to justify behavior that is unethical. Narrow adherence to principle might appear to justify blindly following orders. Concern for consequences can become expediency. A self-righteous man who believes himself to be good may assume that his questionable actions are good. Such a man may feel that the normal rules do not apply, as in the rationalization "I can't be bought by a free meal" for ignoring restrictions on gratuities. Moving out from the triangle narrows the basis for ethical choice and may even permit such unethical actions. Operating from within the triangle reinforces the bases for ethical action and helps to prevent the shortcomings of underutilizing any single approach. It is much more difficult to underutilize all three models simultaneously.

In Chapter 7, we will use the elements of the model as distinct filters that reveal different aspects of a situation requiring an ethical choice. This method helps to clarify the options and ethical considerations associated with each approach. Using all the approaches together helps to prevent the shortcomings of using any of the approaches alone. The use of all three approaches also balances different ways of thinking about ethical issues. The virtue-based approach relies on feeling and reflection, the principle-based uses reason, and the consequentialist approach stresses analysis. Individual weaknesses in one of these ways of thinking can be offset by strengths in others.

What is the advantage of using the ethics triangle over relying on the basic components of ethics (from Chapter 2) to which persons in public administration commonly adhere? If one examines the tenets listed by students in their implicit codes of ethics, there are differences in level and depth of ethical reasoning compared to the ethics triangle. The statements based on simple defini-

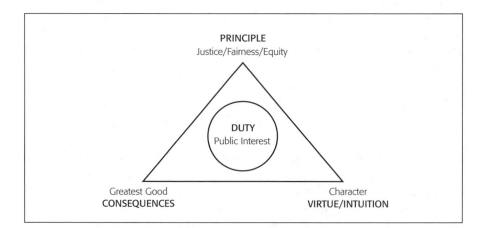

Figure 4–1 *The Ethics Triangle: Key Elements and Central Ideals*
Source: Adapted from Svara (1997). Used with the permission of the Council of State Governments.

tions of duty and public service do not include references to the relationship to elected officials, promoting the democratic process, or seeking to improve policy, and they give relatively little attention to the overarching goal of advancing the public interest. All of these are part of the refined sense of duty elaborated in Chapter 3. The statements based on virtue do not mention benevolence or the pursuit of excellence nor the overarching goal of displaying character. The principle-based statements do not include universal principles such as the sanctity of life, treating each person as an end in him- or herself, basic human rights or Constitutional principles, or challenging improper or illegal orders. Although there is concern for fairness, the broader principle of justice is not included. Finally, as noted previously, the consequentialist perspective is largely missing from the ethical tenets, and there is no reference to promoting the greatest good for the greatest number as a standard. As a public administrator, you may choose to include these standards in your own professional code of ethics, but you should at least consider them and decide whether these standards or others best define your professional values and responsibilities.

The ethics triangle combines standards that reflect a universal-values or postconventional stage of ethical reasoning. For each of the elements, you are challenged to think about what you should do and what qualities you should display based on an assessment of the ideal pursuit associated with that element—the public interest, character, justice, and the greatest good. You are not simply reacting to standards set by authority figures or conforming to prevailing expectations. It is important to consider what you are expected to do or how you are expected to be as determined by others, but the ethics triangle encourages you to go beyond these considerations and form judgments that reflect broader considerations. The administrator who deals with an ethical problem caused by an inappropriate order from a superior using the Stage 4 level of reasoning may be uncomfortable with the order and wish there were an alternative but carry out the order based on a sense of obligation to obey a superior. Using the ethics triangle helps the administrator to approach the problem at the universal-values level. Thinking in terms of a higher sense of duty and drawing on the three approaches will help the administrator to see alternatives and also to justify using the alternative course of action. This administrator is better able to exercise independent judgment and display ethical autonomy. The following three specific cases help to illustrate the interaction among the three points of the triangle.

Case 1:

A candidate for a city manager's position is asked by the council to agree to fire the public works director and told that the other finalist for the job has agreed to do so. The beneficial consequences of getting a job the candidate really wants and having the opportunity to do good work may tempt her to agree to the condition. Recognizing her loss of integrity if she accepts such a demand and considering the principles of fairness in personnel decisions and upholding the city manager's authority over management decisions restrain her. Upon further reflection, even the consequentialist approach cannot justify accepting this incursion on her authority and opening the possibility for similar inappropriate demands in the future. The short-term gain of getting the position is offset by the long-term negative consequences to herself, the organization, and the city.

Case 2:
Proper sting operations by law enforcement agencies reflect a balancing that is consistent with using the triangle. Although the organizers of the operation may feel uncomfortable about being deceptive and principles of fairness and due process are stretched by such operations, the beneficial consequences are the deciding factor. Concern for principle helps to ensure, however, that the operation is not carried out in such a way that it represents entrapment.

Case 3:
A data analyst in a community college becomes aware that enrollment figures are being padded to increase the state allocation. Although he feels that the college is severely underfunded and that the extra revenue will improve the performance of the college, his personal sense of honesty and concern about violating the professional principles of providing complete and accurate information compel him to disclose the abuse.

In all these cases, using the triangle helps to modify decisions that might have been made based on a single approach.

Promoting Use of the Ethics Triangle

The ethics triangle suggests that the valuable aspects of each approach should be incorporated in one's own ethical reasoning without ignoring that any of the approaches used alone can produce problems. This broad-based strategy supports what York Willbern (1984, 107) has called the "ethic of compromise and social integration." It both helps the administrator determine how far to stray from principle to make a deal and also provides the perspective to help arbitrate between "saints" who, Willbern warns, may be intent on cutting each other's throats over differing interpretations of what is ethical.

In order to draw out key ideas associated with each approach, students and managers should internalize these ideas. Questions to guide the discussion would include the following:

- How can the public interest be advanced in general and in particular situations? What are my responsibilities to the organization, political superiors, and to the public?

- What virtues should public administrators generally or persons working within a specific field or agency have? What do these virtues mean, and how does one act in terms of each? In general, what does it mean to have integrity and character?

- What should one do to promote justice, to ensure fairness, and to expand equity? What are the most important principles that should guide any public administrator and a person working in a specific field or agency? How would one prioritize the principles? Are there any that can never be set aside to advance another principle? What does it mean to apply these principles to specific situations?

- How can the greatest good for the greatest number be achieved in making a specific decision? What ends should public administrators or persons working within a specific field or agency seek to advance? How should one ensure that all stakeholders have been identified and that the calculation of benefits and costs is universal, equal, and complete? Can the means to be used be reconciled with the standards of the public interest, virtue, and principle?

Answering these questions promotes the grasp of a wide range of ethical behavior and reasoning. For example, a city manager could develop an ethical profile using the triangle. He would identify those traits that define his character and assess how well they are developed and displayed. He would consider the principles—universal, constitutional, and professional—that must be followed even if unpopular with elected officials or the public. These might include promoting justice, treating each person in the organization and the community as an end in themselves, a commitment to telling the truth, a defense of basic freedoms, support for the democratic process, and upholding the integrity of professional practice. He would think about how to advance the public interest in the community and how to achieve the most beneficial consequences. Finally, he could think about whether any of these various commitments might conflict with others, and how those conflicts might be resolved.

In conclusion, examination of the bases for administrative ethics is challenging and complex, but it should not confuse the student or the administrator. It should help to broaden learning and self-awareness and, in so doing, promote a renewed commitment to meeting obligations, being good, doing what is right, and promoting the best possible consequences. Whereas debates over why one approach is superior and others are deficient can muddy the ethical waters, using the ethics triangle can help to clarify the different ways to promote ethics and give the public administrator solid, mutually reinforcing, and universal grounds for action.

Chapter 5

Codifying Duty and Ethical Perspectives:

Codes of Ethics

Codes of ethics bring together the expectations that apply to persons who work in government or nonprofits or who belong to professional associations. In government, codes convey how the public interest will be advanced. Nonprofit organizations are voluntary associations of people that promote a mission to accomplish some social good. In nonprofit organizations, a code asserts the kinds of values that they seek to advance in order to be true to their purpose.

In the discussion of codes of ethics in this chapter, references will be made to the following codes of ethics, which will be included in the appendices:

- Code of Ethics for Government Service (**Appendix 2**)
- American Society for Public Administration (ASPA), Code of Ethics (**Appendix 3**)
- International City Management Association (ICMA), Code of Ethics with commentary (**Appendix 4**)
- Independent Sector (IS), Code of Ethics for Nonprofit and Philanthropic Organizations (**Appendix 5**)
- American Institute of Certified Planners (AICP), Code of Ethics and Professional Conduct (**Appendix 6**)

The code listed first contains minimum standards and is included to compare with the more elaborate codes. The others represent important statements for generalist administrators in government from the ASPA and ICMA, a comprehensive statement for administrators in nonprofit organizations from the IS, and a code for a group of professionals who often work in public settings from the AICP. References will also be made to the code of the National Association of Social Workers, but because of its length and specialized nature it is not presented in full in an appendix.

When examining codes, one finds five different kinds of statements. The distinctions are useful because the style used reflects differences in the degree of specificity and clarity that can be found in codes of ethics.

1. "Don't" statements.

   These tenets cover prohibited activities or behaviors. These statements tend to be the most specific but do not do much to elevate ethical thinking. Although based on duty or principles, these are typically rule-based tenets. It is clear what one should not do, but it is not necessarily obvious what the larger aspect of duty or principle is to be advanced. These tenets are intended to reduce misbehavior, but they do not necessarily promote positive ethical behavior. Over all the codes, these are the second most common form of statement. Examples include:
   - Code of Ethics for Government Service: Four of the 10 are don't statements.
   - ICMA 12: Seek no favor.

2. Obligations and responsibilities.

   These tenets set forth the things one must or should do. They are based on duty and/or principle. They tend to be somewhat general and subject to interpretation. They are the most common type of statement overall. Examples include:
   - ASPA I, 6: Respond to the public in ways that are complete, clear, and easy to understand.
   - ICMA 10: Resist any encroachment on professional responsibilities, believing the member should be free to carry out official policies without interference, and handle each problem without discrimination on the basis of principle and justice.
   - AICP A, 1, f: We shall seek social justice by working to expand choice and opportunity for all persons, recognizing a special responsibility to plan for the needs of the disadvantaged and to promote racial and economic integration. We shall urge the alteration of policies, institutions, and decisions that oppose such needs.

3. Virtues, personal qualities, and/or values.

   Like the virtue-based approach to ethics, these tenets are essentially statements about how one should be rather than what one should do. They are even more general than obligations and require translation of *being* into *doing*.

- ASPA I-5: Exercise compassion, benevolence, fairness, and optimism.
- ICMA 3: Be dedicated to the highest ideals of honor and integrity.

4. *Aspirations* (desirable conditions one seeks to promote as opposed to actions or personal qualities)

    These are the most general statements. As with virtues, one must think about what actions should be taken in order to achieve these conditions.

    - ICMA 1: Be dedicated to the concepts of effective and democratic local government by responsible elected officials.

To provide another illustration of the types of statements, examine a classic and stirring statement of ethical standards: the Athenian Oath.[33] Although not a code of ethics per se, it has the same purpose as a code—to set standards of behavior for members of an association, in this case, citizens of the city of Athens. The statements in the oath represent each of the five categories.

- Don't/Virtue: We will never bring disgrace on this our City by an act of dishonesty or cowardice.
- Obligation: We will fight for the ideals and sacred things of the City both alone and with many.
- Obligation: We will revere and obey the City's laws, and
- Obligation: will do our best to incite a like reverence and respect in those above us who are prone to annul them or set them at naught.
- Obligation: We will strive increasingly to quicken the public's sense of civic duty.
- Aspiration: Thus in all these ways we will transmit this City, not only not less, but greater and more beautiful than it was transmitted to us.

The oath is not a complete statement of values. It assumes that one knows the "ideals and sacred things" mentioned in the second bullet for which one is obligated to fight as well as knowing what is required in the laws. It is also not very precise. Still, the oath offers guidance about how one should behave and is the basis for in-depth consideration of what it means to be ethical. If individuals and groups were to seriously examine what the oath means and their responsibilities in following it, this short, general statement could provide the foundation for highly ethical behavior.

With these examples, it is possible to offer an initial view of the purpose of codes of ethics. Bowman (1990) suggests that codes may be designed to be regulatory, educational, or inspirational. Stated differently, codes serve to *constrain* and set limits by identifying behaviors that should be avoided. They *guide* or instruct by identifying obligations and desirable qualities. It is helpful when there is commentary that accompanies a code, such as the material provided by ICMA that examines specific situations that illustrate a tenet and explains how the tenet is applied to the situation. Finally, they can *inspire* and set forth the broad goals that the adherents are supposed to promote. The goals expressed in the inspirational tenets in codes are akin to the "internal goods" that associations (or "practices") are supposed to advance (Cooper 1987).

In the discussion that follows, three objections to codes of ethics are examined: Codes of ethics are not necessary, not oriented to broad and significant standards, and not enforced. The first two criticisms will be considered along with a close analysis of the contents of major public governmental and nonprofit codes. Finally, the enforcement processes used by professional associations will be examined to address the third criticism.

Breadth and Purpose of Codes

John Ladd (1980) raises a fundamental question: Why should a code be necessary? Ethics cannot be set by fiat. In this view, having a code contradicts the notion of ethics itself. This approach, like the ethics requirements often found in organizational policies, reflects a "low road" to ethics (Rohr 1989) by spelling out exactly what one should do or should not do. Ethics involves reflective choice, not simply following rules.

This criticism implies that codes operate only at the Stage 4 level of ethical reasoning (the sense that one should follow law and established conventions in society). In actuality, codes differ in the mix of tenets that are negative, narrow, and rule-based and those that are broader in scope. As noted previously, the Code for Government Employees (in Appendix 2) has many "don't" statements and generally sets minimal standards. The other codes, however, have a balance of statement types. As noted in the examples of types of statements, most of the statements in the other codes include numerous and fairly wide-ranging obligations and responsibilities.

A counterargument can be offered to support including some rule-based statements in a code. The behavior that is proscribed or prescribed may be obvious to all persons covered by the code but its inclusion is a signal to those outside the association of what are the basic standards of the association. Other statements may cover areas in which the standards are not completely clear. There may be benefits for some staff members in government and nonprofit organizations in specifying what seems obvious to others. A tenet that spells out the inappropriateness of taking an action when experiencing a potential conflict of interest or that requires that confidential information be protected are possible examples. The clarity may be useful for persons operating at Stages 3 or 4 of moral development, because such persons may engage in behaviors unless they are prohibited and not undertake certain behaviors unless they are required. These staff members are not ethical exemplars to be sure, but they are not necessarily inclined to be unethical. The presence of narrow statements may make them more ethical than they would be in the absence of the code.

A related but distinct criticism is that codes focus on micro- rather than macroethics. The latter refers to the "social responsibilities of professionals as a group" and what they can and should do "to influence social policy" (Ladd 1980, 156). Once again, a question to be answered in examining a particular code is whether its tenets include macro responsibilities. For example, after reviewing the ICMA code (in Appendix 4), these questions could be raised (Svara 1987, 14):

- Does the city manager have an obligation to protect basic values of American society and the community served? For example, if constitutional rights are threatened by restrictive parade control that the city council wants to adopt, does the manager have an obligation to raise objections?

- Does the city manager have the obligation to promote equity in proposing goals and policies and in delivering services?

- What are the quality standards of completeness and objectivity in presenting alternatives in policy proposals? In other words, is the manager required to present objective information about all alternatives and compare them fairly?

- Should the manager be expected to give active encouragement to citizen participation and offer assistance to those less likely to participate based on their own resources and level of interest? Should the manager affirmatively seek out the poor and the powerless and encourage them to get involved? Should the manager help persons participate who disagree with the council?

- Should the manager promote efficiency and effectiveness and periodically reexamine whether existing programs should be continued and how they should be delivered (for example, whether by the city staff or through contracting out)? Should the manager be willing to ask whether a program should be terminated?

One could argue that all of these questions refer to responsibilities that public administrators should observe and I would agree. Still, none of these questions or the responsibilities related to them is explicitly addressed in the ICMA code. Does this mean that the ICMA code is too narrow in scope?[34] Does it fail to guide managers in handling complex and demanding issues?

The ASPA code is comprehensive (with five sections and 32 specific tenets), but it also overlooks some macro issues. Looking at the same issues raised with regard to the ICMA code, the ASPA code (in Appendix 3) has a section entitled Respect the Constitution and Law, which urges administrators to "respect, study, and support government constitutions and laws." However, it specifically mentions only the Constitutional principles of "honesty, fairness, representativeness, responsiveness, and due process" and not, for example, protecting freedom of speech or forbidding unreasonable searches. The ASPA code does not mention equity or social justice and limits the expected policy contributions of administrators (in Section II, tenet 2) to working to change laws that are "counter-productive and obsolete" rather than more generally to changing laws to advance the public interest. (This tenet is not included in Section I in the code that pertains to the Public Interest.) The code asserts that administrators should "take responsibility for their mistakes" but not more generally take responsibility for their actions. The code specifies that administrators should "involve citizens in policy decision-making" but makes no references to affirmative efforts directed at those with fewer political resources. The ASPA code does refer generally to applying "ethics, efficiency and effectiveness in serving the public," but it does not refer to reexamining the efficacy of established programs and practices.

There is strong emphasis on the social responsibilities of professionals in the Code of the American Institute of Certified Planners (in Appendix 6). AICP distinguishes between the opening section of the code which presents a "statement of aspirational principles that constitute the ideals" to which members of the association are committed. The members pledge to "strive to act in accordance with our stated principles" but the failure to meet these principles "cannot be the subject of a misconduct charge or be a cause for disciplinary action." The second section presents rules of conduct to which all members are held accountable. Failure to comply with these can result in ethics charges and investigations.

Overall, the members of AICP espouse the goal of "building better, more inclusive communities." The aspirational section spells out responsibilities to the public, clients and employees, and to the profession and colleagues. The public responsibility is grounded in the obligation to serve the public interest.

> We, therefore, owe our allegiance to a conscientiously attained concept of the public interest that is formulated through continuous and open debate. We shall achieve high standards of professional integrity, proficiency, and knowledge.

To meet this obligation, the members aspire to meet principles that include the following:

a. We shall always be conscious of the rights of others.

b. We shall give people the opportunity to have a meaningful impact on the development of plans and programs that may affect them. Participation should be broad enough to include those who lack formal organization or influence.

c. We shall seek social justice by working to expand choice and opportunity for all persons, recognizing a special responsibility to plan for the needs of the disadvantaged and to promote racial and economic integration. We shall urge the alteration of policies, institutions, and decisions that oppose such needs.

d. We shall promote excellence of design and endeavor to conserve and preserve the integrity and heritage of the natural and built environment.

e. We shall deal fairly with all participants in the planning process. Those of us who are public officials or employees shall also deal evenhandedly with all planning process participants.

In their responsibility to clients and employers, the members aspire to "exercise independent professional judgment on behalf of our clients and employers," to accept the directions of clients or employers regarding the objectives and the services performed "unless the course of action is illegal or plainly inconsistent with our primary obligation to the public interest," and to avoid actual or apparent conflicts of interest. Finally, in the responsibility to the profession and colleagues, the members aspire to promote the integrity of the profession, educate the public about planning issues, share knowledge from experience and research, critically examine theories and practices, support development of colleagues and students, develop themselves, examine ethical issues, and provide pro bono assistance to groups lacking adequate planning resources. The code acknowledges that these principles can compete with each other and that "an ethical judgment often requires a conscientious balancing, based on the facts and context of a particular situation and on the precepts of the entire Code." To a greater extent than the ICMA or ASPA codes, the AICP code addresses a wide range of macroethical issues.

The enforceable section of the code consists of 25 don't statements involving a wide range of professional practices that impact the public, the profession and peers, clients, employers, public officials, and other decision makers. In a way not found in the other codes for public officials that we have examined, the AICP code balances the rule-based and broad ethical principles.

Another statement with two elements is the Independent Sector's extensive code of ethics for nonprofit and philanthropic organizations, building on its statement regarding the social responsibility of nonprofit organizations in the report *Obedience to the Unenforceable* (IS 2002). It begins with the statement of values listed in Chapter 4, which includes advancing the broad but not defined values of the public good, respect for the worth and dignity of individuals, and social justice. The code is organized in 11 ethical principles dealing with personal and professional integrity, mission, governance, legal compliance, responsible stewardship, openness and disclosure, program evaluation, inclusiveness and diversity, and fundraising. These are positive in orientation and in the areas of governance, stewardship, and fundraising contain detailed specifications of how the principle is to be carried out.

The National Association of Social Workers also grounds ethical tenets in broad statements of principle. The complete code statement including introductory material is not included in the appendices with the other codes because of its length. Some key features, however, are worthy of note. The NASW code provides an outstanding example of one that is broad and challenging in its scope and depth. It begins by linking the code to the practice: "professional ethics are at the core of social work" and affirms that the profession has the "obligation to articulate its basic values, ethical principles, and ethical standards" (NASW 1999). Similar to the AICP, the code organizes standards in the areas of responsibilities to clients, to colleagues, in practice settings, as professionals, to the social work profession, and to the broader society. The code is distinctive compared to the others examined by starting with a full elaboration of the profession's core values and a set of broad ethical principles based on them. They are presented in **Figure 5.1**.

The code goes on to specify in great detail (over 50 general statements and over 150 detailed substatements) the ethical standards that apply to the activities of social workers. Like AICP, it makes the distinction between standards that are enforceable guidelines and standards that are aspirational but leaves it to the individual to decide which is which rather than separating the code into two types of statements.

In sum, when examining a code, one can usefully analyze the following features:

- types of statements
- focus and scope: whether excessively narrow and rule oriented or balanced with such statements and others that require reflection and judgment
- coverage: whether the statement is comprehensive or omits important responsibilities; whether it is sufficiently detailed or too detailed
- breadth and reach: whether broad social responsibilities—macroethical issues—are included
- clarity: whether the code clearly sets forth standards that can be used to judge the behavior of administrators if their actions are challenged

Value: *Service*

Ethical Principle: *Social workers' primary goal is to help people in need and to address social problems.*
Social workers elevate service to others above self-interest. Social workers draw on their knowledge, values, and skills to help people in need and to address social problems. Social workers are encouraged to volunteer some portion of their professional skills with no expectation of significant financial return (pro bono service).

Value: *Social Justice*

Ethical Principle: *Social workers challenge social injustice.*
Social workers pursue social change, particularly with and on behalf of vulnerable and oppressed individuals and groups of people. Social workers' social change efforts are focused primarily on issues of poverty, unemployment, discrimination, and other forms of social injustice. These activities seek to promote sensitivity to and knowledge about oppression and cultural and ethnic diversity. Social workers strive to ensure access to needed information, services, and resources; equality of opportunity; and meaningful participation in decision making for all people.

Value: *Dignity and Worth of the Person*

Ethical Principle: *Social workers respect the inherent dignity and worth of the person.*
Social workers treat each person in a caring and respectful fashion, mindful of individual differences and cultural and ethnic diversity. Social workers promote clients' socially responsible self-determination. Social workers seek to enhance clients' capacity and opportunity to change and to address their own needs. Social workers are cognizant of their dual responsibility to clients and to the broader society. They seek to resolve conflicts between clients' interests and the broader society's interests in a socially responsible manner consistent with the values, ethical principles, and ethical standards of the profession.

Value: *Importance of Human Relationships*

Ethical Principle: *Social workers recognize the central importance of human relationships.*
Social workers understand that relationships between and among people are an important vehicle for change. Social workers engage people as partners in the helping process. Social workers seek to strengthen relationships among people in a purposeful effort to promote, restore, maintain, and enhance the well-being of individuals, families, social groups, organizations, and communities.

Value: *Integrity*

Ethical Principle: *Social workers behave in a trustworthy manner.*
Social workers are continually aware of the profession's mission, values, ethical principles, and ethical standards and practice in a manner consistent with them. Social workers act honestly and responsibly and promote ethical practices on the part of the organizations with which they are affiliated.

Value: *Competence*

Ethical Principle: *Social workers practice within their areas of competence and develop and enhance their professional expertise.*
Social workers continually strive to increase their professional knowledge and skills and to apply them in practice. Social workers should aspire to contribute to the knowledge base of the profession.

Source: National Association of Social Workers 1999. Used with the permission of the National Association of Social Workers.

Figure 5–1 *National Association of Social Workers Ethical Principles*

An overarching question is how well the code balances elevating ethical thinking with establishing standards for conduct. It stands to reason that the broader and more inspirational the code, the more difficult it may be to use it as a guide to enforcing ethical standards. The AICP and NASW have addressed this issue by having two parts: one aspirational and one a detailed statement of standards that can be the basis for an ethics investigation.

Enforcement of Codes

A fundamental criticism of codes of ethics is that they have no impact because they are not enforced. If it is left to the individual to decide whether they will follow the code, then the idea of shared professional standards is meaningless. This is a serious limitation when it is true, but the nature of the enforcement process varies greatly. There are no enforcement procedures for the Code for Government Employees. The code of the IS is meant to be a guide to individual organizations, which are encouraged to adopt and presumably enforce their own code. The process may be discretionary as in the case of ASPA, which permits the national council to make a decision on its own. The council may terminate membership "when in its sole and absolute discretion the Council determines that any member appears to have acted in violation of the Society's Code of Ethics" (ASPA 2005).[35]

ICMA and AICP both have a detailed process for receiving complaints, investigating them, providing a judgment that can absolve the complainant of wrongdoing or draw on a range of sanctions, and appealing the judgment.[36] In the ICMA process, the executive director advised by the Committee on Professional Conduct (CPC) makes an initial determination about whether a complaint is covered by ICMA's ethical standards and, if so, turns it over to the CPC for investigation. The CPC relies on a fact-finding committee of ICMA members close to the site of the complaint to gather relevant information from all parties involved. The CPC makes its determination and recommends what action should be taken. If the complaint is upheld, the options are private censure (delivered to the respondent, with copies to the complainant and the state association), public censure, expulsion, and membership bar.[37] If the member objects to the action, the case is reviewed by the executive board and its decision is implemented by the executive director.[38]

The process requires careful judgment by both the CPC and the board in assessing whether an ethics violation has occurred, and what action should be taken. There is not an automatic link between action and sanction. The executive board has established rules of procedure that cover the factors that may be considered in determining the kind of sanction that will be applied:

- Nature of the violation
- Prior violations by the same individual
- Willfulness of the violation
- Level of professional or public responsibility of the individual
- Any other factors that bear on the seriousness of the violation

Former CPC member Curtis Branscome (2005, 4) observes that there is "some generalized concern for precedence, but in my experience, each case is unique." For him, two factors seemed particularly important in choosing a recommended penalty:

> If there are prior violations by the same individual, and this has been brought to the individual's attention, then the reeducation has been attempted and failed. Prior violations make a decision easier. The willfulness of the violation comes into play a lot. Was it someone . . . making a stupid mistake, or what could have been a stupid mistake, or was it someone acting with malice aforethought?

In 2005, the ICMA Committee on Professional Conduct processed 13 cases. In four cases, there was a public censure and a membership bar. Six cases resulted in private censures communicated to the member alone. Three of the cases were closed without issuing any sanctions. In addition, the ICMA responded to 109 ethics inquiries during the year.

The AICP process is similar to that of ICMA. One difference is that the person or persons bringing the complaint—the party that brings the charge—may appeal a dismissal of the ethics charge by the ethics officer either at the start of the process or after the fact-finding stage.[39] The AICP Ethics Committee may either affirm or reverse the dismissal and, if the dismissal is reversed, the ethics committee shall either direct the ethics officer to conduct a further investigation and review the charge again, or issue a complaint that will lead to completing the remaining steps in the review process.

Having a process does not guarantee that it is pursued vigorously or that the interests of members are not given greater weight than those of the person bringing a complaint. Still, it is not correct to assert that no organizations investigate allegations of ethics violations or that complaints never lead to disciplinary action. As the examples show, a thorough process can be established that seeks to respect and protect the rights of all parties in a dispute and to come to a fair and conscientious resolution of the complaint.

Restating the Purpose of Codes of Ethics

Sometimes the criticisms leveled against codes of ethics and enforcement processes are warranted, but in most cases they are not, based on the codes examined here. Codes of ethics provide a summary statement of the standards and expectations of a professional group. In view of the analysis of major codes in public administration, the objectives of codes of ethics can be revised and restated.

First, as noted earlier, codes can constrain, guide, and inspire the administrators themselves. To accomplish these objectives, codes should contain tenets that balance negative and positive approaches, specific or micro- and broad or macrostandards. The more focused and specific aspects of the code set standards for the profession that can be used to discipline members and alert prospective clients of what they can expect. The commentary that accompanies the code can identify potential problem areas and help to deal with complex cases. Broader and aspirational statements can extend the involvement of professionals into areas that touch on the boundaries of professional responsibility in dealings with political superiors and the public. The importance of these kinds of statements should not be underestimated even though the guidance they provide will be very abstract. Persons covered by the code should periodically engage in discussion about what the broader aspects of the codes mean and how they can seek to accomplish challenging goals. If used properly and supported by reflection on the part of members, codes of ethics can alert professionals (and political superiors) to ethical aspects of their work, the limits of acceptable behavior, and the expectations of ethical leadership.

Second, codes can be used as a means of enforcing the shared standards of the profession. In the view of Curtis Branscome, a former president of ICMA, it is the code of ethics that sets administrators in ICMA apart from others, and the Committee on Professional Conduct that investigates ethics complaints "is the 'keeper of the flame' for the profession" (Branscome 2005, 2). Although the enforcement provisions are not the most important part of a code, they must be in place and used to maintain the professional standards and reputation of an organization.

Third, codes alert persons outside of the profession of what they can expect. This includes persons who interact with public administrators in day-to-day activities, clients who seek services or are contacted by public administrators, and the public at-large. For example, one of the explicit purposes of the NASW code is to provide "ethical standards to which the general public can hold the social work profession accountable" (NASW 1999). The public often has a cynical attitude about the performance and motives of governmental staff and in recent years, nonprofit organizations and their staff have been subject to some public criticism for wasting funds or raising money under false pretenses. Simply having a code is not sufficient to convince the public that public administrators are bound by duty, principled, virtuous, and committed to the public interest, but it is a start. One might argue that the absence of a code would lower public estimation of public administrators even more, but there is probably little reason to think that there is much public awareness of the existence of codes and how they are enforced. Public administrators must do more to make the public aware that the codes exist and to demonstrate that they are committed to meeting the standards contained in the code.

Incorporating Codes into Your Own Professional Standards

An ethical public administrator needs a set of values and standards to which he or she is committed. I encourage you to develop your own code of professional ethics that will set forth values and standards to which you are committed. This code should not be a substitute for the official code of the professional group with which you are associated, but it should build on it both to expand the scope of the tenets and also to make it your own.

The expanded personal code of professional ethics could add tenets from other codes. For example, in their code, city managers have only a general commitment to democratic government, informing the community, and encouraging communication with citizens and no statement about fairness in society. They might want to consider the more far-reaching statements in the AICP code about giving people the opportunity to have a meaningful impact in policy making, expanding participation, and seeking social justice. The directors of nonprofit organizations might incorporate and build on tenets from ICMA about responsibilities to their boards of directors in their own personal code.

Furthermore, a personal code could also include values that draw on other sources of guidance and inspiration. The principle to treat all persons as ends in themselves is not explicitly included in any of the codes we have examined, but it is potentially the basis for a tenet that helps ensure a fundamental commitment to fairness and decency in dealings with citizens, clients, and coworkers.

In Chapter 1, there was a pop quiz. Now I will suggest a major assignment: Create your own professional code of ethics. With guidance from these professional codes and the components of the ethics triangle, what tenets will you include in your professional code of ethics? How do you internalize it to make it a "working" code that you will use in real situations? What is suggested is a building process, not one of replacing tenets from established codes but adding to them to make your working code one that is comprehensive and meaningful to you as well as being true to the standards of your professional group. It should also be a work in progress, one that you return to from time to time to update and elaborate further.

The difference between the Stage 4 level of moral reasoning and the universal-values level is the breadth of the norms as well as the extent to which these norms have been internalized. In a similar way, the code of ethics of a professional association—no matter how strong it may be in terms of the criteria considered here—cannot simply be a set of "instructions" to the administrator. The tenets must be understood, accepted at a deep level of commitment, and incorporated into the way one thinks about how he or she practices the profession. The formal code will be even stronger and more meaningful if it is used as the foundation for an expanded personal code of ethics.

Chapter 6

Undermining Duty:

Challenges to the Ethical Behavior of Public Administrators

To this point, the exploration of public administration has taken a generally positive tone. We have stressed that most public administrators and persons who wish to enter the field probably have implicit codes of ethics that cover basic areas of concern. Readers are encouraged to expand and elevate their ethical reasoning by thinking broadly and proactively about the full scope of their democratic responsibilities and by incorporating major philosophical perspectives into their own ethical thinking. The hope and expectation are that public administrators will be able to shift from a reliance on rules and authority figures to develop the capacity for independent ethical reasoning based on universal values. Similarly, they are encouraged to look beyond the sometimes-constraining features of codes of ethics in order to examine the full scope of their responsibilities and the highest aspirations of their profession. They are challenged to develop their own personal code of ethics for their professional work.

These themes may leave some wondering where are the many unethical people who occupy government offices and some nonprofit positions. Even if they are a small minority—as is surely the case, they cannot be ignored. The effort to chart a course to the ethical heights may be fine, but what about the people who prowl the ethical depths of public service?

I will defend the approach taken so far, but then I will address this omission. If, for example, one were writing a book about citizenship and community building—not unlike responsible professionalism and organization building, it would not make sense to start with an examination of the shirkers and the destroyers of civic life. Eventually, however, it would be necessary to address the negative behaviors, note their impacts, and consider how to reduce or eliminate them. In the same way, it is time to examine why some public administrators are unethical.

What are the possible explanations of inappropriate behavior by public administrators? Are bad people or bad systems the primary cause of ethical problems? In some instances, one can find widespread corruption or officials with serious personal flaws. Still, generally—and perhaps more disturbingly—it is decent administrators who have ethical failings in the actions they willingly choose to take or in the actions that are at least in part forced on them or shaped by circumstances they do not fully control. Therefore, we will examine three sets of explanations: those that stress bad people, those explanations that apply to decent administrators who make unethical choices, and those explanations that stress circumstances. Unfortunately, the list of reasons for unethical behavior is depressingly long.

The distinctions among the causes are important. Emphasis on the first leads to efforts to prevent the hiring of ethically deficient persons and to detect and eliminate the "bad apples" from organizations. Emphasis on the latter two leads to the conclusion that promoting high-ethical conduct will take broader and more systemic approaches at the individual and organizational level. For individuals, it is important to broaden the base for their ethical thinking (the focus of Chapters 2–5), to improve their ethical "conditioning" by exercising with the problem-solving model in Chapter 7 and to consider under what circumstances they might defy the organization and blow the whistle examined in Chapter 8. For organizations, the strategies for enhancing ethics in Chapter 9 must come to terms with the individual and circumstantial reasons for unethical behavior presented here. Perhaps it is also useful to impose external legal controls like those examined in Chapter 10, although these may be better designed to constrain bad people than to inspire the decent people in public service. It is also important for administrators to understand why unethical behavior occurs. Knowledge of the causes may provide a defense for those who wish to maintain high ethical standards.

One classification of public administrators by Paula Gordon (2003) divides them into three types, and she offers detailed indicators of each type. The no-ethics administrators or corrupters are the proverbial "bad apples" in public organizations. They use power in Machiavellian ways, play games with information or distort it to advance their purposes, evade responsibility, abuse perquisites of office, allow complex processes to bog down in confusion, fail to be responsive to the public, and contribute to a dog-eat-dog mode of existence. The value-neutral administrators are ethical relativists. They try to observe the law and avoid wrongdoing. They will act with expediency, selectively respond to wrongdoing they observe, take advantage of perquisites of office, focus more on process than purpose, stress productivity and measurable results without common sense and human concern, and address problems only when it becomes pragmatically and politically possible to do so. They abstain from committing illegal acts not because they believe the acts are wrong but rather because they normally do not violate rules or the law. They are indifferent to constitutional and human rights. In contrast, according to Gordon (2003), the "value-based ethicists" see wrongdoing as bad, uncover wrongdoing by others, do not abuse the perquisites of office, do not play games with information or procedure, foster truthful and open communication, act in accordance with constitutional and human rights, are guided by integrity, protect and enhance the public interest, and take mitigative action seeking to prevent problems before they occur. These administrators are exemplars.

The no-ethics types clearly match up with explanations of unethical behavior that stress the deficiencies in public administrators. Presumably the value-neutral types are the typical decent administrators who rely on law and authority to determine what they do; in other words, they rely on conventional or Stage 4 morality. These administrators have weak defenses against conditions that erode their sense of right and wrong or forces including directives from superiors that push them in the direction of unethical behavior. The value-based ethicists are proactively committed to ethics and should be able to resist pressures, but even these administrators can go bad if they lose their ethical compass.

One final approach to classifying the causes of corruption is useful before turning to the specific explanations. Sheldon Steinberg and David Austern (1990, 61–62) argue that corrupt behavior occurs within the interaction of three factors: *incentive* or the size of the benefit, *opportunity* or the ease of access to the corrupt practice, and *risk* or the chance of detection. There are a wide variety of combinations. For example, the higher the incentive to engage in corruption and the lower the chance of detection, the greater the likelihood that corruption will occur. Weak inclination to be unethical and even minor gain may not deter corrupt behavior if the prospect of detection is extremely low. This explanation of corrupt behavior does not necessarily apply to other kinds of unethical behavior (abuse of power or failure to serve may result from different factors), but it is a useful addition to the categories of explanations used here. Extreme levels of unethical motivation are present in the no-ethics group. Decent and good administrators may act unethically under the right "incentive structure"; the combination of benefit and chance of punishment. Finally, officials may be pressured to behave unethically and not receive any benefit, but this circumstance is not covered by the motivation, opportunity, and detection factors.

Explanations Based on
Bad People/Bad "Systems"

The prevalence of decent people in governmental and nonprofit organizations does not mean that there are no evil or dishonest public administrators. The no-ethics corrupters include persons who want to use their power to advance themselves and harm others. Greed and the ability to exploit the system can lead to illegal profiteering by public or party officials through bribes, extortion, bid rigging, and the like. The Knapp Commission investigating police corruption in New York City identified a pronounced form of corruption practiced by the "meat-eaters" who like carnivores on the hunt for big game aggressively seek out opportunities for bribes in narcotics, gambling, and other areas that can yield large payments for protection (GAO 1998, 6).

More prevalent are persons who lack integrity and are willing to take advantage of opportunities for personal gain by taking actions of which they think no one will know. The Knapp Commission asserted that the "grass-eaters" who though like gentle grazing animals accept gratuities and solicit small bribes from contractors, truckers, gamblers, and such, are much more numerous. They take advantage of the opportunity to benefit themselves exploiting the low risk of detection. Although the amounts of money involved are relatively modest, the Knapp Commission (GAO 1998, 6) concluded that these small-time corrupt officers were the main problem because their large number made the practices seem respectable or at least expected because the behavior was so common. If citizens expect that police officers are corrupt, they may offer a bribe to fix a ticket even if it is not solicited. When this happens, the access is high and the risk is low, even if there was little prior motivation to take a payment and not write a ticket. Other officials seek special treatment for family and friends. Perhaps their definition of ethics is deficient and they do not consider this kind of behavior to be corruption. It's just helping people who are close to you. Another form of using public office for personal gain is to make official decisions in ways that intentionally benefit their own personal interests. There is no appreciation that conflicts of interest should constrain official action.

Besides corruption, some no-ethics administrators engage in other kinds of harmful behavior, but the same underlying motivation to benefit personally at the expense of others appears to be present. Arrogance and abuse of power are used to advance one's self and put down others; for example, using power to punish "enemies" or undercut competitors. Abuse of power can also be employed by racists who seek to damage the prospects of persons in minority groups. It is also used by sexists who prey upon and seek to establish their dominance over their victims. The objective may be coercing sexual favors or attacks with sexual connotations may be used as a means of humiliating the target. In either case, sexual harassment involves the imposition of power and victimization.[40]

The explanations thus far focus on individuals who exploit the circumstances in which they work. Even more serious is the condition of systemic corruption. The norms of the system support individual corruption and ethical staff are at risk. When there is systemic corruption, the following conditions identified by Gerald and Naomi Caiden (1977, 306–307) prevail:

(a) the organization professes an external code of ethics which is contradicted by internal practices;

(b) internal practices encourage, abet, and hide violations of the external code;

(c) non-violators are penalized by foregoing the rewards of violation and offending violators;

(d) violators are protected, and when exposed, treated leniently; their accusers are victimized for exposing organizational hypocrisy, and are treated harshly;

(e) non-violators suffocate in the venal atmosphere; they find no internal relief and much external disbelief;

(f) prospective whistleblowers are intimidated and terrorized into silence;

(g) courageous whistleblowers have to be protected from organizational retaliation;

(h) violators become so accustomed to their practices and the protection given them that, on exposure, they evidence surprise and claim innocence and unfair discrimination against them;

(i) collective guilt finds expression in rationalizations of the internal practices and without strong external supports there is no serious intention of ending them;

(j) those formally charged with revealing corruption rarely act and, when forced by external pressure to do so, excuse any incidents as isolated, rare occurrences.

Fortunately, such conditions typically are not found in western democracies, but pockets of systemic corruption can be found.

These bad person/bad system factors provide a partial explanation for corruption, but most ethical lapses are not committed by bad people in government and nonprofit organizations. It is more common to find normal people who commit unethical actions. Why does this happen? What are the factors that can lead good people to be unethical? Why do generally decent officials have ethical lapses or serious violations of ethical (and at times legal) norms? As noted, there are two broad categories of explanations:

1. Failings due to shortcomings by normally good and decent officials
2. Unethical choices shaped by circumstances

The first set of explanations apply to acts of *commission*; choices made by individuals to advance ends they intend to achieve or choices that reflect their personal values. In these actions, the sense of duty may be misdirected or inverted, and ethical perspectives may be distorted to justify unethical behavior. These ethical violators may even be persons who in some respects are or have been exemplary officials.

The second set of explanations applies to acts or failures to act produced by forces or circumstances that lead individuals to make unethical choices. They may blame the actions on others or even fail to recognize that their actions are unethical. It seems plausible that these instances involve ethical "relativists" with a weak sense of ethical commitment and a strong inclination to shift responsibility from self to others, to conform to expectations of others, or to accept the direction of authorities without question. In these cases, a conventional level of moral development may be a contributing factor to the weakness of the individual's ethical commitment in the face of the circumstances they encounter. There are certainly other cases, however, when the external factors exert very powerful pressure. Ethical relativists may put up little resistance and even ethically committed administrators can buckle under the pressure. Each set of explanations is examined in depth. A roadmap to the discussion (and the factors already covered) is offered in **Figure 6.1**.

Failings Due to Shortcomings by Normally Good and Decent Officials

The first cluster of explanations involves so-called "good reasons" why good persons engage in unethical behavior. The unethical official may be driven by ego and overwhelming commitment to accomplish one's own goals. Closely related would be such a strong commitment to ideology or values that an action is justified by ideological or value commitments (self-righteousness that leads to intolerance). Another variation is a distorted consequentialist view of ethics in which the end justifies the means that are taken to accomplish it. Minor deceptions, such as white lies to protect someone or to give someone the answer they are expecting, may seem considerate or harmless. On a larger scale, lies told for the public good may seem justifiable (Bok 1989). Some officials who fall into this category have a lack of respect for the democratic process and feel that the public is not capable of understanding complex arguments for important policies. They must be given, therefore, a simplified view of reality. Similarly, an appointed executive who feels contempt for elected officials may seek to manipulate their decisions by providing selective information.

An attitude of superiority contributes to the conviction that one is above the law, doesn't have to abide by normal rules, or shouldn't be bound by normal restrictions. Self-righteousness may contribute to the feeling that "I can't be bought by a free lunch" or other benefit; therefore, the standard prohibition does not have to be followed. Ironically, some of the most successful administrators can come to feel professional hubris—a conceit, arrogance, or moral superiority fed by their success. An example would be the director of a government agency who believes that her outstanding performance entitles her to benefits that would not normally be provided. Another example is a nonprofit executive whose success leads him to justify lavish perks because he must be able to function on the same affluent level as the business executives he approaches for contributions and commitments.[41] These examples do not indicate a grasping or greedy person who concealed his or her base instincts for decades while building a successful career, and then finally took advantage of the opportunity to benefit personally. Rather, it is the unsettling story of good persons whose drive for accomplishment becomes so self-centered that they violate the trust they have established over the years.

Explanations based on bad people/bad systems

- No-ethics exploiters
- Systemic corruption

Failings due to shortcomings by normally good and decent officials

- Good reasons
- Bias or prejudice
- Ignorance and lack of awareness
- Government context/nonprofit context

Unethical choices shaped by circumstances

- Organizational advantage
- Conformity
- Anticipating actions by superiors; excessive responsiveness
- Pressure and threat
- Following inappropriate orders

Figure 6–1 *Causes of and Factors that Contribute to Unethical Behavior*

A variation on the good reasons argument is to use methods that would not normally be acceptable and justify them because of the good purpose that they serve and/or the negative forces they are combating. The *Malek Manual* (in Richter, Doig, and Burke 1990, 135–38)[42] was written in 1970 in an era of divided government when the Democrats controlled the Congress and Republicans controlled the White House. The methods it espoused could be used against any employee who was not deemed to be sufficiently loyal. The intent is to thwart the possibility of sabotage by career staff that may undermine the initiatives of the president because they follow their own political beliefs or display loyalty to the majority party in Congress rather than to their supervisors in the executive branch. Practices included the frontal assault—offering the choice of resigning with honor or possibly getting forced out with bad references, transfer to an undesirable location, the special assistant technique that turns the staff member with heavy family responsibilities into a traveling salesperson, and the new-activity technique—creating a new but meaningless unit that is designed to contain a large number of "problem" employees. Such techniques were justified in the name of achieving the goals of the organization by undermining those who might obstruct progress.

Another source of unethical behavior that arises from individual shortcoming is *bias* or *prejudice* toward groups that can lead to negative stereotypes and devaluing categories of people. Although extreme forms of racist and sexist attitudes were noted as an example of a serious personal deficiency, these "milder" forms of prejudice are also important. They are likely to be more widespread and harder to detect.

Members of groups who tend to have greater prestige and power may not be overtly discriminatory in their behavior. Still, they may have blind spots when it comes to certain categories of people. They can misperceive or misinterpret behavior, as when a black applicant interviewed by a panel of whites is judged to "lack confidence" in interpersonal relations and lose out to a "self-assured" white applicant. Not considering a woman for a promotion because she "probably wouldn't want additional responsibilities that would interfere with her family responsibilities" or not considering a Hispanic for a management team because "he wouldn't fit in and wouldn't be comfortable" are examples of prejudicial treatment that deny opportunities because of race, gender, or ethnicity. Systematic expressions of stereotypes can take the form of setting different expectations for developed groups. A basic purpose of the performance standards in public schools under the No Child Left Behind Act is to overcome the "soft bigotry of low expectations" (Rothman 2001/02, 6–7) that allows lower performance by children in minority groups to persist without intervention or can even undermine confidence and lower performance by minority children. Racial or ethnic profiling—as opposed to profiling based on more precise and discriminating indicators of likely behavior—leads to the assumption that persons who share racial or ethnic identity will act in similarly antisocial ways.

A third explanation is *ignorance and lack of awareness*. Not knowing that behavior is improper or not knowing that an action is required can lead to inappropriate behavior, but why is the knowledge missing? It may result from shortcomings in training or the topic may be truly complex and hard to understand. *Technical violations* of regulations do not necessarily indicate ethical wrongdoing unless they are persistent and represent an intentional effort to evade the rules.

Still, a serious condition that can contribute to ignorance is the choice some officials make to not be knowledgeable or the preference to be unaware. "I didn't know this was required (or not permitted)" or "I didn't know this was going on" provide convenient excuses. The refusal to be aware can be signaled by the message from managers to staff that they do not want to know about problems or that no one is supposed to come through the manager's supposedly open door with bad news. Managers who rely on information that comes through channels and never get out to talk directly to staff at all levels are essentially resigning themselves to not being aware of important happenings in the organization. Information gets filtered as it goes up the organization's levels and negative reports may get moderated or omitted (Kaufman 1977). Despite this tendency to allow barriers in communication to develop, in cases when the responsible official claims lack of knowledge or awareness, one may ask: "What can an official be reasonably expected to know?" Lack of awareness is not an excuse if one should have known or should have been able to know that improper actions are occurring.

A number of factors can be grouped together as the *governmental context* explanation reflecting conditions that are common in governmental work or prevailing norms in the public sector. The shared element here is that the factors contribute to the notion that individuals can take advantage of the situation or get even for slights they have experienced because they work for government. The circumstances and behavior seem different here than in the bad-people explanations in which officials actively or secretly seek to gain personally from office. The distinction is certainly a narrow one. However, the governmental context factors impact the behavior of persons who are not normally seeking to enrich themselves—nor are they pressured by the governmental context factors to make unethical choices (this is covered in the third set of explanations), but rather they take advantage of the opportunity to do so.

A common sentiment is that behaviors "go with the territory" or are accepted practices. This could include examples of small-scale personal gain; for instance, taking supplies from the office (not simply the occasional pen forgotten in the pocket) or making extensive personal use of the copying machine. A sense of resentment about levels of pay or perquisites or lack of appreciation for efforts could lead to the attitude "I've got it coming." It may seem appropriate to "exploit the exploiters" and get some of the rewards that one is normally denied by practices such as exaggerating claims for travel reimbursement. The use of no-bid and sole-source contracts can provide an opportunity to steer work to friends or associates and even receive a quid pro quo. There are ample sources of insider information that could be put to personal advantage. Although the distinction that George Washington Plunkett of Tammany Hall (Riordan 1995) made between honest and dishonest graft would no longer be accepted, there may still be some who have seen opportunities and taken them out of a misplaced sense of entitlement to special benefits.

Cynicism and low levels of commitment can lead to a failure to serve or slacking. The attitude "it's good enough for government work" can become an excuse for not pursuing excellence. The attitude of "how do they expect me to get anything done with so few resources?" can lead to shirking duties. A grotesque case of failure to serve occurred in New Jersey in 2002 when abused children in foster care were ignored by case workers and one child died. Staff who claimed that they were pressured to increase the rate of resolving cases closed the files on these children even though they did not know where the children were (Purdy 2003).

It seems that these negative conditions are particularly likely to occur in government but anecdotal evidence suggests that there can be a *nonprofit context* as well. Some of the factors that create a possibility for self-serving behavior to emerge are flexibility and lack of controls. These conditions may permit preferences for friends or relatives, exchange of benefits for donations, acting above the law, or developing a sense of ownership of entitlement to organizational resources. The Independent Sector (2002, 22–24) offers examples of behaviors that violate the values of nonprofit organizations. They are presented in **Table 6.1**.

Thus, taking advantage of the nonprofit context is possible. Failings in providing service can occur as well; for example, in a social services board for an organization that serves minority neighborhoods that has no minority members or an organization that year after year talks about its noble goals and plans and does not mention the small number of services provided and the meager accomplishments achieved.

Unethical Choices Shaped by Circumstances

The final set of explanations shift(s) attention to the circumstances surrounding the individual. Unlike the explanations based on the nature of the governmental or nonprofit context, the factors examined here involve pressure from others or organizational forces to do something that an individual official

Table 6–1 *Violations of Values of Nonprofit Organizations*

Commitment beyond self	• Illegal act: The board agrees to sell property to a board member's spouse without competitive bidding and at a price below fair-market value.
	• Unethical behavior: The CEO of a financially strapped organization continues to fly first-class on short business trips while the organization has to lay off staff.
Obedience of the laws	• Illegal act: A solicitation indicates that contributions are tax deductible when they are not.
	• Unethical behavior: Trust fund trustees are paid inflated annual fees for a limited number of meetings and decisions.
Commitment to the public good	• Illegal act: A private foundation does not live up to the minimum payout requirement for grants.
	• Unethical behavior: A foundation's grant guidelines are broad and its application procedures are complicated, but most of the money goes annually to a few institutions with which foundation trustees have affiliation and that submit sketchy applications and reports.
Responsible stewardship of resources	• Illegal act: To deal with a worsening deficit, money withheld from employees' paychecks for federal income tax is not turned over to the IRS.
	• Unethical behavior: Services are targeted to clients with the least amount of needs because the organization wants to show funders high numbers of people served successfully.

Source: Independent Sector 2002. Used with permission of the Independent Sector.

would not choose to do if left alone. The impact may be focused and sudden (for instance, a superior threatens to fire a subordinate if he does not follow an order to commit an act that is unethical) or it may be protracted and gradual, as in the erosion of integrity of "moral attrition" identified by Dobel (1999). It also may be persistently insidious, as in the subtle pressure from peers to conform. Identifying these outside factors does not relieve individuals of responsibility for their actions, but it emphasizes the interaction between self and context that can shape an ethical challenge. Although it is questionable that individuals in these described situations have no choice but to act the way they do, they may claim that they did not intend to be unethical but caused harm without knowing it or because they were forced or pressured into doing so. The latter defense carries the claim that they would not have made the unethical choice if they had been free to act on their own. This is the perceived lack of moral agency presented in Chapter 2. The former situation—unthinking and unintentional harmful actions—is the essence of Guy Adams and Danny Balfour's (1998) "administrative evil."

One factor that leads to unethical behavior is the drive for *organizational advantage*. In contrast to the internal goods of a practice or organization—the essential positive purposes of a practice that are achieved by pursuing its standards of excellence (Cooper 1987), external goods are the resources and benefits that come to the organization or agency. Seeking expanded money, personnel, power, or prestige can cause an organization to engage in practices that undercut the ethical standards of excellence. When vice presidents at Morton Thiokol overruled the safety concerns of engineers to move forward with the launch of space shuttle *Challenger* in 1986, this appears to be a case of putting external goods over standards of excellence. Here is Cooper's (1987, 324) assessment:

> Morton Thiokol's decision to ignore engineering standards of excellence through the imposition of management authority seems clearly to have been a response to expectations generated by NASA. During the decade before the shuttle tragedy, NASA had begun to orient itself increasingly to pressures for short turnaround times and frequent and reliable launch schedules. Safety, an internal good for manned space flight engineering, was sacrificed or at the very least devalued. Redundancy, a standard of excellence for achieving safety in this kind of engineering, was set aside. Prudence, one of the virtues of aerospace engineers involved in maintaining safety for human crew members, was rejected. The external goods of contract security, maintenance of schedules, profit, and marketability appear to have ruled the day.

The pressure to succeed can arise from financial pressures and the sense that the organization must survive at any cost. Even though the circumstances are not dire, some organizations will ignore criticisms and cover up problems to avoid embarrassment or to deflect the need for change. These are all variations on the rationalization called *the false necessity trap* (Josephson Institute of Ethics 2005). This orientation is a perversion of the utilitarian standard that leads some in an organization to put pressure on others to set aside virtue and violate principle.

The transmission of expectations can differ in their explicitness and the amount of pressure involved. With *conformity*, choices about behavior are shaped in the absence of direct orders and the pressures are vague. Nonetheless, they can be powerful. Conformity can take the form of going along and not wanting to make waves. The social pressures from peers to be loyal to the workgroup can be persuasive if you feel that these are the people you depend on and the only ones who can help you when you are in trouble. In a less-obvious way, conformity can arise out of diffused responsibility and the sense that somebody else will do it. If no one else steps forward, you can rational-ize not acting yourself because "no one else seems to think it is important." Not wanting to stand apart from the group can be reflected in the attitude that "it's none of my business." Acting or failing to act in the way that others expect creates complicity. If one feels that they have contributed and could share part of responsibility for problems, they have additional incentive to protect themselves by maintaining solidarity.

A different kind of transmission of expectations occurs when officials decide to take an unethical action "for the good of the organization." This approach involves *anticipating the actions* preferred by someone else before they have issued directions. "I'm taking care of this because I know this is what my boss would want me to do" is such a rationale. This attitude is often accompanied by the assumption that the activity will be condoned because they feel that they are doing something that is expected. Indeed, there may have been subtle indications that the person should take the action. Whether it was implicitly expected, however, if the action goes bad or is exposed, it is likely that the official who takes the action will be left to suffer the conse-quences. Superiors can correctly say that the offending official was acting without authorization. It is important, therefore, for self-protection as well as to clarify the ethical situation for an official to ask that an expectation be made explicit. Clarity does not mean that the action should be taken—indeed it may raise the stakes and the level of pressure,[43] but at least the individual will not have acted on his or her own and find that no one will back up the action.

Another variation on anticipated reactions is excessive policy responsive-ness by staff members (Aberbach and Rockman 1993). Undermining profes-sionalism in order to serve political superiors can be expressed in many ways. These include eliminating options that staff members feel superiors will find objectionable, slanting evidence to support political goals, and pass-ing over qualified staff members for assignments or promotions who are out of favor with superiors. When staff members are excessively responsive, political superiors can rightfully claim that they were simply acting on the recommendation or the information provided by administrators and in so doing give professional credibility to what was in fact a politically inspired action. As stressed in Chapter 3, it is a duty for administrators to be respon-sive to the policy goals of political superiors, but they should not sacrifice principle, standards, and commitment to serve the public. When the full range of options and complete information is provided, political superiors can still choose the option they preferred or act in a way that is not consistent with the evidence, but this is a clear political decision rather than a concealed political decision.

Finally, there is the use of threat or political pressure to induce a staff member to comply or act cooperatively. According to a study in 1993, a large proportion—50 percent—of federal government staff who observed serious problems did not report them because of the fear of retaliation, although this was an improvement over the 70 percent who failed to report problems in 1983 (U.S. Merit Systems Protection Board 1993).[44] In this situation, the individuals were not inclined to remain silent or to accept the conditions they observed but feared that there would be negative consequences if they reported them.

Thus, the kinds of transmission of expectations considered so far are conformity, anticipating preferred actions, being responsive to the extent that instructions do not have to be given, and the threat of retaliation as a signal that an action should not be taken. In none of these types of communication were explicit directions given to the individual under pressure. Now we turn to the hardest form of transmitted expectations: orders and explicit pressure to carry out actions.

In organizations that serve the public, administrators are expected to *follow orders*. They make extensive contributions to the formation of policy and they have considerable discretion in the day-to-day implementation of policy and management of organizational resources, but in the final analysis, they are expected to obey instructions from their political superiors who are directly accountable to the public or from their administrative superiors who have the authority to direct their subordinates. Indeed, in the normal course of administrative affairs, the failure to obey is ethically wrong and constitutes insubordination unless the order is illegal or clearly inappropriate. (See Chapter 3.) One of the most important ethical problems, however, occurs from failing to recognize the limits of obedience and presuming that one is required to obey regardless of what the order entails.

Unlike the other ways that expectations are transmitted, an order makes it clear and explicit what one is supposed to do (although the consequences may not be obvious) and the failure to obey creates a direct confrontation between the subordinate and the superior. The order may be vague as when subordinates are told to protect the executive and preserve his or her ability to deny any knowledge of the action; in other words, achieving a condition of "plausible deniability." The instruction may leave discretion regarding how it is carried out (the command to "take care of this" is often accompanied by the additional proviso "I don't want to know how you did it"). In other cases, the instructions will be more specific. In either case, the ethical dilemma is whether to obey an order.

When facing this dilemma, the official is not without choices. There is the option of resigning instead of obeying; doing so can draw attention to the problem and potentially strengthen political forces that will correct it. When stressed in Chapter 3 that officials typically do not have *only* the options of obeying or resigning, that does not mean that resigning is not an important option. As Dobel (1999, 111) reminds, the fact that resignation is an option "means that a person cannot escape responsibility by pretending he or she had no choice." Still this is a dire consequence that officials would naturally wish to avoid, just as they would prefer not being fired.

There are two ways that the subordinate can perceive the situation. Some may have such a high deference to authority and such a low independent capacity for assessing the implications of actions that they obey without question or reservation. Helping persons in this group starts with altering how they define their duty and sense of professional responsibility and how they think about ethics. Others will doubt whether they should do what they are told.[45] It is this group on which we focus here.

The orders may involve doing something; suppress information, punish a troublemaker, or harm a citizen. Alternatively, the order may be to *not* do something; reporting damaging information to superiors or outsiders. There is ample anecdotal evidence that some officials in governmental and nonprofit organizations choose to obey improper and illegal orders. There is also gripping experimental evidence in the research of Stanley Milgram of the inclination of most ordinary people to obey orders (Milgram 1974).[46] In Kohlberg's (1981, 44) view, this experiment tests "what happens when justice and authority are opposed." In this famous study based on research conducted in the 1960s, subjects believed that they were the "teachers" in an experiment to test the effects of punishment on learning. The teacher was instructed to administer a progressively stronger shock when a learner sitting in an adjoining room made a mistake in an answer to a question. The supposed shock was administered by depressing one of 30 switches that resulted in shocks supposedly ranging from 0 to 450 volts.

Prior to the experiment, when it was described to psychiatrists, students, and middle-aged adults, most predicted that the subjects would refuse to continue with the experiment when the shock reached level 10 labeled "strong shock" (150 volts), and no one predicted that the subjects would go beyond level 20 on the scale marked "extreme intensity shock" (300 volts) (Milgram 1974). In actuality, 65 percent of the adult subjects followed instructions to the end and administered the maximum shock of 450 volts at level 30. No shocks were actually being given, but the setting was realistic enough that the subjects believed they were. Even when the experiment was altered to provide voice feedback with screams and protests that accelerated as the level of supposed shock increased and the "student" complained that his heart was hurting, still 63 percent administered the maximum shock (Milgram 1974).

Many had strong misgivings and voiced them to the experimenter who sat in the same room as the "teacher" and issued instructions, but in the final analysis, most continued to the end. Despite the short-term relationship between the subject and the experimenter, most gave up their own moral agency and ignored the protests of the student. As Stanley Milgram (1974, 57) puts in with chilling understatement: "Probably there is nothing the victim can say that will uniformly generate disobedience; for the teacher's actions are not controlled by him." An *agentic shift* had occurred in which the teacher felt responsible to the person giving orders rather than feeling responsible for the actions taken. For most teachers, the experimenter was in charge, and over three in five of the teachers felt they (including women as teachers in one version) were obligated to follow orders. If the prestige of the experimenter was lowered or if the experimenter was not present in the room, rates of obedience dropped; this also happened when there were three teachers and two dropped out. On the other hand, when there was a second teacher who administered the shock and the subject only asked the questions, 93 percent continued with the experiment to the end. Being one step removed from inflicting the pain produced an even lower sense of responsibility for what was happening to the learner (Milgram 1974).

The experiment approximated conditions observed among some of the German bureaucrats who passively did their part in carrying out the extermination of Jews, staff in the Tuskegee experiment on untreated syphilis that started in the 1930s in which poor black men were denied penicillin after it was developed in the early forties (Jones 1981), and participants in studies with radioactive materials involving mentally retarded children after World War II (Moreno 2001, 213). It is not insignificant that in all these cases the victims were marginal or devalued persons according to the prevailing social mores. It is "easier" to protect oneself and go along with orders when those affected are viewed as less important or worthy, although the argument does not apply to all cases of following orders and harming others. In the Milgram experiment, as far as the teacher knew, only the drawing of lots had put him or her in that role rather than in the learner role—nor was this circumstance present in 1949 when workers at the Hanford nuclear plant in Washington state ignored the potential for harm to residents and intentionally released large amounts of radioactive iodine with the belief that U.S. scientists could locate the location of Soviet plutonium factories by looking for similar atmospheric evidence.[47]

There are countless less dramatic examples of inappropriately following orders—or complying with unspoken expectations—when individuals do nothing. The pressure can come in the form of interference or manipulation by political superiors to get a favorable recommendation, to ignore a violation, to get a benefit for a person who does not qualify, or to hire a person outside the standard personnel process. One of the greatest ongoing challenges that public administrators face is to be aware of the significance of the actions they take and consider the broader consequences of taking or not taking action. It is the heart of responsibility to accept that each official is a moral agent who is capable of taking action—evading or delaying, refusing to obey, whistleblowing, or resigning. Dobel's (1999, 111) comments about the last option are relevant to all these forms of independent action.

> I want to make clear that I am referring to a robust notion of integrity and responsibility. This is not a call for hair-trigger resignations. In public life, no one gets all they want all the time. Most officials lose more battles than they win, and victories are almost always imperfect. So public officials find themselves compromising and contributing to imperfect outcomes.

Officials should not resign for frivolous reasons or refuse to follow orders because they would prefer a different approach or outcome than does their superior. They must be sensitive, however, to situations when important consequences are at stake and when their action or inaction will violate an important principle, break the law, inflict harm on innocent persons, or cause substantial waste of resources. Then they must carefully weigh all the facts, responsibilities, ethical perspectives, and options, and make a reasoned and defensible choice. A systematic approach to thinking through serious ethical dilemmas is presented in the next chapter.

In all the explanations considered here, there is interaction between the contextual conditions and the individual's ethical strength. In the bad-people explanations, the question is whether the external conditions will provide sufficient mechanisms for surveillance and control to limit the ability of those who would exploit the system to do so. In this instance, the restraint must come from the context. In contrast, the ethical strength must come from the individual to curb the zeal and ambition that can lead to good-reason ethical violations when at least some contextual forces may support the actions. Finally, there is tension between self and context when the individual has to decide whether to remain true to high standards even when there are opportunities to take advantage, to provide dedicated service even in conditions of inadequate support, to stand apart from peers and do what is right, and to stand up to superiors and refuse to carry out improper orders. As we shall see in Chapter 8, ethical strength is needed to work through the complexities of situations that may call for blowing the whistle.

Drawing on the ethics triangle, the presence of ethical strength is indicated by the commitment to advance the public interest, to pursue justice, to display character, and to seek the greatest good. *Strength* means the ability to engage in ethical thinking that draws on universal standards and the capacity to take courageous ethical action. It is important to recognize that ethical reasoning at the universal-values stage is no guarantee of ethical action. Kohlberg (1981, 44) found that among persons at Stage 6 who took part in Milgram's experimental test of the limits of obedience, one quarter remained in the experiment to the end and administered the maximum shock. It is hard to reconcile their behavior with their level of moral development. Still, 87 percent of persons at lower stages administered the maximum shock (Kohlberg 1981). They were generally aware of the conflict between following orders and inflicting pain on the learner, but they did not have the universal reasons for defying the strong conventional norm of deferring to authority. The actions of the highest stage subjects highlight the distinction between analysis and action. If their judgment tells them that they should defy convention, they must also find the courage to act knowing they may suffer negative consequences.

In the bad-people explanations, the sense of duty is absent and the other approaches to ethical thinking are missing or distorted. Personal interest takes precedence over the public interest. In the explanations based on decent people with personal shortcomings, the sense of duty may be excessive, misdirected, or warped by personal values that violate public service norms. Alternatively, individual shortcomings and failure to resist external pressures may reflect a weakness in ethical judgment and a narrow definition of professional responsibility. In the view of Adams and Balfour (1998), there are two basic reasons for administrative evil. One is an excessive emphasis on value neutrality and a refusal to assert moral standards in the face of bad laws and improper orders. The second is the absence of the strength of character and principle to resist directions from superiors. From this perspective, administrators have no ethical foundation to object to orders from political superiors because the sense of duty is narrow and reactive, there is a lack of moral agency, or moral judgment has not advanced beyond the conventional stage.

Public administrators overcome these challenges by drawing on a sense of duty, philosophical perspectives, and codes of ethics. They need a high level of ethical awareness to recognize when they are in a problematic situation. It helps to have reinforcement from like-minded persons inside or outside the organization, but ultimately ethical choices are individual decisions. To resolve how to act when confronting an ethical dilemma, careful consideration, deep reflection, and rigorous analysis are required.

Chapter 7

Deciding How to Meet Obligations and Act Responsibly:

Ethical Analysis and Problem Solving

I s it possible to improve the quality of ethical problem solving by using some kind of systematic approach? *Better quality* would mean considering a broader range of issues and making greater use of universal values in ethical decision making. One must be suspicious of any process that attempts to produce a transformation in the way that people think about the world or a checklist that tries to make a complex matter simple. Still, the problem-solving model proposed in this chapter sets forth a series of questions that potentially enable an administrator operating at the postconventional or even the conventional level of moral development to reason through a dilemma they encounter.

Ethical analysis must be coupled with other elements if ethical action is going to occur. To Rest et al. (1999, 100–101), there are four psychological components or processes that all affect ethical decision making and behavior. Moral *sensitivity* includes awareness of the existence of an ethical problem or dilemma as well as being attentive to the consequences that different courses of action could have on persons involved in the situation. Moral *judgment* includes weighing the standards that guide behavior ("judging which action would be most justifiable in a moral sense") (101) and moral *motivation* reflects the inclination to choose the ethically appropriate alternative. The final component is moral *character*, which is needed to convert judgment into action and persist in the face of pressure and opposition. Thus, to act ethically, one must be aware of an ethical problem, judge which course of action is most appropriate, be inclined to accept this alternative, and be able to act on the choice and stick with it.

Some might argue that analytical ethical problem solving is not particularly important. The awareness component of ethical action triggers the need for a response, and there is an affective dimension to action involving feelings and motivations as well as the reasoning and judgment dimension (Walker et al. 1995, 398). As noted, ethical problem solving requires action as well as analysis. If one had to choose between being either aware and in touch with their feelings or rationally systematic, it would presumably be more important to be aware than systematic. The skilled but unaware problem solver will not know that there is a problem to be solved. Still, the person who is capable of broad-ranging ethical judgment may also have heightened awareness and see the ethical implications in a wider array of situations. The two need not be in conflict. Another either/or argument is that it is better to act than to analyze. Analysis by itself may never lead to action. Indeed, it can be confusing or an excuse for delay. Still, analysis can improve the depth of judgment and help ensure that action is based on careful reflection that takes into account relevant considerations. It may also reinforce taking actions that entail risk for the decision maker. The conclusion that "I must take this action for these reasons" combines character and judgment.

These observations support the conclusion that the components of ethical action are not linear; rather, each stage in the decision process can reinforce the others (Rest et al. 1999, 102). The model that is proposed here is a framework for analysis but it depends on awareness. The model does not isolate ethical judgment from ethical action. The model involves the identification of options including a hypothetically "ideal" choice, but it culminates with the actual choice that one is willing to make and its justification to self and to others.

For some, the difficulty in ethical problem solving may come at the beginning. One must first have awareness, and this mental state cannot be automatically triggered. Even administrators with limited awareness, however, may have ethical problems thrust upon them that they cannot miss. Administrators in this circumstance will know that they have a problem to deal with, and a problem-solving model helps to ensure that they do so in a systematic and comprehensive way. It can help to expand sensitivity to encompass all aspects of the situation, guide the identification and analysis of options, and reinforce the inclination to choose the best alternative. The model does not ignore the impact of the choice on the decision maker and the fact that courage is needed to take a risky action; it can help to prevent errors and reduce the unknown aspects of risk. A useful problem-solving model cannot ignore emotions, practical considerations, and consequences for oneself as well as other stakeholders (Walker et al. 1995, 403).

The ethics problem-solving model presented here is a variant of the rational method for decision making.[48] Such models have advantages and disadvantages. They promote an orderly consideration of a problem based on comprehensive information. The decision should be drawn from the full range of relevant options. Some of these positive features, however, are related to the disadvantages. The information needed to support the model is considerable, and one can never have all the information that is related to a complex problem. The progression through stages in an orderly way conflicts with the nonrational way that people commonly approach decisions. The presence of a problem often prompts us to turn to a preformed "solution." The problem provides an opportunity to do something that we have wanted to do for some time. We then work backwards to collect the information needed to justify what we have already decided to do.

Despite the potential shortcomings of the rational approach to policy making, this kind of model is useful when facing complex problems with serious consequences. The context and implications are quite different when using this kind of model to decide how to handle an ethical dilemma as opposed to choosing among proposals to deal with a policy question. In the latter situation, the decision maker may have a preferred solution and must reconcile the use of a model that does not preclude any options with getting acceptance of an option that he or she already prefers. In handling an ethical problem, one faces the challenge of coming up with the best solution when there are no "good" options. Using the model may check an impulse (a "gut reaction") to act precipitously. In a sense, the difference between the policy-making context and the ethical problem-solving context is the difference between saying "I want to do this" and "what am I going to do?" When you know what you want to do, a "rational" analysis may mask this preference, and it would be better to either not use the analysis or to be truly open to all options. When you don't know what you can do or are not certain you can do what you think you should do, there is an incentive and benefit to using a systematic process that helps to identify alternatives and clarifies the consequences of each option.

The ethics problem-solving model can help to determine whether one should actually go through with an action that he or she would prefer not to take because of potential negative consequences. For example, an official may be agonizing over whether to expose a serious problem in the organization and report it to a superior or go outside the organization and blow the whistle. In making this decision, the model seeks to ensure that all factors have been taken into account, all stakeholders have been identified, all ethical approaches have been considered, and all options have been generated. One may have an immediate preference for one course of action, but the model can be used to check that option against others before making a commitment. If the original option still emerges from the analysis as the best option, one has the reassurance that he or she is not acting impulsively.

The model is divided into three stages: description, analysis, and decision.[49] Each major stage and step within it will be described and applied to a case. The model appears in **Figure 7.1**.

The problem-solving model starts with description; identifying the facts of the situation and the stakeholders. It is important to get as much information as possible and to not interpret the information at this stage in the analysis. Rather than trying to determine "why is my boss taking this action?", focus instead on exactly what your supervisor is doing. It is also important to be as inclusive as possible in identifying stakeholders. Ignoring key groups that are affected by the situation weakens the process and increases the likelihood that the analysis will be self-serving.

I. Description

- Clarify the facts of the situation.
- Assess the interests of all parties who have stakes in the outcome of the situation and how they are potentially affected; stakeholder analysis.

II. Analysis

- Determine your duty in this situation considering the obligations and responsibilities of your position and your professional role.
  - Consider one's position and place in the organizational structure and what one is expected to do by the organization
  - Consider any professional obligations that are distinct from what the organization expects; specific standards for one's profession and general obligations, including advancing the public interest and promoting the democratic process.
- Analyze the situation according to each ethical approach.
  - Virtue based: What would a good person do in this situation?
  - Principle based: What principles apply to the situation?
  - Results oriented: How does one promote the best consequences?
- List options.

III. Decision

- Choose the best alternative.
- Provide a reasoned justification for the decision.
- Monitor and evaluate results. Make adjustments if necessary.

Figure 7–1 *Ethical Problem-Solving Model*

The analysis stage examines the situation from different perspectives in order to identify options. It is important to first determine one's duty from an internal and external perspective; what are the obligations and responsibilities one has based on his or her position in the organization and what are the obligations and responsibilities based on external professional standards? The overall question here is based on duty: "How can the public interest be advanced in this situation?" Further analysis is guided by using each of the three ethical approaches guided by these questions:

- What would a person of character do in this situation?
- What principles are at stake in this situation and what actions would follow from these principles?
- What are the best consequences that could be achieved in this situation, and what actions would be taken to achieve them?

From the answers to these questions, a set of options can be developed. It is possible that the alternate perspectives will all reinforce the same option. When this happens, using duty and the three approaches will have produced beneficial reinforcement. In other situations, the different analytical questions may generate options that conflict with or are at odds with each other. Even when this happens, the use of all the approaches helps to ensure that one does not choose among a limited or skewed set of options that ignores an important ethical perspective.

The final stage in the model is to make an informed ethical choice and to be able to explain and justify it. Choosing among conflicting options is difficult, but at least one can feel confident that the choice did not ignore an important alternative. It will also be easier to explain the basis for the decision if duty and all three ethical approaches have been considered.

It is useful to work through the model using a case. Consider the situation presented in **Case 7.1**. In this situation, the initial impulse is probably to keep the former employee from getting another job and to protect your colleague. This response, however, could easily have serious negative implications for the city manager in North Carolina and his government. He might also feel helpless thinking that the legal settlement precludes any action on his part and has removed all flexibility.

Forcing oneself to systematically analyze the dilemma using the problem-solving model can help to produce responsible and creative options. In the description stage of the model, one seeks to clarify the facts and collect additional information to understand the situation as fully as possible. Insofar as possible, one should not try to interpret the facts at this stage but treat them objectively. Similarly, one should try to distinguish what is known and what is speculation. In this case, the manager considers the facts of the employee's

Case 7.1   *The Troubling Reference*[50]

You are a city manager in North Carolina. You check your voice mail messages and find that one of your colleagues in Georgia has just called you to inquire about a job applicant for a mid-level management position who once worked for your town. You can feel your blood pressure begin to rise and beads of sweat break out on your forehead. This job applicant was charming and produced good results in units he directed, but he had to be fired after numerous allegations of sexual harassment. You reviewed the case and were convinced that the firing was fully justified. He promptly hired a lawyer and sued the town. To save embarrassment for their families, the victims of the alleged harassment did not want the case to go to trial. Without their testimony, the city's position was untenable. So, reluctantly, the city settled the case out of court for several thousand dollars, a carefully worded letter of reference, and an agreement not to talk about the agreement. Your colleague, who attended graduate school with you, is now asking you some detailed questions. Many of these questions cannot be answered with the letter of reference. Do you answer the questions or not?

tenure in the city and the legal settlement. He cannot know whether the former employee will engage in the same behavior, but he feels certain that the employee was sexually chauvinistic and harassed at least three female subordinates. His challenge to the city's firing indicates that he was unrepentant. The legal agreement restricts what the city manager can say about the former employee. The city manager does not know whether his former employee will get the job, but he knows that the man can make an extremely positive impression in an interview setting and that his experience looks impressive on paper.

The stakeholders are numerous and include the former employee/job applicant, you and your colleague, employees in the Georgia city (in particular, the female staff the applicant would supervise), and the employees and citizens of your city. If the former employee were damaged by revealing information that went beyond the agreed-to letter of recommendation, the city could be forced to pay a substantial sum to compensate the employee. The city manager could be personally liable. If he were hired, some of his female subordinates could be severely harmed. The city manager's Georgia colleague would blame him for not warning him about the applicant's past behavior.

In the analysis stage, there are two separate but potentially overlapping elements. First, one determines the obligations of his or her actual position as well as the obligations of his or her professional role. Second, one applies each of the ethical perspectives to the situation. In the first element, there may be a distinction between what the organization expects an official to do and what one's profession would expect. This aspect of the analysis involves examining the duties of the position and the profession. A key potential difference in these two ways of looking at your role will involve what the organizational or political superiors want an official to do as opposed to what the profession would expect you to do. Expectations of organizational and political superiors are important given the emphasis on accountability in public administration, but they are not necessarily binding. Their preferences must be weighed against the professional standards, which reflect the recommended practices of the professional group, and an assessment of how to best serve the public interest. For example, policy analysts may encounter the tension between pressures to make a favorable case for a proposal favored by political superiors and the standards of cost-benefit analysis. A nonprofit director may have to reconcile a decision by her board of directors to undertake a project that does not meet professional standards for effective use of funds.

In this situation of the former employee, the obligations of the city manager's position are shaped by the legal settlement and his fiduciary responsibility to his city government. He cannot expose his city to financial harm by ignoring the terms of the settlement. The broader obligations of his professional role, however, based on tenets in the ICMA code of ethics would stress objective consideration of merit in hiring and support for members of the profession. At this step in the analysis, there are two obvious options: (a) do not share any information beyond the letter of recommendation and (b) reveal additional information about the former employee's past behavior. A possible option (c) is to warn the colleague without violating the terms of the agreement, but it is not clear how this could be done.

When one analyzes a problem according to each ethical perspective, there are three key questions. In the virtue-based perspective: What would a person of character do? A good person would be honest (how could he withhold such important information?), be beneficent and protect others from harm, and be loyal to his colleague. The second or third options are supported by this perspective. In the principle-based perspective: What principles apply to the situation? The principles that apply to the situation are drawn from the legal dimension. The city manager should adhere to the legal agreement in the settlement. Option (a) is supported as is option (c) if it can be developed. In the results-oriented perspective: How does one promote the best consequences? The manager considers how to promote the best consequences for the greatest number. An inherent limitation of this perspective becomes apparent: How does one compare the intense suffering of a few women possibly mistreated in the future by the applicant in Georgia with the potentially large but widely spread fiscal pain of the legal settlement to the taxpayers or the citizens denied services in the city in North Carolina? There is a differing level of uncertainty about outcomes. If the manager remains silent and the applicant gets the job, he may sexually harass women in his new position. If the applicant does not get the position because of information from the manager that goes beyond the legal settlement, the applicant is very likely to sue the city. Also, how much weight should the city manager give to the loss of his professional reputation (and personal regard) in eyes of his colleague? In the absence of a clear way to resolve these competing calculations, the results-oriented perspective does not clearly support or preclude option (a) or (b). It would be supportive, however, of option (c) because it promotes good outcomes in Georgia without negative outcomes in North Carolina.

To review the options, there are three: (a) do not share any information beyond the letter of recommendation, (b) reveal additional information about the former employee's past behavior, and (c) warn the colleague without violating the terms of the agreement.

The third option is the best because it meets the conditions of each aspect of the analysis. The question is how it can be accomplished. To use duplicity to call the colleague at home and give him some friend-to-friend advice or to send a message through another person would raise other ethical issues. To state that he cannot answer the questions because of a legal settlement would violate the spirit of the agreement. One method would be for the city manager to read the letter in response to each question his colleague asked. This method would be consistent with the letter of the agreement and, after several repetitions, his colleague would probably get the message that there is something that the North Carolina city manager cannot tell him. The manager would have met his clear obligation as a responsible member of the city manager profession, as a virtuous person, and as a person who seeks to achieve the best outcomes to both protect staff members in the city in Georgia and to protect his own city. The drawback is that the colleague in Georgia would not know the nature of the misconduct but simply get the impression that there is a problem with this applicant.

The manager should monitor the situation and evaluate results. If, for example, he were to learn that the applicant had been hired after all, he would once again face the dilemma of whether to somehow warn his colleague in Georgia. At this point, he should go through the model again to assess options under these changed conditions.

Use the model again to consider a decision in a nonprofit organization. Examine **Case 7.2**. The stakeholders in this case are the organization itself and its commitment to the causes it supports, the board members and their ability to establish policy, the director and staff whose integrity and security

Case 7.2   *The Big Donor*[51]

Yours is an advocacy organization, and funding is always difficult for such nonprofits, because most foundations are leery of supporting them. You have a donor who has been very generous; indeed, her gifts have underwritten a substantial portion of your budget. The organization takes a position on a local controversy in furtherance of and consistent with its mission. It turns out that the donor will be adversely affected if the organization prevails, and the donor makes it clear that support will stop if the organization doesn't mute, or at least moderate, its position. It is possible to modify the position significantly without looking as if you have backed off, so other supporters will not know that you have bowed to the pressure. There is no way to make up for the loss of income in the short term, and you will have to fire three long-time staff members if the donor terminates support. What do you do?

are affected, and of course the major donor. A consideration of the responsibility of the director would stress commitment to mission and resistance of the use of financial pressure to force a change in policy. According to the ethical approaches, honesty and integrity would also be linked to resisting pressure, as would the related principle of promise keeping. The consequentialist approach offers conflicting perspectives. There is a great potential risk to credibility if the change in position were to become known. Supporters and future contributors would likely be repelled by the action. Even if the reasons for the change in position were not known, the organization would be vulnerable to pressure from this donor again in the future if the director caved in on this issue. On the other hand, the short-range consequences of losing the funding from the major donor are dire. Staff members would have to be dismissed, and the capacity of the organization to maintain its program of work would be lost for some time to come. The major options then are to stand firm and give up the contribution or to quietly move away from the position that is offensive to the donor. The latter course of action could be acceptable only if it were accompanied by a major effort to diversify support. You would need to inform key members of the board of the actions and be held accountable for achieving results. You also need to inform the staff members that the action you are taking is buying time, but there is uncertainty about their future prospects because the director will not give in to the large donor again. I believe that either course of action is defensible—the virtuous, principled approach of standing firm or the consequentialist choice of modifying the position and undertaking a major effort to broaden support. If you choose the latter approach to save the organization's resources in the short run, you must be accountable to the key members of the board for success in diversifying the funding for the organization and to resisting pressure from any funding source in the future.

Problem Solving and Action

What kind of risk and cross pressures did the administrators experience in these cases? The city manager faced with deciding how to handle the disturbing reference did not need courage so much as cunning to discern an approach that would signal a warning without violating the legal agreement as well constraint to keep from revealing the details about the applicants that might have been the impulsively right thing to do. The nonprofit director who chose to let her organization and a number of its key staff members live to fight another day while taking long-term steps to strengthen organizational capacity and independence experienced the inner turmoil of deciding not to be fully honest and not to stand on principle. All these emotional reactions are part of the process of analyzing and deciding what to do. As Walker and his colleagues (1995, 397) put it, "real-life moral conflicts are hardly experienced in the same way as . . . idle intellectual exercises." I do not suppose that the decision maker uses the model with *Star Trek* Vulcanian detachment. The mixture of analysis and emotion (the interaction of the cognitive and affective dimensions) is to be expected. The importance of the model is to force one to consider aspects of the situation that might be lost in a purely intuitive response and to incorporate both one's own responsibilities and consequences, including the emotional impact of the decision. The analysis incorporates consideration of the qualities needed to act. The analysis clarifies which options are satisfactory or unsatisfactory for different reasons. It will be obvious if one does not choose the hypothetical ideal (standing firm in the nonprofit case) and it calls on the decision maker to justify whatever option is chosen, to review the impact of the decision, and to consider when a different choice should be made if the consequences are bad.

The dilemma of choosing among options that differ greatly in their impact on the decision maker is dramatically highlighted in whistleblowing cases. What can be learned from whistleblowers about making tough decisions is considered in the next chapter.

Chapter 8

Acting on Duty in the Face of Uncertainty and Risk:

Responsible Whistleblowing

The act of whistleblowing involves special complications. It is the classic act of deviance for an administrator, but is sometimes taken behind the cloak of anonymity. It can be a noble gesture taken at great personal risk, but it is not always the ethically appropriate action to take. When is whistleblowing a heroic action that serves the public interest, and when is it an act of disloyalty that weakens the organization and indirectly harms those the organization is supposed to be serving?

It is useful to start with a definition of whistleblowing, even though this precise definition is commonly ignored. When a staff member becomes aware of a problem within a public organization, the active responses are to raise the matter internally or to alert someone outside the organization. Technically, the former action is an internal complaint, and only the latter is actual whistleblowing or sounding an alarm outside the organization. The distinction is critically important because a major decision that the staff member must make is whether to take the internal or external path and how long to stay on the internal path if nothing positive seems to be happening. Furthermore, the distinction is important because there is typically a much stronger negative reaction from the organization when actual whistleblowing occurs as opposed to staying inside. Although negative consequences can result from internal complaints as well, the full force of organizational retaliation often accompanies going public with the complaint; in other words, whistleblowing precisely defined.

Despite these arguments about the distinctions, there are definitions in use that break down the differences. A major report from the Merit System Protection Board deals with *internal* complaints by federal employees, but the report is entitled "Whistleblowing in the Federal Government." The Government Accountability Project (GAP)—a major advocacy group that supports whistleblowers—combines internal and external reporting in its standard definition of a whistleblower. Blowing the whistle may include reporting the wrongdoing to authorities in government, refusing to take part in activities that involve wrongdoing in the workplace, providing testimony in a legal proceeding, and leaking information about wrongdoing to the media.[52] It would seem obvious that publicly reporting a problem, as opposed to "leaking" it anonymously to the media or to other outside sources such as an elected official or board member, would also constitute whistleblowing but it is not included in the list for reasons that will be examined shortly.

Despite these combined uses of the term, we will maintain the distinction between internal complaints and whistleblowing that reveals a problem outside the organization. However, be mindful that whistleblowing is often viewed as any complaint activity by staff regarding allegedly serious organizational misconduct. It is distinguishable from resisting an order to bury a negative report, even though an action of that kind can produce a similar response from a superior and GAP considers this behavior to be whistleblowing as well.

It is helpful to recognize one other aspect of both practices. When we discuss strategies for complaints and whistleblowing, it is assumed that there is organizational reluctance and even resistance to change. The complaint is threatening to the organization, and it acts defensively. A concern expressed internally that is resolved through positive action will not lead to whistleblowing and may not even be perceived by either the initiator or the superiors as a complaint. This condition adds an element of uncertainty at the front end. When a problem area is identified and/or an idea about change is introduced, will it be welcomed or snag a trip-wire that produces an explosion? What constitutes a "complaint," therefore, is partly in the eye of the beholder. In this regard, the distinction between complaints and whistleblowing holds up. It can be taken for granted that a report taken outside the organization despite efforts to show the organization in a favorable light is going to be considered as whistleblowing and produce a negative response.

Conditions for Responsible Whistleblowing

Staff members owe loyalty to their organization. They should try to help make it strong and encourage internal improvement. Consequently, one does not casually go public with concerns about the organization. Certain conditions should be met before blowing the whistle. First, be certain that a true, serious problem exists that clearly warrants corrective action. Second, have facts about the problem, which usually means that you are close to the situation. It is not appropriate to go outside based on unsubstantiated rumors about problems that may be occurring in some other part of the organization than your work area. Third, focus on the abuse that is occurring, not the people or personalities involved. Whistleblowing is not for personal attacks on people you do not like. Fourth, be certain your motives are to serve the public, not advance your own or your unit's agenda. Finally, exhaust internal channels to see if the problem can be solved internally before going outside of the organization with the problem.

There is one additional set of conditions: Be above reproach with regard to the problem, in your work life, and possibly in your personal life. This is important for two reasons. First, do not use whistleblowing to pin the blame on others if you are partly responsible for the problem. It is likely to be ineffective, because you may be singled out as the primary source of the problem. Second, when you blow the whistle, be prepared for negative reactions, which we examine later. If there are deficiencies in your work performance, these could be used as the reason for taking disciplinary action against you, and you will be in a gray area in trying to establish the claim that you were a victim of retaliation. If there are aspects of your personal life that make you vulnerable to attack or embarrassment, it is unwise to open yourself to the possibility that information will be used to discredit you or hurt your family. If you do not meet the "above-reproach" test, it is better to work on the inside even if the prospects for effective resolution of the problem are more limited.

Let us return to one of the key conditions: exhausting internal channels to correct the problem. There are strong reasons why this should be done—and unfortunately, there are also strong reasons for not doing this. The arguments for exhausting internal channels build on the condition of loyalty to the organization. You should normally alert others in the organization to give them a chance to correct the problem. One should not assume that the organization would condone the behavior or activity that you have observed and would not want to correct it. If it happens that your supervisor is involved in the problem, this does not mean that persons above him or her would allow the behavior to continue if they knew about it. It is possible that corrective efforts are already underway and bringing public attention could interfere with the actions being taken as well as embarrass the organization. Finally, exhausting internal channels may be a requirement for employees in the organization and going outside could bring about disciplinary action for failure to meet this requirement (or could be the reason given for disciplinary action). If you are clearly identified with the problem and its identification, there is nothing lost in trying the internal approach first.

There are also many reasons to blow the whistle before exhausting all internal channels. The biggest unknown is how others in the organization will respond. If they are part of the problem or aware and condone the practices that created the problem, you have exposed yourself to persons who may have the power to retaliate. Alerting superiors on the inside gives time for a cover-up and possibly a counterattack that implicates you in the problem. If there is no one who will receive your complaint other than your superior whom you believe is part of the problem, you may put yourself in jeopardy by taking the complaint to this person. Finally, pursuing the complaint first inside the organization may preclude being an anonymous whistleblower later. If information is leaked about a problem you have already raised internally, you are likely to be identified as the source.

The agonizing reality of the whistleblowing options is that you probably will not be able to have full information on which to make your choice, even if you use a systematic problem-solving model to analyze your options. You will take a chance whether you stay in or go out. It is safer to keep quiet but that means ignoring the situation. If the problem is serious enough, you may be compelled to act.

A method of reducing the risk to yourself is to engage in "The Art of Anonymous Activism," the title of a report from the Government Accountability Project (GAP), Project on Government Oversight (POGO), and Public Employees for Environmental Responsibility (PEER). Anonymous leaks serve the purpose of getting the word out, but they rule out any engagement by a staff member who seeks change in dialogue within the organization. The leak may cause the organization to hunker down and create an atmosphere of suspicion that affects all staff as the effort is made to identify the leaker, but at least it may be pressured by embarrassment and outside pressure to make reforms. GAP/POGO/PEER (2002) equate anonymous whistleblowing with "serving the public while surviving public service," the subtitle of their report. The three organizations support this approach to counter the likelihood of retaliation of public agencies against whistleblowers and the perceived weakness of whistleblower-protection provisions.

The revelation of the identity of the mysterious and infamous "deep throat" of the Watergate scandal has focused the spotlight on the anonymous whistleblower and produced a controversy about how to interpret the actions of the number two official in the FBI who chose to reveal information to the reporter Bob Woodward. Mark Felt's behavior also raises a question not considered up to this point: Do the motives of the whistleblower make a difference? Although there is still considerable uncertainty about the circumstances surrounding Felt's actions, these points can be made (Hitchens 2005, 8):

- Felt sought to expose abuse of power and illegal activity at the same time as a large scale criminal investigation of the Watergate break-in was going on.

- Felt settled a score after being passed over as the new director of the FBI.

- Felt feared that the independence of the FBI was threatened by the White House, but he also resisted changes in the FBI.

- Felt assisted the media but also took advantage of it. In the words of one reviewer, his disclosure "ranks as the single most successful use of the news media by an anonymous unelected official with an agenda of his own."

- By going outside, Felt helped to prevent suppression of the investigation which was being closely monitored by the White House. His superiors already knew the information that Felt was leaking.[53]

Ethical ambiguities surround Felt's behavior. Some contend that he acted disloyally by revealing information that undermined the president, and he had to actively conceal his behavior by lying to acting director L. Patrick Gray III (Dobbs 2005; Corn and Goldberg 2005). He carried out investigations of other FBI personnel in sham efforts to identify who was leaking information. He appears to have acted out of a combination of self-interest and protecting the public interest, but he apparently believed sincerely that the Constitution was threatened by the coverup.[54] David Schultz (U.S. Newswire 2005) characterizes Felt as a "qualified patriot."

Generalizing from this spectacular case, the practice of anonymous leaking may be the only way to reveal problems inside an organization without risking great personal sacrifice. The practice, however, frees leakers from any accountability for the veracity of the information they reveal and increases the possibility that motives other than safeguarding the public will drive the action. The leaker may not be contributing to any internal solution of the problem, which might have been correctable without great public embarrassment to the organization. Anonymous whistleblowers, if successful at concealing their identities, never have to justify their actions.

Despite acknowledging these reservations about anonymous activism, the likelihood and severity of retaliation often makes it a prudent act.

Retaliatory Techniques

Whistleblower-protection groups urge officials to be aware of the risks and costs of whistleblowing. They warn potential whistleblowers to be aware of the tactics of retaliation that organizations may use against whistleblowers.

1. Spotlight the whistleblowers: Make the whistleblower, instead of his or her message, the issue.
2. Manufacture a poor record.
3. Threaten them into silence.
4. Isolate or humiliate them.
5. Set them up for failure.
6. Prosecute them.
7. Eliminate their jobs, paralyze their careers, or fire the whistleblower.[55]

Although these kinds of retaliation may seem particularly relevant to government, variations on any of the tactics can be found in the nonprofit sector. The job security for nonprofit staff is low—most are at-will employees—and there are no legislated whistleblower protections like those found in government. These circumstances could mean that options 2 through 6 from the list may be bypassed and a retaliating organization would go directly to number 7 and dismiss the staff member. Although there are many nonprofit organizations, the effect of blackballing the dismissed employee could be dire, especially within a specialized mission area, such as child advocacy or the arts. It is always hard to get another job without a satisfactory recommendation from one's last employer, and top staff in organizations doing similar work are likely to know each other.

When the organization is challenged, retaliation and the ensuing battle between the organization and the whistleblower may progress through a number of stages (Truelson 1987). First, the organization closes ranks against the whistleblower, and even peers and associates may shun the whistleblower as a troublemaker. The retaliation stage can involve the steps listed previously and result in the demotion, expulsion, and/or defamation of the whistleblower. Although in simplest terms, supervisors are not permitted to take reprisal against a staff member for whistleblowing, if managers are not punished for their retaliatory actions, they may be unrestrained in the actions they take. (This issue is explored further later in this chapter.) The effort to get back one's job or lost status often involves frequently delayed and prolonged lawsuits. The organization has far greater resources to survive during this extended process than does the whistleblower. Even if the final court decision is positive, there may be little or no victory for the whistleblower.

"The Art of Anonymous Activism" offers a set of recommendations for considering the whistleblowing option. They are presented in **Figure 8.1**.

Given these points of guidance, it seems unlikely that any rational administrator would choose to take the option to openly blow the whistle.

If you do become identified as a whistleblower, the GAP adds some additional recommendations.[56] As noted in the list of steps, try to create a support network to provide both personal and professional support. Even if the organization turns a cold shoulder or worse, others likely will share your concern about the problem you have brought to light. At the same time, it is a mistake to assume that even sympathetic supporters will share the same level of intensity—the same moral indignation—that the whistleblower does and the general public is going to be even less engaged. Keep others informed and make judicious use of public relations but don't let your cause become a crusade that is

---

1. **Consult your loved ones.** . . . Blowing the whistle is a family decision. Before taking any irreversible steps, talk to your spouse, your family or close friends—the support group you will need to depend upon in the coming days—about your decision to blow the whistle. If they are not with you, you may want to rethink your path.

2. **Check for skeletons in your closet.** Any personal vulnerability or peccadillo you possess can, and most likely will, be used by the agency against you. . . . One practical step is to make a copy of the complete contents of your personnel file as insurance that new but backdated "dirt" cannot be later slipped in.

3. **Document, document, document.** Keep copious records and a daily diary of relevant information, memorialize conversations with letters to the file and maintain a separate set of documents outside of work in a safe place. Your chances of success will likely depend on how powerful a paper trail you produce. After you blow the whistle, your access to agency records may be immediately cut off.

4. **Do not use government resources.** Do not engage in whistleblowing activity on agency time, even to defend yourself in a retaliation case unless you have specific approval, such as through a union collective bargaining agreement. . . .

5. **Check to see who, if anyone, will support your account.** Gauge the level of concern among your co-workers for the concerns you might raise. If you can't count on others to later testify as supporting witnesses, you may be well advised to wait before challenging misconduct. Try to stay on good terms with administrative staff members who may be in a position to know of impending agency actions.

6. **Consult an attorney early.** Do not wait until you are in the "career emergency room" before seeking professional help. . . .

7. **Choose your battles.** Pick favorable terrain for highlighting your issue. Don't sweat the small stuff. . . . In any personnel action, the advantage is with the employer, not the lone employee.

8. **Identify allies.** There is strength in numbers. Do not wait to be isolated by the agency. . . . If possible, line up the assistance of sympathetic interest groups, elected officials or journalists. The strength of your support coalition may determine the outcome of the battle ahead.

9. **Have a well thought-out plan.** Be clear-headed about precisely what you expect to accomplish and how. . . . Try to prepare for agency counter-moves by anticipating agency responses to your charges and mapping out the counter to those charges. . . .

10. **Get yourself a little career counseling.** Map out where your actions will leave you a year from now, two years from now, five years, etc. Plan out the route you want to take and how you reasonably expect your professional path to proceed. There is no doubt that you are about to embark upon a professional journey.

Source: POGO/GAP/PEER 2002, 4–7. Used with the permission of the Government Accountability Project.

Figure 8–1 *Ten Tips for Potential Whistleblowers*

all-consuming. It is possible to seek assistance from whistleblower support groups. In addition, be careful not to exaggerate or embellish your charges in order to gain more attention or support. If part of your story can be shown to be inaccurate, your whole position can be discredited. When working with authorities in the organization or in agencies that deal with your complaint, don't wear your cynicism on your sleeve. Staff who could be sympathetic or at least neutral may be turned against you. The experiences of whistleblowers show that you should prepare for the long haul, and you need to make wise use of your personal, professional, and financial resources.

A coalition of whistleblower advocacy groups (POGO/GAP/PEER 2002, 1–7) presents anonymous whistleblowing as "A Better Way." Their preference is evident in the Chapter 1 title, "Blowing the Whistle May Be Hazardous to Your Professional Health" and subheadings like "Downsides Are Apparent," "It Is Not a Fair Fight," and "It Often Takes the Best and Brightest Out of the Agencies." Rather than drawing attention to the complainant, this approach involves leaking information in a way that will not identify the source. For these groups, the risks of public whistleblowing are simply too high: "Throwing away your entire career, particularly if there are other ways to ventilate the problem, is imprudent and counterproductive" (POGO/GAP/PEER 2002, 7). The alleged ineffectiveness comes, in their view, from the tendency of organizations to focus on the disgruntled employee rather than the substance of the problem that has been identified. They argue that by making the employee invisible, more attention is given to the issue. Even leaks do not necessarily preserve the anonymity of a source if only a very small number of staff have access to a document that is given to the media. The methods of anonymous whistleblowing must be flexible and include the following (POGO/GAP/PEER 2002, ch. 2):

- Stay under cover and feed information to an outside advocacy group. Using an advocacy partner who negotiates the way that the document can be used is safer than contacting the reporter directly.

- Use a collective voice such as an employee union or other employee organization as the source to raise the complaint. It is harder to retaliate against an organization.

- Publication of "white papers" that explain complex issues in understandable language is often a better approach than using the original internal documents which are full of jargon and technical language. The paper should be written by anonymous employees and edited by the staff of an advocacy partner that releases the paper and handles media relations.

- Ghost writing by agency staff tells advocacy groups or the staff of legislative committees what to ask for in requests to the agency for explanations of actions or requests for release of documents under the Freedom of Information Act.

Steps to Protect Whistleblowers

The U.S. government and many states have enacted laws designed to protect whistleblowers from reprisal and also to define how complaints are to be made. The Whistleblower Protection Act of 1989 contained these provisions:

- Disclosures can be made to anyone inside or out of an agency of actions that the employee reasonably believes evidences (a) a violation of any law, rule, or regulation, or (b) mismanagement, a gross waste of funds, an absence of authority, or a substantial and specific danger to public health or safety.

- If the disclosure of information is prohibited by law and if the information is classified as secret by Executive Order, disclosure must be made to
  - Special Counsel
  - Inspector General of the agency or
  - Another employee designated by the head of the agency to receive such disclosures.

- Office of Special Counsel (OSC) was made an independent agency whose mandate includes protecting whistleblowers.

- OSC may request a delay, or "stay," of 45 days in carrying out an adverse personnel action, pending investigation of the action by OSC.

- Softened the burden of proof for establishing that one was a victim of reprisal: the employee simply needs to show that a complaint was a "contributing" rather than a "significant" or "predominant" factor in dismissal, harassment, or other reprisal.

The central provision of the act establishes whistleblower protection as one of the key merit system principles on which the federal civil service is based. If the employee believes that he or she has been the victim of *reprisal* (a prohibited personnel practice), a written complaint can be filed with the U.S. Office of Special Counsel.[57] The primary mission of the OSC is to protect federal employees and applicants from prohibited employment practices, with a particular emphasis on protecting whistleblowers from retaliation.

When a claim is filed by a federal employee, the OSC investigates the allegation to determine whether there are reasonable grounds to believe that a prohibited personnel practice has occurred. If there is reason to believe that a prohibited personnel practice has occurred, the special counsel sends a report to the head of the employing agency, stating the OSC's findings and requesting that the agency remedy the illegal action. If an agency does not do so, the OSC is authorized to file a petition for corrective action with the Merit System Protection Board. The number of cases investigated is small compared to the number of complaints received. For example, in 2003, of the 2385 complaints on file including cases carried over from the previous year, 7 percent (162 cases) were referred for field investigation. Two thirds were processed and closed and just over one quarter were carried to the next year (OSC 2004, Table 1).[58]

The OSC investigation and intervention can restore the work conditions of an employee who has suffered reprisal and generally when a case is referred to an agency, corrective action is agreed to through a voluntary process (OSC 2004, 7).[59] Still, very few cases are investigated. In response to a survey of staff members who have submitted complaints, over four out of five were dissatisfied with the results of the OSC service in 2002 (OSC 2003, 25) and 2003 (OSC 2004, 22).

Four aspects of the Whistleblower Protection Act (WPA) limit what actions are permissible and the likelihood of receiving protection. First, although the law as amended in 1994 seems clear and straightforward in its coverage and protection, significant limitations exist—some resulting from the provisions of the law itself and other from interpretations by the federal circuit court, which has exclusive jurisdiction for handling WPA cases. The kind of actions that qualify as whistleblowing and, therefore, are suitable for protection have been limited in practice. If the conduct is part of one's normal responsibilities or involves a supervisor rather than someone outside the chain of command or outside the organization, it is not protected. Elaine Kaplan (U.S. Congress 2003), a former special counsel who opposes this interpretation, offers this example:

> Suppose that a security screener at National Airport who works for the Transportation Security Administration notices that the X-ray machines are malfunctioning on a regular basis. He suspects that, because of these malfunctions, a number of passengers may have been permitted to board airlines without being screened. It is part of his job to report such malfunctions to his supervisor. The screener goes to his supervisor and tells him about the malfunctioning machines. The supervisor tells the employee not to write up a report but to go back to work—he does not want to do the paperwork and does not want it to get out that the X-ray machines at National Airport don't work properly. He tells him, don't worry, we will get the problem fixed. One week later, the employee returns and the problem has not been fixed. This time, he tells his supervisor, if nothing is done, he will report the supervisor's inaction up the chain of command, or perhaps to the Inspector General. The supervisor fires the employee.

"Under current law," Kaplan concludes, "this employee has no recourse. Because he made his disclosure as part of his regular job duties, he is not protected by the anti-retaliation provisions of the Whistleblower Protection Act" (U.S. Congress 2003).

Second, another questionable aspect of interpretation is the extent of misconduct alleged by whistleblowers and the evidence they have to support it. Although an extremely high standard of evidence is apparently not required,[60] it appears that complaints that are based on subjective opinion alone (even if believed by other staff) or which do not represent serious mismanagement are not considered to be disclosures that will be treated as whistleblowing that qualifies for protection. For example, a recent Merit Systems Protection Board (MSPB) publication provides qualitative standards for what constitutes gross mismanagement or waste of funds, serious abuse of authority, or substantial and specific danger to public health. Thus, other elements of uncertainty are added to whistleblowing: Am I complaining to the right person, will my complaint rise to the level of seriousness expected, and does the complaint have sufficient reasonableness to warrant protection from reprisal?

Third, another important limitation of whistleblower protection is restrictions on the kinds of material that can be released. Classified material may not be released, but other kinds of reports are restricted by law as well. For example, Robert Sullivan, a criminal investigator with the General Services Administration (GSA), took three GSA audit reports and six FBI reports to the *Boston Globe* in 1975.[61] Sullivan insisted the reports revealed a pattern of corruption in construction contracting at the Boston GSA office. Both GSA and the Civil Service Commission considered Sullivan's activity as a threat to agency authority. He was discharged for the unauthorized release of documents and for failing to report what he considered to be irregularities to appropriate GSA officials. The appeals officer for the Civil Service Commission described Sullivan's activity as personal, unofficial, and smacking of anarchy. This is an interesting case but it occurred before the passage of the WPA of 1989. Would Sullivan's actions be protected today? The documents Sullivan released, although not classified as secret, are restricted under the Freedom of Information Act (FOIA). The FOIA exempts interagency and intraagency communications protected by legal privileges and information compiled for law enforcement purposes. Although the documents in question might be obtained today if the investigation were completed, they would be released only after review by the agency and removal of sensitive information. Thus, it is likely both the GSA internal audits and the FBI investigations would be excluded from release by these two exemptions.

A final limitation in the law pertains to the disciplining of supervisors who engage in reprisal. Just as the protection of whistleblowers seems straightforward, reprisal appears to be a clearly prohibited personnel action. Federal civil service law specifies that a supervisor may not take a personnel action against an employee because of whistleblowing. The examples of disciplinary actions, however, contained in annual reports of the special counsel seem light in view of the actions taken by supervisors.[62]

In 2002 and 2003, the OSC reports, respectively, 13 and 12 disciplinary actions negotiated with agencies (Office of the Special Counsel 2003; 2004). If the agency does not agree, however, the OSC can file a complaint requesting disciplinary action with the MSPB.[63] It is necessary for the OSC to demonstrate that if the whistleblowing activity had not occurred, then that manager would not have taken the adverse personnel action (U.S. Congress 2005). It is important to note that this is not the test that is applied to the whistleblower under WPA; the whistleblower must simply show that the complaint was a contributing factor to the reprisal. The law, however, did not address disciplinary actions. If the supervisor can offer other reasons why the whistleblower was disciplined, the action is not considered to be reprisal. As a Senate committee report concluded, the MSPB has often agreed with the whistleblower that he or she was a victim of reprisal and should get relief, but the OSC rejected the claim that the managers should be disciplined.[64] Generally organizations defend the action that they have taken against the whistleblower's charges of inappropriate reprisal. It is to be expected, therefore, that the agency will view the actions of their managers as appropriate, and the managers will not be penalized for their actions.

Although little systematic research has been done on state whistleblower-protection laws, it is likely that similar limitations would apply to their coverage and effectiveness as well.

Who Are Whistleblowers?

Some observers criticize ethics reform on the grounds that it makes government even more complex and impairs effective performance. The critics are likely to see whistleblowing as a disruptive activity and whistleblowers generally as malcontents who exploit efforts to protect them. Frank Anechiarico and James Jacobs (1996) argue that the benefits of disclosing information are immeasurable but the negative impact of protection provisions in undermining the disciplinary process are obvious. The "apparent premise" that supports provisions to protect staff "is that whistleblowers' allegations are generally true," but Anechiarico and Jacobs (1996, 66) have doubts about this. Whistleblower protection provisions may provide an incentive to employees with performance problems to protect themselves from disciplinary action by filing a complaint about an organizational problem.

Former Special Counsel Kaplan (U.S. Congress 2003) notes this rationale but refutes it as follows:

> As the head of OSC I frequently heard this old canard trotted out—that the law protects bad employees or that employees

cynically invoke the law's protection in order to make themselves immune from legitimate personnel actions. This is pure urban legend. The fact is, weak claims pressed by bad employees are weeded out through the administrative process. The majority of the cases filed with OSC get closed because the law is clear that it is not illegal to take appropriate action against bad employees, even if they are whistleblowers.

Despite these possibilities of self-serving behavior, the overwhelming evidence is that whistleblowers and internal critics are conscientious and public serving in their motivation (Jos, Tompkins, and Hays 1989; Brewer and Seldon 1998). Indeed, they are likely to suffer negative consequences for their action despite the presence of whistleblower-protection provisions. Their behavior can be viewed as contrary to their own self-interest. As noted earlier, whistleblower advocacy groups take the position that alternatives to whistleblowing should be found so as not to endanger one's career. They do not have faith in the protection process.

Responsible whistleblowing and internal complaining provide dramatic examples of behavior based on duty, adherence to principle, and personal and professional integrity. Whistleblowers may also feel that they are preventing negative consequences and helping the organization avoid the higher level of public opposition that comes from covering up problems rather than acknowledging and correcting them. Whistleblowers and internal critics accept a personal responsibility to act and stress their accountability to the public rather than organizational superiors. They are inspired by duty and are reinforced by each of the philosophical perspectives. This reinforcement includes the virtue of courage to act.

One must wonder whether it is inevitable that the individual must be pitted against their organization in serving the public. Meaningful protections should be put in place so that staff members do not have to face this choice. Despite these possibilities of self-serving behavior, most whistleblowers and internal critics seek to serve and protect the public. They choose to take an action that experience should tell them is not in their self-interest and that may lead to reprisal—large or small, formal or informal—even when there are whistleblower protections in place. If there is sincere concern about the negative effects of having an outside body investigate the possible wrongdoing that gives rise to blowing the whistle or alleged retaliation against whistleblowers, it is important for organizational leaders to create open and responsive organizations that renew themselves from within. This comes in part by being receptive to those who identify problems and by being committed to taking positive corrective action. This is part of the approach to elevating the ethical climate examined in the next chapter.

Chapter 9

Elevating Ethical Behavior in the Organization

I n this chapter, the attention shifts from challenges and choices that individuals face regarding their own behavior to how they can enhance the prospects of ethical behavior from others in the organization. The review of factors that contribute to unethical behavior in Chapter 6 identified many organizational features that have a negative impact. How can these be removed or reduced and how can a positive climate be created?

The discussion is obviously directed to the leaders of the organization who have broad-ranging opportunities for setting direction and priorities. It also applies to individual staff members at all levels as they take actions and exert responsibilities that have an impact on others. You may be a mid-level manager who can shape the conditions for a work group and guide how staff members interact with citizens, a supervisor who assesses and helps shape the performance of subordinates, or an analyst who develops proposals or procedures or evaluates how the organization performs. Street-level administrators of all kinds who have face-to-face contact with citizens and clients in delivering services— teachers, social services eligibility specialists, inspectors, and police officers— and staff members in nonprofit organizations who conduct outreach efforts or evaluate grant proposals are the public face of their organization. Their actions shape the operational meaning of concepts for openness, fairness, and public service and impact public perceptions of the integrity of the organization.

There are six major approaches to leadership and management that elevate the ethical climate in public organizations[65]:

1. Strong organization and management culture
2. Clear standards and expectations and effective training

3. Effective mechanisms for control
4. Positive management practices
5. Channels for complaints and values that encourage dissent
6. Commitment to equity and involvement in dealings with the public

Each will be examined in depth. It is not assumed that the task of creating a coherent organizational approach to enhancing ethics is an easy task to accomplish. In assessing ethical approaches in the organizations of a sample of ASPA members in 1996, James Bowman and Russell Williams (1997, 519) found that only one in 10 felt that most organizations have a "proactive, human-development, problem-solving approach that focuses on encouraging ethical behavior and deterring unethical behavior." Over one in five views organizations as taking a reactive, legalistic, and blame-punishment approach, whereas a majority—58 percent—felt that most organizations have no consistent approach (Bowman and Williams 1997), a slight improvement from the 64 percent who held this view in 1989 (Bowman 1990, 347). The challenge to the managers in public organizations is to develop a consistent and positive approach.

Strengthening Organization and Management Culture

The Office of the Public Sector Standards Commissioner in the state of Western Australia offered this observation about leadership:

> An important contributing factor to an agency's ability to build public trust and enable employees to better serve the public interest is a strong and demonstrable ethical base. Whilst all employees, including managerial staff, are contributors to building a strong ethical base, it is the managers who have a key role in making explicit the organisation's values and modeling the behaviour implicit in the ethical codes. In this sense, managers have greater scope and capacity to effect the cultural and systemic changes necessary to build public trust (Commissioner for Public Sector Standards 2005, 48).[66]

It can be argued that nothing is more important to enhancing the ethical climate of an organization than strong principled leadership that is credible and visible or, in other words, "management by example" (Bowman and Williams 1997, 519). These qualities are based on the personal example of the top administrator and supervisors at every level in the organization. These qualities reinforce the behavior of the vast majority of staff in public organizations who have a respect for leadership and a basic sense of duty and commitment to ethical practice. It is likely, as discussed at several points, that typical public service staff members have limited independent capacity for ethical action. Their ethical inclinations are embedded in a rule-oriented approach and constrained by the expectations of superiors and coworkers. Principled leadership provides a positive influence just as unprincipled leadership has a negative impact. An organizational culture that reinforces taking responsibility for actions, honesty, integrity, fairness, and openness in effect creates a tailwind that pushes staff in the positive direction they are generally inclined to go.

The idea of organizational culture suggests that there are widely perceived and shared norms that shape the way members interact with each other and guide behavior for good or ill.[67] It is a mix of formal policies and procedures and the unwritten "rules" that can be particularly powerful because they are not made explicit. All divisions in the organization may be equally important on the organization chart but one may be actually dominant because more of the resources and top officials tend to be drawn from it. There are specified standards and processes for promotion and salary but some people may get ahead more than others based on factors that are not part of the formal criteria. Official standards and actual decisions are not necessarily at odds with each other in an organization. Indeed, the level of consistency between policy and practice is a key indicator of the kind of organizational culture that exists with an agency. When there is a discrepancy, however, staff members tend to pay more attention to actions than to the rules, and cynicism is likely to be pervasive. For staff members who operate within the boundaries of rules, a culture in which the rules are variable or slippery encourages ethical relativism. It is easy to conclude that actions are OK if _____. You can fill in your own rationalization: the organization gets ahead, you make your superior look good, you shield the organization from criticism, and so forth.

To provide a positive and supportive culture, leaders and supervisors must seek in their public statements and policies and also in their day-to-day actions to promote positive norms. The leaders must follow the same rules and hold themselves to the same standards that others are expected to meet. They obviously enjoy enhanced power, prestige, and benefits by virtue of their position, and it is easier for them to bend the rules for still more benefits, shift blame to others, and claim credit for themselves that should be given to others. Furthermore, they may seek to be kept informed about what is really going on in the organization. As noted in Chapter 6, top-level officials cannot know everything that happens, but they can be more or less committed to openness and accepting of bad news as well as good. If leaders make negative choices, others see these behaviors as validated and look for the opportunity to behave in the same way themselves. Powerful signals are sent such as who gets ahead in the organization and what kinds of behavior are rewarded. If success at any cost gets one promoted, a higher salary, better assignments, or greater recognition, this is the behavior that will be emulated and actions that benefit others or put public interest over organizational interest will be slighted. If real accomplishment, sharing credit, helping out when you don't have to, and other positive behaviors are recognized, they will be encouraged.

Top officials should not simply avoid breaking the rules or making unjustified exceptions to policy. They should also be positive role models. Admired leaders do not have a shining image because it has been buffed by public relations specialists. They are ethical exemplars (Cooper and Wright 1992) who offer guidance and inspiration to others in the organization (and often to persons outside as well). They represent the best expression of the ideals to which the organization is committed. The exemplar is not on a pedestal; indeed the opposite is often the case. They are engaged in the same kinds of activities and deal with the same challenges as other staff members. Although a hackneyed expression, the illustrious leader will not ask others to do things he or she would not do him- or herself. By extension, such leaders also would not apply different standards to themselves and to others.

Leaders cannot always count on selfless behavior from members of the organization. Difficult circumstances arise when the organization is strapped for resources and cuts must be absorbed. Top leaders should not expect that some units or individuals will volunteer to sacrifice themselves to help the organization as a whole. Leaders should be transparent in their decisions and fair in the criteria that are used to impose burdens. Across-the-board cuts with the same percentage reduction for all serve to reward those who have not been as resourceful and whose programs are less important. No one is happy to get less than others but when leaders take the heat for hard decisions and act on clearly articulated principles, they can engender more support than they can by evading difficult decisions or obscuring (or concealing) the reasons for them.

Providing leadership by example and promoting positive norms are behaviors that persons at all levels of the organization can encourage. Anyone with supervisory responsibilities is a leader to those who report to him or her and can provide guidance. Staff members who encourage peers to maintain high standards are making a positive contribution to the ethical climate of the organization. Simply filling one's responsibilities in a conscientious way and refusing to cut corners or deviate from expectations set an example for others. Demonstrating the initiative to behave in this way without depending on the direction of superiors or the influence of coworkers presumes that the individual official, whether director or member of the rank and file, has and acts on a sense of ethical autonomy based on universal grounds, such as those summarized in the ethics triangle. Thus, we come full circle. Positive organizational culture reinforces ethical behavior by the members of the organization, but it ultimately depends on individuals who are willing to assert their own values to help shape that culture.

Clear Standards and Expectations and Effective Training

A question for organizational leaders to consider is whether it is useful to have an organizational code of ethics. Over the past decade, there appears to be a substantial increase in the adoption of codes of ethics by organizations as well as expanded emphasis on existing codes and standards.[68] Between 1992 and 2002, the proportion of city governments over 50,000 in population with codes increased two in five to three in five (West and Berman 2004, 195), although it appears that codes are less common in smaller cities. The Independent Sector promotes the adoption of codes in nonprofit organizations and provides guidelines and a suggested set of values and standards (see Chapter 5 for discussion). The United Way requires that its affiliates adopt and adhere to a locally developed code of ethics for volunteers and staff, and all of the members in the two highest categories of contributions must submit a copy of their current code of ethics to the national United Way.

Can a code contribute to widespread awareness of and commitment to ethics in the organization? Administrators generally feel that an agency-specific code is needed to supplement the ASPA code to make it effective (Bowman and Williams 1997, 521). West and Berman (2004) find that in city governments it is not the presence of a code but rather monitoring adherence to a code and the use of relevant ethics training that contribute to a greater sense of commitment and openness by staff. Presumably, the impact of having an organizational code would depend on its content. As noted in the discussion of professional codes of ethics, if a code is negative and focuses narrowly on microethical issues, it does little to elevate ethical thinking or behavior. It seems more appropriate to put specific rules of conduct into a personnel handbook. A code of ethics should be used to convey shared values, responsibilities, and expectations. It should help staff members move into a universal-values level of ethical thinking with specific reference to the organization for which it is created.

The way the code is developed is probably as important as its content. The process should include extensive discussion by staff members. Rather than having a code imposed on them, the members of the organization should be involved in its creation. If one accepts the logic of this approach, however, there is another challenge. How do you make the code relevant to those who inherit it after the period of formation, and how do you keep it current? Part of the answer is to periodically repeat general discussions of what the code is and what it means. As in the original process of forming the code, small focus groups can be used to generate ideas and solicit input. It might be useful to start with a blank slate and ask again: What should be included in the code of ethics for members of this organization? When the answers have been compiled, they could be compared to the existing code. Discrepancies or additions could be identified and collected for a summary discussion that might lead to revision of the code. A process such as this could promote a sense of ownership by current staff.

The other way to make the code relevant and current is effective training. Standards of integrity and excellence can be explicitly articulated and disseminated by means of formal training within the organization whether the organization has its own code. Organizations without their own code would rely on general themes in ethics awareness and examination of the codes of appropriate professional associations. Organizations with a code would integrate examination of it with these other topics. The extent of ethics training is somewhat hard to estimate. It appears that most cities now use ethics training, although the amount of time devoted to it is limited (West and Berman 2002). There are examples of organizations with large-scale training efforts in cities and counties such as Chicago, Tampa, King County in Washington, and Utah's Salt Lake County (Menzel 2006). The National Institutes of Health requires online training for new employees and additional annual training for all staff. In 2005, all NIH employees were required to complete online modules on outside activities, awards from outside organizations, and prohibited financial interests (National Institutes of Health Ethics Program 2006).[69] Other organizations avoid these kinds of efforts. Whether they are embarrassed with the topic, assume it is not necessary to address the topic, or do not think that it will do any good, some organizations spend little time talking about ethics.[70]

A useful preliminary step to designing a training program is to conduct an ethical climate survey. A sample survey is provided in **Appendix 7**. A survey of this kind uncovers what staff members think about organizational practices and standards, the personal qualities regarding integrity and honesty of themselves and others in the organization, the commitment of organizational leaders to ethics, and the levels of trust, fairness, and responsiveness. The results could be used to guide the development of training and repeated periodically to monitor progress. The Australian Public Sector

Standards Commission noted earlier in this chapter has such a comprehensive program of monitoring and training. The compliance report for 2004–2005 provided comparison of survey results collected annually since 1999 (Commissioner for Public Sector Standards 2005). It appears, however, that the use of such surveys to guide training and support monitoring is rare. For example, it was found in less than 10 percent of U.S. cities (West and Berman 2004, 197).

Effective training should address conditions within the organization—possibly guided by a climate survey—and include agency-specific cases.[71] Simply providing drills on the content of law and regulations pertaining to employee conduct is a narrow approach that reinforces a rule-based orientation. It provides a useful foundation of knowledge, but it does not promote judgment and problem solving.[72]

Case studies broaden the scope of training and increase its relevance. Cases from the organization itself can be drawn from a number of sources. Supervisors can identify areas that have been particularly important in disciplinary actions with staff, and elected officials or board members can be asked about elements of organizational performance that have ethical implications. In addition, individuals in focus groups can be asked to anonymously identify a situation in which they experienced an ethical dilemma in the organization and describe it without revealing the identity of the unit or the persons involved. The group can then discuss the situations and decide which ones are most important. These cases then are available for use in the training session.

In addition, staff members should have the opportunity to submit questions anonymously about any matter concerning standards and expectations in the organization. Officials from various levels in the organization should be available to provide answers, commentary, and encourage discussion. Finally, effective training requires assessment by the participants to determine whether the experience expanded their knowledge, awareness, and ability to handle ethical problems.

The content of training should include legal emphases, the behavior of public administrators, and policy and service area linkages for staff from specific departments; for instance, what are the ethical dimensions of a community development program or a fiscal policy, and what are the ethical issues in law enforcement (West, Berman, Bonczek, and Kellar 1998, 6–8).

Mechanisms for Control

Despite the importance of creating a positive culture and providing effective training, measures to assure internal control are also needed. The old adage that "you expect what you inspect" is consistent with the generalization that reducing the prospect of detection increases the likelihood that some officials will choose to act unethically. Accounting and audit systems are needed to do routine checks on performance and behavior, and the capacity for surveillance and investigation must be available to ensure that suspicions of corrupt behavior are not ignored.

Supervisors should consider what kinds of ethical problems can arise in their area of responsibility and develop appropriate mechanisms for checking and controlling staff. They need to examine the potential for corruption and unethical behavior within their units and to consider how common a potential problem is and how serious it could be. A basic concern is whether staff members are failing to perform at acceptable levels (*shirking*). The supervisor needs to make certain that reporting systems accurately reflect their level of activity in accomplishing key tasks. Less common but moderately to very serious areas include conflict of interest and taking favors in exchange for providing services or favorable decisions. A screening and disclosure approach can be used to identify any staff members who may have a potential conflict (for instance, interest in a company that has contracts with the organization) and then focus attention on these staff members to ensure that proper safeguards are in place. Serious ethical lapses include favoritism or lower quality service based on bias, slanting evidence to push a preferred policy position, or succumbing to partisan pressure or giving partisan advantage. Specialized areas with potential problems include staff positions that receive money and disperse funds. The list could go on. Supervisors need to consider what activities of these kinds occur within their area of responsibility, and what kinds of reports and checking are needed to control them or prevent unacceptable deviations for standards.

An unethical practice like favoritism in dealing with clients and citizens has consequences that are serious enough that special efforts such as spot checks through soliciting feedback from randomly selected clients are appropriate, even though it is a costly procedure. Supervisors should be mindful of the impact of checking certain actions and not checking others and possibly shift the areas of emphasis over time.

It is also useful for supervisors to assess their staff members and their ethical orientation. As discussed in Chapter 6, some staff members seek to evade the rules and will do whatever they can get away with. Most are rule oriented and will comply unless they conclude that no one pays any attention. With very low risk of repercussions, not much of a reward is needed to convince some to violate the rules. Finally, the principled or value-based staff member would normally be expected to adhere to the spirit as well as the letter of the rules. They may be offended by intrusive surveillance. Still, even this group, as seen, may come to conclude that noble ends permit inappropriate means, especially if no one is checking.

Mechanisms for control and investigation are needed to address instances of pervasive corruption. The Public Integrity Division (PID) was launched in 1995 to combat endemic corruption in the New Orleans Police Department (NOPD).[73] The underlying philosophy was early warning and intensive surveillance (Walker, Alpert, and Kenney 2001). Established in a partnership between the Federal Bureau of Investigation (FBI) and Louisiana law enforcement officials, it represents a high-control strategy with three elements. First, there are aggressive criminal and administrative investigations of any complaints received using undercover personnel to detect wrongdoing. Second, as early intervention, intensive training is offered to any officer who receives multiple complaints. Finally, there are random integrity "stings" aimed at the police department itself to ensure officers are complying with the department's policies and procedures, and state and federal laws. This is an extreme example of using checks and controls, presumably compelled by circumstances that led the leadership in the department to want everyone in the department to know that they are being checked.

When "bad" persons are rare, less punitive approaches are more appropriate as long as there is not the general perception that no one ever checks. Even though control mechanisms create a mild atmosphere of mistrust, this may help to prevent rule-abiding employees from developing the corrosive attitude that some staff members are getting away with flaunting the rules.

Positive Management Practices

Elevating the ethical climate is promoted by using positive management practices. In part, using positive practices reflects the leadership and shapes an engaged organizational culture. Beyond simply setting the tone for the organization, the specific components of positive management reinforce the qualities that promote ethical behavior. Effective management practices are the topic of many courses in an MPA degree and the focus of a wide array of continuing professional development activities. There is wide support among public administration scholars for using participative management techniques, improving productivity, organizational innovation, focusing on results and performance measurement, and human resource development.

One could argue that good management supports a strong ethical climate. Giving staff members a voice in making decisions and setting objectives reinforces the realization that they are responsible for their actions. These measures give staff a sense of "ownership" of their work even in a large organization. Reducing inefficiencies and wasted effort make better use of scarce resources and foster a sense of stewardship. Incorporating successful practices from other jurisdictions can improve performance and effectiveness and elevate morale. Staff members who receive appropriate training and have opportunities for professional development expand their sense of competence and control. Finally, using the performance-appraisal process to promote development of staff rather than simply to reward or punish them encourages staff to identify weaknesses and pursue training. If staff members feel that they have a say in what the organization does and how they can expand their capabilities, they are more likely to play an active rather than passive role in dealing with ethical issues.

The linkage between management practices, ethics, and organizational climate has been examined by West and Berman (2004) in their research on city government. It is a rare quantitative analysis of the origins and impact of ethics training. They find an association between providing training and developing other innovative programs within the organization. Strong moral leadership by top managers is a key starting point to finding other important attributes of a commitment to ethics including monitoring adherence to a code of ethics (which presumes that the organization has a code), examining ethics in hiring and promotion, and applications-oriented ethics training.[74] This kind of training is related to positive labor-management relations. Training is also one contributor to a more positive organizational culture that stresses putting forth one's best effort, creativity, openness and dialogue, taking on new challenges, and rewarding commitment to accomplishment. Finally, the positive organizational culture—on a path that starts with leadership and training—is linked to higher employee productivity, which in turn is related to citizen trust. Their results suggest that the theoretical connection between positive management practices that incorporate ethics and improved organizational climate and performance can be demonstrated with quantitative evidence. The thrust of this discussion is that a commitment to ethics plays a key role in the overall approach to management.

Adequate Channels for Complaints and Values that Encourage Dissent

If a lack of awareness on the part of managers and supervisors is a condition that allows unethical behavior, learning to listen can help to promote a higher level of ethics. It is important to have honest open-door policies and encourage staff to come through them, even if they are bringing bad news. Getting out to observe first hand what is going on in the organization can both help to make a supervisor aware of problems and also encourage openness and sharing by staff. The practice labeled *management by walking around* (Peters and

Waterman 1982) helps to ensure that officials at any level in the organization are not limited to information and reports received through official channels.

There should be multiple channels for complaints so that a staff member does not have to report problems to his or her supervisor or others in the chain of command if he or she feels that these direct superiors are contributing to the problem. It is critical that leaders pay attention to, and act on, complaints. In federal studies of internal complaints, the most common reason for not reporting a problem noted by 59 percent of officials was the feeling that it would do no good because nothing would be done about it (U.S. Merit Systems Protection Board 1993).

Leaders should be committed to protection of complainants, because fear of retaliation is the other leading reason for not reporting problems. It is natural that organizational leaders want to prevent whistleblowing because it brings public criticism and internal relations are strained when the organization must deal with an external investigation. The best strategy for dealing with whistleblowing seems to be a proactive one of making it unnecessary to go outside the organization with complaints. Despite the inconvenience and embarrassment that may come from whistleblowing, when it does occur, it is still important to protect those who go outside the organization. This includes a clear message that supervisors who harass staff members who expose problems to outsiders will be punished. It is also important that the same protection should be given to internal complaints that are available to external disclosures. This is not currently the case under court interpretations of the federal Whistleblower Protection Act. Elaine Kaplan (2003), former Special Counsel, offers this comment:

> I think it is counterintuitive to protect people only when they go outside their chain of command—one would think that it is in management's interest to encourage people to stay in their chain of command, rather than going, for example, to the *Washington Post* or the *New York Times*.

Organizational leaders must avoid the practice of "killing the messenger" and encourage active participation by staff members both in the form of positive proposals and also through dissent.

Equity and Involvement in Dealings with the Public

To reinforce positive interactions with citizens, leaders can adopt a two-pronged strategy by promoting equity and encouraging citizen participation.

Fairness and the absence of discrimination are important not only as aspects in the behavior of individual staff members. It is important for the organization to model a commitment to social equity and ensure that it is meeting standards of equity in its practices. Social equity means:

> The fair, just and equitable management of all institutions serving the public directly or by contract, and the fair, just and equitable distribution of public services, and implementation of public policy, and the commitment to promote fairness, justice, and equity in the formation of public policy (NAPA 2000).[75]

Criteria for measuring equity are divided into four areas: procedural fairness, access, quality, and outcomes (NAPA 2005). *Procedural fairness* involves examination of problems or issues in procedural rights (due process), treatment in procedural sense (equal protection), and application of eligibility criteria (equal rights) for existing policies and programs. This criterion includes examination of fairness in management practices involving areas such as hiring, promotion, and award of contracts. *Access*—distributional equity—involves a review of current policies, services, and practices to determine the level of access to services/benefits and analysis of reasons for unequal access.[76] *Quality*—process equity—involves a review of the level of consistency in the quality of existing services delivered to groups and individuals. Process equity requires consistency in the nature of services delivered to groups and individuals regardless of the distributional criterion that is used. Finally, equity in *outcomes* involves an examination of whether policies and programs have the same impact or achieve equal results for all groups and individuals served.

Part of the difficulty of achieving equal results is that government action is not the sole determinant of most important social outcomes. Social and economic conditions (for example, poverty) that are broader than the policy problem being examined may explain the differences in outcomes in areas such as education or health. Furthermore, individual behavior is often a critical element in explaining social outcomes. Still, a critical issue in consideration of equity at this level is how much inequality is acceptable and to what extent government can and should intervene to reduce the inequality in results. The focus on performance management is an effort to align the use of organizational resources with achieving intended outcomes.

Department directors or the heads of small agencies can examine the ways that their organization addresses equity issues. Using the input of staff and citizens or clients served, the director can uncover actual or potential problem areas and identify corrective strategies. Equity is a key ethical principle and managers should pay attention to whether it is being incorporated into organizational practices. The steps in **Figure 9.1** offer guidelines for conducting an equity inventory.

The results of an equity inventory can be varied in scope and the nature of remedial action that would be required to address the problems identified. For example, if the department identified lapses in procedural fairness and failure to distribute a service to all those entitled to receive it (or differences in the quality of the service provided), the department director should be able to initiative corrective actions within his or her existing policy mandate and administrative authority. If the problems involved inappropriate distributional criteria to achieve equal results[77] or a deficiency in the number and training of staff members who were capable of communicating competently with a minority group, the department director would need to raise these issues as matters that should be taken to elected officials in order to

---

1. What is the purpose of the department, what services does it provide, and whom does it serve? Identify any equity issues that have arisen recently. Meaningful citizen input should be included in the assessment process. What are the equity areas that are likely to be relevant to the department and its programs?

   - procedural equity
   - access and distributional equity
   - quality and process equity
   - equal outcomes

2. Assess agency *procedures* to identify any equity issues.

   - How well does the agency meet the procedural fairness standard in its current operations?
   - What changes are needed to improve procedural fairness?

3. Assess the nature and *distribution* of benefits and services distributed externally (services, benefits, enforcement activities, etc.) or internally (hiring, promotions, access to training, etc.).

   - What criteria for distribution equity are currently followed: equal distribution, distribution to compensate for special needs or conditions, or distribution oriented to achieving the results?
   - What criteria should be followed? Can the criteria be changed within existing policies?
   - How well is the agency performing in terms of the preferred criteria?
   - What impact is the agency having on equity outcomes relevant to its purpose?

4. Assess the *quality* of services provided.

   - Are there differences in quality by area of the city or characteristics of the client?
   - What changes are needed to improve the uniformity in quality?

5. Assess the outcomes impacted by the department's performance (sense of security, cleanliness of area, job placement, or health).

   - Are there systematic differences in outcome indicators?
   - What changes are needed to reduce disparities in outcomes?

Source: NAPA 2005. Used with permission of the National Academy of Public Administration.

Figure 9–1 *Equity Inventory at the Departmental or Agency Level*

change existing policy or considered in developing the budget for the organization as a whole. The ethical requirement for the administrator is to be committed to social equity and to find meaningful ways to incorporate that commitment into management practices. The organizational inventory is one way to do that.

Organizational leaders at all levels should also take measures to encourage public participation in the policy-making process and in the other work of the organization. Citizen participation "closes the loop" of public service by encouraging citizen feedback. A number of approaches can be used to expand citizen participation. Organizations should consider how they can meaningfully incorporate citizens in developing policies, guiding implementation, and evaluating results. Citizens can be included in task forces or advisory committees, invited to meetings, and systematically surveyed. The level and kind of participation by citizens should be related to the kind of decision that is being made (Thomas 1995). Not all decisions necessitate full involvement. For example, sometimes simply soliciting needed information from citizens is sufficient. If officials, however, want to be fully informed and get support from citizens for a decision, they should open the process to permit citizens to help define the problem and make the decision, not simply provide input about needs and preferences.

The most numerous and active links are established to measure citizen assessment of the services they receive. Citizens are not only consumers of organizational services,[78] but they do consume services from public organizations and their assessment of these services is important. Customer-feedback methods should be available that enable citizens to assess the quality of the services received and the behavior of staff members in service delivery. It should also be easy and secure for citizens to make complaints. In the case of the New Orleans PID, locating the PID office outside of the department's central administration building helped to make citizens feel more comfortable about registering complaints against officers. A toll-free 24-hour hotline where one could report police misconduct or offer feedback was also available. Beyond the information received, the ongoing interaction with citizens through service assessment and accessible channels for suggestions and complaints is a reminder that "serving the public" is not a one-way relationship.

In sum, strong leadership, clear standards, effective training, targeted control and investigation, sound management practices, and equitable and inclusive management build a positive climate for ethics and reinforce the best inclinations of staff members. There is evidence that staff members in public service and nonprofit organizations were attracted to their work by a sense of duty to serve the public (Perry and Wise 1990). By themselves, they are likely to have a correct but confined set of ethical standards. Individual staff members are strongly influenced by their organization setting: the behavior of superiors, attitudes of peers, organizational policies and procedures, and the pervasive attitudes about how to relate to citizens and clients. The approaches discussed in this chapter use these factors to promote the development of individual staff members and broaden their ethical competence and autonomy. A local government official summed up his perception of what ethics training can accomplish, and his conclusion can be extended to cover all six areas of organizational practice (West, Berman, Bonczek, and Kellar 1998, 6):

> Ethics trainings helps to move the passive majority of workers in the middle into a more active posture, in which they are more willing to notice and report unethical conduct and to model ethical behavior.

This kind of movement to a higher level of ethical development is enhanced by a positive ethical climate and helps to strengthen it.

Chapter 10

Mandating Duty:

External Measures to Promote Ethics

S tructural features and legal requirements have been established in national, state, and local government to promote ethics and reduce unethical behavior. These approaches represent measures outside the organization designed to control activities and to open up operations for external review. The effort represents an attempt to mandate adherence to duty from the outside. In this chapter, three approaches are reviewed: open meetings laws and freedom of information requirements, inspectors general, and ethics laws. After describing the approaches, the issue of their likely effectiveness and limitations will be considered.

Open Meetings Laws and Freedom of Information Requirements

There is ongoing tension between the public and organizations over access to information about the internal affairs of organizations. Despite the broad expectation that officials should inform the public, there is disagreement about how much information should be made available and when it should be provided. Sharing information is a basic duty and essential to supporting the democratic process. Citizens cannot participate meaningfully if they do not know what public organizations are doing and how they are doing it. This is also an important responsibility for nonprofits as they seek to maintain public trust through transparency and responsiveness to requests for information. The legal requirements for disclosure of information are limited to those needed in completing forms required by the Internal Revenue Service (the 990), but the ethical expectation of openness is much broader.[79]

The public information requirements of federal government agencies are quite extensive. In general, the requirements seek to promote a culture of openness and accountability across the federal government.[80] Among other types of information, each agency shall make available to the public information about the agency's organization, rules of procedure, generally applicable substantive rules, and statements of general policy adopted by the agency. They shall make available for public inspection and copying key documents such as administrative staff manuals and instructions to staff that affect a member of the public. Furthermore, agencies should make available other records that are requested in a reasonable period of time.

There are exceptions. Information that is protected for national security reasons can be withheld. When giving names would invade personal privacy, they can be deleted from documents although a justification for the deletion is to be explained fully in writing. More troublesome are restrictions that can be interpreted in such a way that information the public may feel it has a right to know is withheld. In local government, details about personnel matters generally should not be revealed, but the factors that led to a city council's decision to dismiss a city manager may be important for the public to know— either because the details shed light on the city manager or on the council members who made the decision. Negotiation of contracts is protected for good reason, but should the public be able to know what economic incentives were provided by a government agency in order to persuade a company to come to a particular state or city? Citizens may have to take legal action to get records released, and even if the citizens win the lawsuit, a judge may not require the government agency to pay the legal bills.[81] The State of North Carolina Commerce Department withheld details of $242 million in tax breaks and other incentives to Dell Computers in 2004 until news organizations sued to get the information 2 months after the negotiations were completed. The state legislature in North Carolina passed a law in 2005 that requires the state and local agencies to publicly release all non-confidential information about the tax and other incentives given to a business in a specific deal within 25 days of completing an agreement (General Assembly of North Carolina 2005).

An ASPA workbook on *Applying Ethical Standards* provides commentary and diagnostic questions on handling public information issues in a balanced way. It is displayed in **Figure 10.1**.

Inspectors General and Auditors

In 1978, the Inspector General (IG) Act was approved. Independent audit and investigative offices were created originally in 12 federal agencies. They are now present in 58 agencies,[82] and comparable offices with an auditing function

A. Background

The administrator must be cognizant of the public's right to know about the actions of government agencies and the information they obtain, unless information sharing would be harmful to the security and welfare of the nation or its citizens.

We continue to be guided by the need to be responsive to legitimate citizen information requests, to cooperate with the private and not-for-profit sectors, and to abide by democratic values of participation, representativeness, and free speech and association.

Because we live in a democratic society, we understand that we cannot be arrogant about the breadth and accuracy of our knowledge. Further, we have an obligation to share that knowledge with the public in a manner that promotes an understanding of their rights and opportunities to participate. These rights sometimes come into conflict with laws that protect confidentiality or create zones of privileged information . . . , causing ethical dilemmas for public employees. Each person, whether a citizen-at-large or a government employee, has rights of privacy which should be safeguarded. Included are protections against illegal domestic surveillance, unauthorized sharing of credit information, unauthorized access to confidential personal and medical files, and the like.

B. Some Self-Diagnostic Questions

1. How do I resolve conflicts between the public's right to know and the need for confidentiality that is needed to protect individuals or my organization?

2. Am I aware of how Freedom of Information Acts, government in the sunshine laws, Privacy Acts, and associated laws and regulations relate to me?

3. Do I respond fully and promptly to legitimate requests for information from citizens, organizations, and the media?

4. Do I use informal techniques and procedures to circumvent the spirit or specific requirements of freedom of information? Under what circumstance, if any, could such behavior be justified?

5. When I take part in decisions that affect the public welfare, are the issues presented to the public in sufficient time and in such a way that questions can be raised?

6. Am I careful not to divulge privileged information to enhance my own importance?

Source: Mertins et al. 1998, 13–14. Used with permission of the American Society for Public Administration.

Figure 10–1 *The Public's Right to Know*

are found in many state and local governments. The offices of IG and auditor represent an external check on the operation of a public agency. According to the Inspector General Act of 1978, as amended, the inspector general's mission is to conduct independent and objective audits, investigations, and inspections; prevent and detect waste, fraud, and abuse; promote economy, effectiveness, and efficiency; review pending legislation and regulation; and keep the agency head and Congress fully and currently informed. Similar to these independent audit offices at the national level is the Government Accountability Office (GAO) which serves as an independent, nonpartisan agency that works for Congress and investigates how the federal government spends its money and performs. Offices of this kind and their counterparts at the state and local level—sometimes with the title of auditor—can be a powerful ally to citizens in knowing how well government is performing. Mark Funkhouser, the city auditor of Kansas City, Missouri, observes that auditors deal with "real people being hurt by a poorly performing government program, the difficulty of changing the situation, and the role of successful performance auditing in making a positive difference in people's lives" (National Association of Local Government Auditors 2005).

At the federal level, inspectors general are appointed on the basis of ability in accounting, auditing, and financial analysis as well as the general fields of law, management analysis, and public administration.[83] They are to be nonpartisan and supposed to be persons of integrity. The president nominates the IGs in cabinet-level departments and major agencies with confirmation by the Senate. These IGs can only be removed by the president. In 28 other federal agencies (e.g., Amtrak, National Science Foundation, and the U.S. Postal Service), the IG is appointed by and can be removed by the agency head. It is required by law, however, that both houses of Congress must be notified if an IG is removed by the president or an agency head.

The IG system is designed to ensure independence. IGs have in-depth knowledge of their organization and work under the general supervision of the head of the agency. Still, no one in the agency can prevent or prohibit an IG from conducting an audit or investigation. By law, IGs report independently both to the agency head and to the Congress. The IGs have broad authority to inspect all records and information of the agency, issue subpoenas for information and documents outside the agency, administer oaths for taking testimony, and hire and control their own staff and contract resources. The IGs conduct such investigations and issue such reports as the IG thinks appropriate (with limited national security and law enforcement exceptions). Any allegations of misconduct against an IG are referred to the Integrity Committee of the President's Council on Integrity and Efficiency (PCIE) rather than to the agency head.

The GAO and most state and local level inspectors general or auditors are usually linked to the legislature or city council rather than to the executive or operate as an independent official directly elected by the voters (e.g., in Idaho, Michigan, New Mexico, and North Carolina).

In the nonprofit sector, financial auditing is a standard practice. There are some distant analogues to external reviewing bodies in the form of watchdog groups that rate nonprofits such as the Wise Giving Alliance (www.give.org). Outcomes measurement has become an important theme in nonprofits as well as in governments and is encouraged by umbrella organ-

izations such as United Way.[84] Organizations that receive funds from government agencies can expect to have external scrutiny of how they use the
funds and what they accomplish.

An important question for administrators is what kinds of external-review
agencies may examine the work of their organization. Officials should avoid a
cautious and reactive approach, holding on to information unless and until it
is required by the reviewing office. These offices provide a check on the operation of public organizations and can use the law or public opinion to subject
organizations to scrutiny. The process is not necessarily pleasant or easy, but
administrators should remind themselves of the importance of transparency
and the commitment they should have to sharing information with the public.

State Ethics Laws

Most states (and countless local governments) seek to promote ethics of government officials by passing ethics laws (Menzel 2005, 153). The New York
State Ethics in Government Act passed in 1987 is used as an example to
illustrate the kinds of provisions that are included in these laws.[85] In the following sections, an ethics bill proposed in North Carolina in the early 1990s
is reviewed for comparison.[86] The sections examine the areas typically
included in an ethics law.

Those Covered by Provisions

The 1987 New York act gave the New York ethics commission jurisdiction
over only officers and employees of the executive branch. Other states covered legislators and local government officials, both elected and administrative. The draft bill in North Carolina illustrated the latter approach. One consideration in deciding on coverage is that the larger and more diverse the
scope of employees covered, either the more resources that will be required
for an ethics commission to do its work *or* the less work the commission will
be able to take on and the less depth the commission will be able to achieve.
For example, an underfunded commission relative to the number of staff
members to cover may do fewer self-initiated investigations and less staff
education (assuming these are allowed functions—see the section on administration and enforcement later).

Conflict of Interest

Ethics laws identify conflict of interest as a potentially harmful influence on
the behavior of officials and attempt to restrict it. The New York act states

that officials "may not engage in activities that would create or appear to create a conflict with their public duties" (New York State Ethics Commision, no date). Some of the specific restrictions include:

- they may not sell goods or services to the State or any agency of the State except through a competitively bid contract;
- they may not appear before any State agency or render services for compensation in a matter before any State agency in connection with such subjects as the purchase or sale of goods, rate making, funding or licensing.
- More generally, State officers and employees should not have any interest in or engage in any business or activity "in substantial conflict" with the discharge of their public duties. This restriction prohibits them from:
  - disclosing confidential information acquired in the course of their official duties or using such information to further their personal interests;
  - using or attempting to use their official positions to secure unwarranted privileges or exemptions for themselves or others;
  - giving reasonable basis for the impression that any person can improperly influence them or unduly enjoy their favor in the performance of their official duties, or that they are affected by the kinship, rank, position or influence of any party or person.
- Finally, State officers and employees should endeavor to pursue a course of conduct which will not raise suspicion among the public that they are likely to be engaged in acts that are in violation of their public trust (New York State Ethics Commision, no date).

The North Carolina act had a similar intent but broadened the scope to include members of the public servant's immediate family or a business with which the official is associated. If an actual or potential conflict is present, the official is expected to abstain from participating in the discussion and voting on any official action (recusal or removing themselves from the decision).

Disclosure

Financial disclosure complements conflict-of-interest restrictions. By publicly disclosing interests and holdings, it is possible for third parties to make a judgment about whether a potential conflict may exist. The ethics commission can be asked to provide an advisory opinion about whether the official should participate in the decision based on analysis of the disclosed information. The New York act requires annual statements of financial disclosure by staff members who occupy policymaking positions and of those who—unless exempted by the Commission—are in a salary grade that pays more than $74,621 in 2005. The drafted North Carolina act specifies certain high-ranking officials and the chief deputy or chief administrative assistant to these officials, the members of state boards and commissions, and members of local policy-making boards. In both cases, the disclosure statement lists major assets, sources of income, liabilities, and names of spouses and children. The New York disclosure also asks whether the official is licensed by or does business with a state agency and holds offices with a political party.

Prohibitions and Controls

Ethics laws usually prohibit certain activities or impose controls on others. Prohibited activities may include use of public position for private gain, representing persons or organizations before your agency, nepotism, and disclosing confidential information or using it for private gain. "Honest graft" based on insider information is not permitted.

Outside activities or honoraria fall into the controlled category. In New York, the commission's regulations restrict certain high-level officials, including all policymakers, from serving as an officer of any political party or organization or as a member of a political party committee. The commission also requires either agency approval or ethics commission approval before earning outside income. No salaried state officers or employees may engage in any outside activity that interferes or is in conflict with their duties. To avoid conflicts of interest and the appearances of such conflicts, state officers and employees may accept reimbursement of travel expenses or honoraria only under certain circumstances. The North Carolina proposal would have restricted honoraria if the work was part of official duties or used official time and resources to perform the service.

The controls over accepting gifts vary widely. In New York, state officers and employees may not accept or solicit a gift under circumstances in which it could be inferred that the gift was intended to influence or reward the recipient for performing official duties. New York uniformly applied these restrictions to gifts over $75 in value, but warns that even gifts of lower value may be illegal if their receipt produces clear conflict with the job duties of the official. The North Carolina act would not have permitted gifts of any value from persons who sought business from the state or were regulated by the agency. The drafted bill, however, also exempted gifts in the form of meals and beverages or tickets or free admission for charitable, cultural, or political events. The intent of these restrictions is to prevent conflict of interest or inducements that could influence employees to give special treatment.

Postemployment Restrictions

Another prohibited or controlled activity of special importance in the public sector is work after leaving a government position. There is a pervasive concern about the "revolving door" between government and business or special interests based on two practices. Those practices include (1) officials making decisions in government in order to curry favor from a future employer and (2) former officials using their insider knowledge and contacts to give special advantage to their private employer. Still, it is difficult to determine the proper balance between controls that are necessary to protect the public interest and what is fair and reasonable. Postemployment restrictions should not be so broad and punitive that public officials have no possibility of leaving a government job and going into an area that is somewhat related to the work that was done on the public payroll. Another question in designing postemployment provisions is whether the same restrictions should apply to administrators and elected officials.

The New York restrictions apply to administrators but not elected officials. Depending on the nature of the activity, there is a 2-year bar and a lifetime bar. For 2 years, former state officers or employees can not make presentations before their former agency or receive compensation for performing services related to any matters being considered by their former agency. The lifetime bar applies to specific cases, projects, or transactions with which they were directly involved during their public service. Presumably, over time activities in which the former employee was actively engaged will be completed, but as long as these activities are ongoing, a former employee cannot have any connection with them.

In North Carolina, the restriction was simpler and shorter, but the coverage was broader. For 1 year, former public servants would not have been permitted to represent another person before their former employer. The coverage was broader because the restriction would have applied to legislators as well as administrators. Thus, a favorite activity of former legislators—lobbying— would not have been permitted for 1 year. Is this an important and necessary restriction? How would you design a reasonable postemployment restriction?

Whistleblower Protection

This may be another feature of an ethics law or related legislation. Neither the New York ethics act nor the proposed North Carolina bill, however, included this provision.

Administration and Enforcement

The final element of an ethics law is the provision for an ethics commission. Questions concerning this provision include:

> How will members be appointed and supported?
> What duties and authority will it have?
> What sanctions can it impose?

The appointment process is usually designed to ensure impartiality. The governor and legislature may share appointments and partisan balance may be required. The New York board, perhaps because it focuses on executive department personnel alone, is appointed entirely by the governor, although one of the members is nominated by the state attorney general and another by the state comptroller. The North Carolina draft bill, which would have covered a wider range of officials, divided appointments among the chief justice of the state supreme court, who appointed the chair; the governor who appointed four members with no more than three coming from the same political party; and the state house and senate that each appointed two members.

The duties of an ethics commission can range widely from offering advisory opinions only to being both educator and investigator. In New York, the ethics commission's duties include:

- receiving and investigating complaints alleging violations by officials;
- investigating possible violations on its own initiative;
- providing advisory opinions that interpret and apply the laws with regard to present and former state officials;
- collecting and auditing financial disclosure statements;
- issuing rules and regulations needed for the implementation and enforcement of the Ethics in Government Act; and
- proposing legislation designed to reform and strengthen the ethics law.

The North Carolina commission would have been similar but limited to investigating complaints, not undertaking investigations at its own initiative. In both cases, the commissions could conduct studies and make recommendations, but neither had an explicit function to educate the public or officials regarding public ethics.

A final issue is the extent to which the commission has the power to impose settlements and penalize those who violate the law. The New York commission can impose a civil penalty not to exceed $10,000 for certain violations. Instead of imposing a civil penalty, the commission may refer violators to prosecutors for a possible trial. Officials may also be subject to disciplinary action, including a fine, suspension, or dismissal by their agency for which they work. The proposed North Carolina commission would have been limited to referring violators to the state's attorney general for possible prosecution for violations of criminal law (which are beyond the scope of ethics bill) or referring the matter to the appointing authority for appropriate action. The latter approach would not affect former employees who could no longer be disciplined by their previous employer.

Assessment of Ethics Laws

In view of this description of how ethics laws can be constructed, what value is an ethics law? It can codify and clarify expectations, including expectations of administrators about what is acceptable practice. It can raise awareness among officials and the public. It can send a positive message to the public about the importance of standards and the consequences of violating them, although it is not clear whether this message is reassuring or simply confirms public suspicions that unethical behavior is widespread. The chief limitation is that ethics laws are essentially negative in approach and do not do much to raise the level of ethical behavior. These measures might be more properly called anticorruption or antiabuse laws rather than ethics laws because the focus is a negative one and the purpose is to prevent abuse of office. This has been the explicit focus of laws passed in many other countries (Menzel 2005, 158).

An ethics law may be well-matched with Stage 4 ethical reasoning. By elevating ethics to the level of law, ethics may have greater validity for these administrators. The legal approach may offer little, however, to administrators who demonstrate universal-values reasoning. The criticisms of codes of ethics considered earlier in Chapter 5 are more appropriately directed at ethics laws: They tend to be narrow and negative. When this logic is carried to the extreme, the "pursuit of absolute integrity," as Anechiarico and Jacobs (1996) call it, may hamstring the governmental process and create the negative organizational conditions that can contribute to unethical practices. One could ask whether states without ethics laws or nonprofits that operate on the basis of voluntary observance of ethical standards are truly disadvantaged. Should a state without a comprehensive ethics law such as North Carolina reconsider this issue and establish an ethics law? It does seem clear that the process of formulating ethics laws should involve administrators and not simply be imposed on them.

In conclusion, external measures can be important as protection for the public and a check on the behavior of public officials. It is important, however, for these measures to be combined with positive organizational strategies.

Chapter 11

Conclusion:

The Duties of Public Administrators

At the end of this book, we revisit the definition of administrative ethics offered at the beginning:

> Administrative ethics refers to well-based standards of right and wrong that prescribe what public administrators ought to do, in terms of duty to public service, principles, virtues, and benefits to society.

The highest duty of public administrators is to embrace a broad set of obligations and responsibilities that promote the public interest, demonstrate character, advance justice, and seek the greatest good.

Various ways exist to articulate these obligations and responsibilities. The statements that follow reflect my own approach drawing on the themes developed in this book. It does not describe how all public administrators typically behave, although I believe that most administrators incorporate many of these recommendations in their behavior. It is similar to a code, but the list is presented as a set of obligations and responsibilities that summarize the key points covered in the discussion.

Public administrators should:

1. Be accountable to the law and organizational mission.
   - Obey and implement the law.
   - Protect Constitutional principles.
   - Be accountable to the organization of which they are a part and seek to advance its mission.
2. Defend the integrity of public service.
   - Do not use public office for personal gain or to advance personal or private interests.

- Avoid conflict of interest, recognizing that their own view of what constitutes a conflict may be more narrow and self-serving than would an objective observer.
- Disclose any interests that may affect objectivity in making decisions and recuse themselves from participation in those decisions.

3. Be dedicated to the public interest.
   - Serve the public in their one-on-one interactions with individuals and in their commitment to service over self.
   - Advance the public interest following basic precepts of public administration, including fairness, consistency, impartiality, neutrality, and equity.
   - Seek to create the greatest good for the greatest number over the long term while protecting the rights of minorities.

4. Accept individual responsibility for their actions and the consequences of their actions.

5. Provide leadership in ways appropriate to their position to improve policy, programs, methods, and procedures.

6. Respect and strengthen the democratic process and the values of the democratic system in ways appropriate to their position. For example:
   - Offer complete and unbiased information in support of recommendations.
   - Support political superiors with honesty and independence.
   - Be honest, open, and responsive to the public.
   - Strengthen citizen participation in the development, implementation, and assessment of programs.

7. Promote ethics in their organization.
   - Set a good example and pursue excellence.
   - Encourage and support ethical behavior by others.
   - Report wrongdoing and correct problems that are brought to their attention.
   - Support criticism and organizational renewal.
   - Seek to strengthen the ethical climate in their organization through positive management practices and equitable treatment of the public.

8. Identify the codes of ethics that cover their professional work and commit themselves to observe them. Support the enforcement of these codes of ethics.

9. In a balanced way, be virtuous, act on principles, and promote positive consequences.

10. Approach problems with informed ethical reasoning; think through a dilemma and make a morally reasonable decision.

- Get all the facts and interpret them objectively.
- Identify all potential stakeholders.
- Balance the requirements of law and policy, organizational expectations, and professional standards.
- Apply considerations drawn from distinct ethical approaches:
  What would a person of character do in this situation?
  What principles apply to the situation?
  How does one promote the best consequences for the greatest number?

You are encouraged to develop a list and incorporate these items into your own professional code of ethics. It should be organized in ways that are most useful to make it accessible and meaningful as you encounter specific situations. You may choose to drop some of these items, although you should provide a thoughtful basis for doing so and think about how those responsibilities are met in different ways. You may choose to add additional responsibilities or more specific indicators. The purpose of constructing a list is to elevate and expand your own individual capacity for ethical commitment and action.

I hope that you will find it useful to reflect on the general themes that were developed in this book. Ethical public administrators do their duty. They encounter pressures to curtail their duty or experience temptations to exceed the appropriate bounds of duty. They are often isolated in wrestling with ethical issues and feel at odds with the prevailing culture and standards of their organization. Ethical administrators are guided and sustained by their understanding of what ethics means. They have refined their understanding of what duty entails to encompass a broad range of responsibilities and balance the inherent tensions between the accountability owed the public and superiors and the independence that must be preserved to be an ethical agent. This approach to duty goes far beyond simple adherence to the law or narrow accountability to one's superiors that would be part of a law and order level of ethical reasoning. Their sense of duty is further broadened and elevated by virtue, adherence to principles, and a commitment to positive consequences for the greatest number. These perspectives expand the meaning of duty and reinforce it with ideas from outside the world of public affairs. Taken together, these approaches shape universal ethical values for administrators by blending a definition of role that transcends a specific position or organization and standards of right and wrong that are grounded in philosophical traditions.

The ethics triangle from Chapter 4 provides a graphic representation of this complete model of administrative ethics. Operating within the triangle helps to ensure that a comprehensive and balanced approach is taken in dealing with ethical opportunities and ethical challenges. Questions such as the following focus attention on the ideals derived from duty, virtue, principle, and consequences:

- How can the *public interest* be advanced in general and in particular situations? What are my responsibilities to the organization, my political superiors, and to the public? Is my definition of the public interest compatible with the expectations of principle, virtue, and the greatest good?
- What does it mean to display *character*? What virtues should public administrators or persons working within a specific field or agency have? What do these virtues mean? How does one act in terms of each? How do the dictates of conscience match with serving the public, advancing principle, and achieving the best consequences?
- What should one do to promote *justice, fairness, and equity*? What are the most important principles that should guide any public administrator and a person working in a specific field or agency? How would one "order" the principles? Are there any which can never be set aside to advance another principle? What does it mean to apply these principles to specific situations? Is my use of the chosen principle guided by the public interest, virtue, and consequences?
- How can the *greatest good for the greatest number* be achieved in making a specific decision? What ends should public administrators or persons working within a specific field or agency seek to advance? How should one ensure that all stakeholders have been identified and that the calculation of benefits and costs is universal, equal, and complete? Do the means chosen stand up to the standards of the public interest, virtue, and principle?

These questions help to focus attention on the requirements of each approach, and also suggest how each approach may be expanded and modified by considering the other approaches. This is the essence of what it means to operate within the ethics triangle.

The ethics triangle consists of approaches that differ in the content of ethical thinking. In addition, a different orientation and mode of action are associated with each approach. Promoting the public interest entails reflection: What is in the public interest, both in the abstract and within the Constitutional and legal institutions in which I work? Developing virtue and expanding character requires practice; by being virtuous, one becomes more virtuous. Advancing justice and acting on principle is based on the expansion of knowledge about principles and discernment of how to apply principles in specific situations. Advancing good ends requires analysis to determine what would constitute the greatest possible benefits for the society along with recognition that this question cannot be answered definitively. Put simply, the ethics triangle combines reflecting, feeling, reasoning, and analyzing. All presuppose an inclination that is elevated into commitment. One must want to—and become dedicated to—incorporating each of the approaches into one's practice as a public administrator.

Public administrators have a duty to act in a public-serving, virtuous, and principled way. As this book ends, I hope that you have a better understanding of how much is encompassed by this statement. Most important, I hope that you have an expanded commitment based on a broader range of values to put duty into action.

Let us end by returning to an extension of John Gaus' (1950) views about the political nature of public administration noted in the preface. I suggested that a theory of public administration in the political process is also a theory of ethics. This has been true since the origins of modern, democratic administrative practice in the nineteenth century. For professional staff members to fulfill their part of the relationship with elected officials and with the lay leaders of nonprofit organizations, they must have an independent commitment to serve the public, promote democracy, and achieve the highest possible level of ethical attainment balancing virtue, principle, and beneficial consequences. They use this commitment to universal values not to supplant political leaders but to challenge them to govern wisely and to do their best to accomplish the goals that political leaders have set. Without ethics, public administration is merely an instrument and administrators are simply the tools of their political masters. The founders of public administration would never have accepted these characteristics nor should we now. Without a dedication from public administrators to advance the public interest, the public loses the benefits of the distinctive expertise and values that administrators bring to the political process. When administrators have a dedication to duty and independent ethical standards, government and nonprofit organizations are better able to govern and to serve the public.

Standards of Ethical Conduct for Employees of the Executive Branch

(a) Public service is a public trust. Each employee has a responsibility to the United States Government and its citizens to place loyalty to the Constitution, laws and ethical principles above private gain. To ensure that every citizen can have complete confidence in the integrity of the Federal Government, each employee shall respect and adhere to the principles of ethical conduct set forth in this section, as well as the implementing standards contained in this part and in supplemental agency regulations.

(b) General principles. The following general principles apply to every employee and may form the basis for the standards contained in this part. Where a situation is not covered by the standards set forth in this part, employees shall apply the principles set forth in this section in determining whether their conduct is proper.

(1) Public service is a public trust, requiring employees to place loyalty to the Constitution, the laws and ethical principles above private gain.

(2) Employees shall not hold financial interests that conflict with the conscientious performance of duty.

(3) Employees shall not engage in financial transactions using nonpublic Government information or allow the improper use of such information to further any private interest.

(4) An employee shall not, except as permitted by subpart B of this part, solicit or accept any gift or other item of monetary value from

any person or entity seeking official action from, doing business with, or conducting activities regulated by the employee's agency, or whose interests may be substantially affected by the performance or nonperformance of the employee's duties.

(5) Employees shall put forth honest effort in the performance of their duties.

(6) Employees shall not knowingly make unauthorized commitments or promises of any kind purporting to bind the Government.

(7) Employees shall not use public office for private gain.

(8) Employees shall act impartially and not give preferential treatment to any private organization or individual.

(9) Employees shall protect and conserve Federal property and shall not use it for other than authorized activities.

(10) Employees shall not engage in outside employment or activities, including seeking or negotiating for employment, that conflict with official Government duties and responsibilities.

(11) Employees shall disclose waste, fraud, abuse, and corruption to appropriate authorities.

(12) Employees shall satisfy in good faith their obligations as citizens, including all just financial obligations, especially those—such as Federal, State, or local taxes—that are imposed by law.

(13) Employees shall adhere to all laws and regulations that provide equal opportunity for all Americans regardless of race, color, religion, sex, national origin, age, or handicap.

(14) Employees shall endeavor to avoid any actions creating the appearance that they are violating the law or the ethical standards set forth in this part. Whether particular circumstances create an appearance that the law or these standards have been violated shall be determined from the perspective of a reasonable person with knowledge of the relevant facts.

Source: Code of Federal Regulations, Title 5—Administrative Personnel, Chapter XVI—Office of Government Ethics, Part 2635. Standards of Ethical Conduct for Employees of the Executive Branch, Subpart A_General Provisions, Sec. 2635.101, Revised as of January 1, 2004.

http://a257.g.akamaitech.net/7/257/2422/12feb20041500/edocket.access.gpo.gov/cfr_2004/janqtr/5cfr2635.101.htm (accessed June 16, 2006).

Code of Ethics for Government Service

Resolved by the House of Representatives (the Senate concurring), That it is the sense of the Congress that the following Code of Ethics should be adhered to by all Government employees, including officeholders.

CODE OF ETHICS

Any person in Government service should:

1. Put loyalty to the highest moral principles and to country above loyalty to Government persons, party, or department.
2. Uphold the Constitution, laws, and legal regulations of the United States and of all governments therein and never be a party to their evasion.
3. Give a full day's labor for a full day's pay; giving to the performance of his duties his earnest effort and best thought.
4. Seek to find and employ more efficient and economical ways of getting tasks accomplished.
5. Never discriminate unfairly by the dispensing of special favors or privileges to anyone, whether for remuneration or not; and never accept for himself or his family, favors or benefits under circumstances which might be construed by reasonable persons as influencing the performance of his governmental duties.
6. Make no private promises of any kind binding upon the duties of office, since a Government employee has no private word which can be binding on public duty.
7. Engage in no business with the Government, either directly or indirectly which is inconsistent with the conscientious performance of his governmental duties.

8. Never use any information coming to him confidentially in the performance of governmental duties as a means for making private profit.

9. Expose corruption wherever discovered.

10. Uphold these principles, ever conscious that public office is a public trust.

(Passed July 11, 1958.)

Source: http://usgovinfo.about.com/blethics.htm (accessed June 16, 2006).

American Society for Public Administration's Code of Ethics

I. Serve the Public Interest

Serve the public, beyond serving oneself. ASPA members are committed to:

1. Exercise discretionary authority to promote the public interest.
2. Oppose all forms of discrimination and harassment, and promote affirmative action.
3. Recognize and support the public's right to know the public's business.
4. Involve citizens in policy decision-making.
5. Exercise compassion, benevolence, fairness and optimism.
6. Respond to the public in ways that are complete, clear, and easy to understand.
7. Assist citizens in their dealings with government.
8. Be prepared to make decisions that may not be popular.

II. Respect the Constitution and the Law

Respect, support, and study government constitutions and laws that define responsibilities of public agencies, employees, and all citizens. ASPA members are committed to:

1. Understand and apply legislation and regulations relevant to their professional role.
2. Work to improve and change laws and policies that are counterproductive or obsolete.

3. Eliminate unlawful discrimination.

4. Prevent all forms of mismanagement of public funds by establishing and maintaining strong fiscal and management controls, and by supporting audits and investigative activities.

5. Respect and protect privileged information.

6. Encourage and facilitate legitimate dissent activities in government and protect the whistleblowing rights of public employees.

7. Promote constitutional principles of equality, fairness, representativeness, responsiveness and due process in protecting citizens' rights.

III. Demonstrate Personal Integrity

Demonstrate the highest standards in all activities to inspire public confidence and trust in public service. ASPA members are committed to:

1. Maintain truthfulness and honesty and to not compromise them for advancement, honor, or personal gain.

2. Ensure that others receive credit for their work and contributions.

3. Zealously guard against conflict of interest or its appearance: e.g., nepotism, improper outside employment, misuse of public resources or the acceptance of gifts.

4. Respect superiors, subordinates, colleagues and the public.

5. Take responsibility for their own errors.

6. Conduct official acts without partisanship.

IV. Promote Ethical Organizations

Strengthen organizational capabilities to apply ethics, efficiency and effectiveness in serving the public. ASPA members are committed to:

1. Enhance organizational capacity for open communication, creativity, and dedication.

2. Subordinate institutional loyalties to the public good.

3. Establish procedures that promote ethical behavior and hold individuals and organizations accountable for their conduct.

4. Provide organization members with an administrative means for dissent, assurance of due process and safeguards against reprisal.

5. Promote merit principles that protect against arbitrary and capricious actions.

6. Promote organizational accountability through appropriate controls and procedures.

7. Encourage organizations to adopt, distribute, and periodically review a code of ethics as a living document.

V. Strive for Professional Excellence

Strengthen individual capabilities and encourage the professional development of others. ASPA members are committed to:

1. Provide support and encouragement to upgrade competence.

2. Accept as a personal duty the responsibility to keep up to date on emerging issues and potential problems.

3. Encourage others, throughout their careers, to participate in professional activities and associations.

4. Allocate time to meet with students and provide a bridge between classroom studies and the realities of public service.

Source: www.aspanet.org/scriptcontent/index_codeofethics.cfm (c) 2005 ASPA, all rights reserved. Used with permission of the American Society for Public Administration.

International City/County Management Association Code of Ethics with Guidelines

The ICMA Code of Ethics was adopted by the ICMA membership in 1924, and most recently amended by the membership in May 1998. The Guidelines for the Code were adopted by the ICMA Executive Board in 1972, and most recently revised in July 2004.

The mission of ICMA is to create excellence in local governance by developing and fostering professional local government management worldwide. To further this mission, certain principles, as enforced by the Rules of Procedure, shall govern the conduct of every member of ICMA, who shall:

1. Be dedicated to the concepts of effective and democratic local government by responsible elected officials and believe that professional general management is essential to the achievement of this objective.

2. Affirm the dignity and worth of the services rendered by government and maintain a constructive, creative, and practical attitude toward local government affairs and a deep sense of social responsibility as a trusted public servant.

Guideline

Advice to Officials of Other Local Governments. When members advise and respond to inquiries from elected or appointed officials of other local governments, they should inform the administrators of those communities.

3. Be dedicated to the highest ideals of honor and integrity in all public and personal relationships in order that the member may merit the respect and confidence of the elected officials, of other officials and employees, and of the public.

Guidelines

Public Confidence. Members should conduct themselves so as to maintain public confidence in their profession, their local government, and in their performance of the public trust.

Impression of Influence. Members should conduct their official and personal affairs in such a manner as to give the clear impression that they cannot be improperly influenced in the performance of their official duties.

Appointment Commitment. Members who accept an appointment to a position should not fail to report for that position. This does not preclude the possibility of a member considering several offers or seeking several positions at the same time, but once a *bona fide* offer of a position has been accepted, that commitment should be honored. Oral acceptance of an employment offer is considered binding unless the employer makes fundamental changes in terms of employment.

Credentials. An application for employment or for ICMA's Voluntary Credentialing Program should be complete and accurate as to all pertinent details of education, experience, and personal history. Members should recognize that both omissions and inaccuracies must be avoided.

Professional Respect. Members seeking a management position should show professional respect for persons formerly holding the position or for others who might be applying for the same position. Professional respect does not preclude honest differences of opinion; it does preclude attacking a person's motives or integrity in order to be appointed to a position.

Reporting Ethics Violations. When becoming aware of a possible violation of the ICMA Code of Ethics, members are encouraged to report the matter to ICMA. In reporting the matter, members may choose to go on record as the complainant or report the matter on a confidential basis.

Confidentiality. Members should not discuss or divulge information with anyone about pending or completed ethics cases, except as specifically authorized by the Rules of Procedure for Enforcement of the Code of Ethics.

Seeking Employment. Members should not seek employment for a position having an incumbent administrator who has not resigned or been officially informed that his or her services are to be terminated.

4. Recognize that the chief function of local government at all times is to serve the best interests of all of the people.

Guideline

Length of Service. A minimum of two years generally is considered necessary in order to render a professional service to the local government. A short tenure should be the exception rather than a recurring experience. However, under special circumstances, it may be in the best interests of the local government and the member to separate in a shorter time. Examples of such circumstances would include refusal of the appointing authority to honor commitments concerning conditions of employment, a vote of no confidence in the member, or severe personal problems. It is the responsibility of an applicant for a position to ascertain conditions of employment. Inadequately determining terms of employment prior to arrival does not justify premature termination.

5. Submit policy proposals to elected officials; provide them with facts and advice on matters of policy as a basis for making decisions and setting community goals; and uphold and implement local government policies adopted by elected officials.

Guideline

Conflicting Roles. Members who serve multiple roles—working as both city attorney and city manager for the same community, for example—should avoid participating in matters that create the appearance of a conflict of interest. They should disclose the potential conflict to the governing body so that other opinions may be solicited.

6. Recognize that elected representatives of the people are entitled to the credit for the establishment of local government policies; responsibility for policy execution rests with the members.

7. Refrain from all political activities which undermine public confidence in professional administrators. Refrain from participation in the election of the members of the employing legislative body.

Guidelines

Elections of the Governing Body. Members should maintain a reputation for serving equally and impartially all members of the governing body of the local government they serve, regardless of party. To this end, they should not engage in active participation in the election campaign on behalf of or in opposition to candidates for the governing body.

Elections of Elected Executives. Members should not engage in the election campaign of any candidate for mayor or elected county executive.

Running for Office. Members shall not run for elected office or become involved in political activities related to running for elected office. They shall not seek political endorsements, financial contributions or engage in other campaign activities.

Elections. Members share with their fellow citizens the right and responsibility to vote and to voice their opinion on public issues. However, in order not to impair their effectiveness on behalf of the local governments they serve, they shall not participate in political activities to support the candidacy of individuals running for any city, county, special district, school, state or federal offices. Specifically, they shall not endorse candidates, make financial contributions, sign or circulate petitions, or participate in fund-raising activities for individuals seeking or holding elected office.

Elections in the Council-Manager Plan. Members may assist in preparing and presenting materials that explain the council-manager form of government to the public prior to an election on the use of the plan. If assistance is required by another community, members may respond. All activities regarding ballot issues should be conducted within local regulations and in a professional manner.

Presentation of Issues. Members may assist the governing body in presenting issues involved in referenda such as bond issues, annexations, and similar matters.

8. Make it a duty continually to improve the member's professional ability and to develop the competence of associates in the use of management techniques.

Guidelines

Self-Assessment. Each member should assess his or her professional skills and abilities on a periodic basis.

Professional Development. Each member should commit at least 40 hours per year to professional development activities that are based on the practices identified by the members of ICMA.

9. Keep the community informed on local government affairs; encourage communication between the citizens and all local government officers; emphasize friendly and courteous service to the public; and seek to improve the quality and image of public service.

10. Resist any encroachment on professional responsibilities, believing the member should be free to carry out official policies without interference, and handle each problem without discrimination on the basis of principle and justice.

    Guideline

    Information Sharing. The member should openly share information with the governing body while diligently carrying out the member's responsibilities as set forth in the charter or enabling legislation.

11. Handle all matters of personnel on the basis of merit so that fairness and impartiality govern a member's decisions, pertaining to appointments, pay adjustments, promotions, and discipline.

    Guideline

    Equal Opportunity. All decisions pertaining to appointments, pay adjustments, promotions, and discipline should prohibit discrimination because of race, color, religion, sex, national origin, sexual orientation, political affiliation, disability, age, or marital status.

    It should be the members' personal and professional responsibility to actively recruit and hire a diverse staff throughout their organizations.

12. Seek no favor; believe that personal aggrandizement or profit secured by confidential information or by misuse of public time is dishonest.

    Guidelines

    Gifts. Members should not directly or indirectly solicit any gift or accept or receive any gift—whether it be money, services, loan, travel, entertainment, hospitality, promise, or any other form—under the following circumstances: (1) it could be reasonably inferred or expected that the gift was intended to influence them in the performance of their official duties; or (2) the gift was intended to serve as a reward for any official action on their part.

    It is important that the prohibition of unsolicited gifts be limited to circumstances related to improper influence. In *de minimus* situations, such as meal checks, some modest maximum dollar value should be determined by the member as a guideline. The guideline is not intended to isolate members from normal social practices where gifts among friends, associates, and relatives are appropriate for certain occasions.

Investments in Conflict with Official Duties. Member should not invest or hold any investment, directly or indirectly, in any financial business, commercial, or other private transaction that creates a conflict with their official duties.

In the case of real estate, the potential use of confidential information and knowledge to further a member's personal interest requires special consideration. This guideline recognizes that members' official actions and decisions can be influenced if there is a conflict with personal investments. Purchases and sales which might be interpreted as speculation for quick profit ought to be avoided (see the guideline on "Confidential Information").

Because personal investments may prejudice or may appear to influence official actions and decisions, members may, in concert with their governing body, provide for disclosure of such investments prior to accepting their position as local government administrator or prior to any official action by the governing body that may affect such investments.

Personal Relationships. Member should disclose any personal relationship to the governing body in any instance where there could be the appearance of a conflict of interest. For example, if the manager's spouse works for a developer doing business with the local government, that fact should be disclosed.

Confidential Information. Members should not disclose to others, or use to further their personal interest, confidential information acquired by them in the course of their official duties.

Private Employment. Members should not engage in, solicit, negotiate for, or promise to accept private employment, nor should they render services for private interests or conduct a private business when such employment, service, or business creates a conflict with or impairs the proper discharge of their official duties.

Teaching, lecturing, writing, or consulting are typical activities that may not involve conflict of interest, or impair the proper discharge of their official duties. Prior notification of the appointing authority is appropriate in all cases of outside employment.

Representation. Members should not represent any outside interest before any agency, whether public or private, except with the authorization of or at the direction of the appointing authority they serve.

Endorsements. Members should not endorse commercial products or services by agreeing to use their photograph, endorsement, or quotation in paid or other commercial advertisements, whether or not for compensation. Members may, however, agree to endorse the following, provided they do not receive any compensation: (1) books or other publications; (2) professional development or educational services provided by nonprofit membership organizations or recognized educational institutions; (3) products and/or services in which the local government has a direct economic interest.

Members' observations, opinions, and analyses of commercial products used or tested by their local governments are appropriate and useful to the profession when included as part of professional articles and reports.

Source: ICMA, www.icma.org/upload/library/2004-10/{718F9BFF-DCEA-46CD-A888-4F0FEAB92625}.doc (accessed June 16, 2006). Used with permission of the International City/County Management Association.

The Code of Ethics for Nonprofit and Philanthropic Organizations

Approved by the Independent Sector Board of Directors on January 29, 2004

A. Personal and Professional Integrity

All staff, board members and volunteers of the organization act with honesty, integrity and openness in all their dealings as representatives of the organization. The organization promotes a working environment that values respect, fairness and integrity.

B. Mission

The organization has a clearly stated mission and purpose, approved by the board of directors, in pursuit of the public good. All of its programs support that mission and all who work for or on behalf of the organization understand and are loyal to that mission and purpose. The mission is responsive to the constituency and communities served by the organization and of value to the society at large.

C. Governance

The organization has an active governing body that is responsible for setting the mission and strategic direction of the organization and oversight of the finances, operations, and policies of the organization. The governing body:

- Ensures that its board members or trustees have the requisite skills and experience to carry out their duties and that all members understand

and fulfill their governance duties acting for the benefit of the organization and its public purpose;

- Has a conflict of interest policy that ensures that any conflicts of interest or the appearance thereof are avoided or appropriately managed through disclosure, recusal or other means; and

- Is responsible for the hiring, firing, and regular review of the performance of the chief executive officer, and ensures that the compensation of the chief executive officer is reasonable and appropriate;

- Ensures that the CEO and appropriate staff provide the governing body with timely and comprehensive information so that the governing body can effectively carry out its duties;

- Ensures that the organization conducts all transactions and dealings with integrity and honesty;

- Ensures that the organization promotes working relationships with board members, staff, volunteers, and program beneficiaries that are based on mutual respect, fairness and openness;

- Ensures that the organization is fair and inclusive in its hiring and promotion policies and practices for all board, staff and volunteer positions;

- Ensures that policies of the organization are in writing, clearly articulated and officially adopted;

- Ensures that the resources of the organization are responsibly and prudently managed; and,

- Ensures that the organization has the capacity to carry out its programs effectively.

D. Legal Compliance

The organization is knowledgeable of and complies with all laws, regulations and applicable international conventions.

E. Responsible Stewardship

The organization and its subsidiaries manage their funds responsibly and prudently. This should include the following considerations:

- It spends a reasonable percentage of its annual budget on programs in pursuance of its mission;

- It spends an adequate amount on administrative expenses to ensure effective accounting systems, internal controls, competent staff, and other expenditures critical to professional management;

- The organization compensates staff, and any others who may receive compensation, reasonably and appropriately;

- Organizations that solicit funds have reasonable fundraising costs, recognizing the variety of factors that affect fundraising costs;

- Organizations do not accumulate operating funds excessively;
- Organizations with endowments (both foundations and public charities) prudently draw from endowment funds consistent with donor intent and to support the public purpose of the organization;
- Organizations ensure that all spending practices and policies are fair, reasonable and appropriate to fulfill the mission of the organization; and,
- All financial reports are factually accurate and complete in all material respects.

F. Openness and Disclosure
The organization provides comprehensive and timely information to the public, the media, and all stakeholders and is responsive in a timely manner to reasonable requests for information. All information about the organization will fully and honestly reflect the policies and practices of the organization. Basic informational data about the organization, such as the Form 990, reviews and compilations, and audited financial statements will be posted on the organization's website or otherwise available to the public. All solicitation materials accurately represent the organization's policies and practices and will reflect the dignity of program beneficiaries. All financial, organizational, and program reports will be complete and accurate in all material respects.

G. Program Evaluation
The organization regularly reviews program effectiveness and has mechanisms to incorporate lessons learned into future programs. The organization is committed to improving program and organizational effectiveness and develops mechanisms to promote learning from its activities and the field. The organization is responsive to changes in its field of activity and is responsive to the needs of its constituencies.

H. Inclusiveness and Diversity
The organization has a policy of promoting inclusiveness and its staff, board and volunteers reflect diversity in order to enrich its programmatic effectiveness. The organization takes meaningful steps to promote inclusiveness in its hiring, retention, promotion, board recruitment and constituencies served.

I. Fundraising
Organizations that raise funds from the public or from donor institutions are truthful in their solicitation materials. Organizations respect the privacy concerns of individual donors and expend funds consistent with donor intent. Organizations disclose important and relevant information to potential donors.

In raising funds from the public, organizations will respect the rights of donors, as follows:

- To be informed of the mission of the organization, the way the resources will be used and their capacity to use donations effectively for their intended purposes;
- To be informed of the identity of those serving on the organization's governing board and to expect the board to exercise prudent judgment in its stewardship responsibilities;
- To have access to the organization's most recent financial reports;
- To be assured their gifts will be used for the purposes for which they were given;
- To receive appropriate acknowledgment and recognition;
- To be assured that information about their donations is handled with respect and with confidentiality to the extent provided by the law;
- To expect that all relationships with individuals representing organizations of interest to the donor will be professional in nature;
- To be informed whether those seeking donations are volunteers, employees of the organizations or hired solicitors;
- To have the opportunity for their names to be deleted from mailing lists that an organization may intend to share; and,
- To feel free to ask questions when making a donation and to receive prompt, truthful and forthright answers.

J. Grantmaker Guidelines

Organizations that are grantmakers have particular responsibilities in carrying out their missions. These include the following:

- They will have constructive relations with grantseekers based on mutual respect and shared goals;
- They will communicate clearly and on a timely basis with potential grantees;
- They will treat grantseekers and grantees fairly and with respect;
- They will respect the expertise of grantseekers in their fields of knowledge;
- They will seek to understand and respect the organizational capacity and needs of grantseeking organizations; and,
- They will respect the integrity of the mission of grantseeking organizations.

February 3, 2004

The full statement includes four sections: Introduction, Statement of Values, Code of Ethics, and Process and Afterword.

Source: www.independentsector.org/members/code_ethics.html (accessed June 16, 2006).

American Institute of Certified Planners Code of Ethics and Professional Conduct

We, professional planners, who are members of the American Institute of Certified Planners, subscribe to our Institute's Code of Ethics and Professional Conduct. . . . The principles to which we subscribe in Sections A and B of the Code derive from the special responsibility of our profession to serve the public interest with compassion for the welfare of all people and, as professionals, to our obligation to act with high integrity.

As the basic values of society can come into competition with each other, so can the aspirational principles we espouse under this Code. An ethical judgment often requires a conscientious balancing, based on the facts and context of a particular situation and on the precepts of the entire Code.

As Certified Planners, all of us are also members of the American Planning Association and share in the goal of building better, more inclusive communities. We want the public to be aware of the principles by which we practice our profession in the quest of that goal. We sincerely hope that the public will respect the commitments we make to our employers and clients, our fellow professionals, and all other persons whose interests we affect.

A: Principles to Which We Aspire

1. Our Overall Responsibility to the Public

Our primary obligation is to serve the public interest and we, therefore, owe our allegiance to a conscientiously attained concept of the public interest that is formulated through continuous and open debate. We shall achieve high standards of professional integrity, proficiency, and knowledge. To comply with our obligation to the public, we aspire to the following principles:

a) We shall always be conscious of the rights of others.

b) We shall have special concern for the long-range consequences of present actions.

c) We shall pay special attention to the interrelatedness of decisions.

d) We shall provide timely, adequate, clear, and accurate information on planning issues to all affected persons and to governmental decision makers.

e) We shall give people the opportunity to have a meaningful impact on the development of plans and programs that may affect them. Participation should be broad enough to include those who lack formal organization or influence.

f) We shall seek social justice by working to expand choice and opportunity for all persons, recognizing a special responsibility to plan for the needs of the disadvantaged and to promote racial and economic integration. We shall urge the alteration of policies, institutions, and decisions that oppose such needs.

g) We shall promote excellence of design and endeavor to conserve and preserve the integrity and heritage of the natural and built environment.

h) We shall deal fairly with all participants in the planning process. Those of us who are public officials or employees shall also deal evenhandedly with all planning process participants.

2. Our Responsibility to Our Clients and Employers

We owe diligent, creative, and competent performance of the work we do in pursuit of our client or employer's interest. Such performance, however, shall always be consistent with our faithful service to the public interest.

a) We shall exercise independent professional judgment on behalf of our clients and employers.

b) We shall accept the decisions of our client or employer concerning the objectives and nature of the professional services we perform unless the course of action is illegal or plainly inconsistent with our primary obligation to the public interest.

c) We shall avoid a conflict of interest or even the appearance of a conflict of interest in accepting assignments from clients or employers.

3. Our Responsibility to Our Profession and Colleagues

We shall contribute to the development of, and respect for, our profession by improving knowledge and techniques, making work relevant to solutions of community problems, and increasing public understanding of planning activities.

a) We shall protect and enhance the integrity of our profession.

b) We shall educate the public about planning issues and their relevance to our everyday lives.

c) We shall describe and comment on the work and views of other professionals in a fair and professional manner.

d) We shall share the results of experience and research that contribute to the body of planning knowledge.

e) We shall examine the applicability of planning theories, methods, research and practice and standards to the facts and analysis of each particular situation and shall not accept the applicability of a customary solution without first establishing its appropriateness to the situation.

f) We shall contribute time and resources to the professional development of students, interns, beginning professionals, and other colleagues.

g) We shall increase the opportunities for members of underrepresented groups to become professional planners and help them advance in the profession.

h) We shall continue to enhance our professional education and training.

i) We shall systematically and critically analyze ethical issues in the practice of planning.

j) We shall contribute time and effort to groups lacking in adequate planning resources and to voluntary professional activities.

B: Our Rules of Conduct

We adhere to the following Rules of Conduct, and we understand that our Institute will enforce compliance with them. If we fail to adhere to these Rules, we could receive sanctions, the ultimate being the loss of our certification:

1. We shall not deliberately or with reckless indifference fail to provide adequate, timely, clear and accurate information on planning issues.

2. We shall not accept an assignment from a client or employer when the services to be performed involve conduct that we know to be illegal or in violation of these rules.

3. We shall not accept an assignment from a client or employer to publicly advocate a position on a planning issue that is indistinguishably adverse to a position we publicly advocated for a previous client or employer within the past three years unless (1) we determine in good faith after consultation with other qualified professionals that our change of position will not cause present detriment to our previous client or employer, and (2) we make full written disclosure of the conflict to our current client or employer and receive written permission to proceed with the assignment.

4. We shall not, as salaried employees, undertake other employment in planning or a related profession, whether or not for pay, without having made full written disclosure to the employer who furnishes our salary and having received subsequent written permission to undertake additional employment, unless our employer has a written policy which expressly dispenses with a need to obtain such consent.

5. We shall not, as public officials or employees; accept from anyone other than our public employer any compensation, commission, rebate, or other advantage that may be perceived as related to our public office or employment.

6. We shall not perform work on a project for a client or employer if, in addition to the agreed upon compensation from our client or employer, there is a possibility for direct personal or financial gain to us, our family members, or persons living in our household, unless our client or employer, after full written disclosure from us, consents in writing to the arrangement.

7. We shall not use to our personal advantage, nor that of a subsequent client or employer, information gained in a professional relationship that the client or employer has requested be held inviolate or that we should recognize as confidential because its disclosure could result in embarrassment or other detriment to the client or employer. Nor shall we disclose such confidential information except when (1) required by process of law, or (2) required to prevent a clear violation of law, or (3) required to prevent a substantial injury to the public. Disclosure pursuant to (2) and (3) shall not be made until after we have verified the facts and issues involved and, when practicable, exhausted efforts to obtain reconsideration of the matter and have sought separate opinions on the issue from other qualified professionals employed by our client or employer.

8. We shall not, as public officials or employees, engage in private communications with planning process participants if the discussions relate to a matter over which we have authority to make a binding, final determination if such private communications are prohibited by law or by agency rules, procedures, or custom.

9. We shall not engage in private discussions with decision makers in the planning process in any manner prohibited by law or by agency rules, procedures, or custom.

10. We shall neither deliberately, nor with reckless indifference, misrepresent the qualifications, views and findings of other professionals.

11. We shall not solicit prospective clients or employment through use of false or misleading claims, harassment, or duress.

12. We shall not misstate our education, experience, training, or any other facts which are relevant to our professional qualifications.

13. We shall not sell, or offer to sell, services by stating or implying an ability to influence decisions by improper means.

14. We shall not use the power of any office to seek or obtain a special advantage that is not a matter of public knowledge or is not in the public interest.

15. We shall not accept work beyond our professional competence unless the client or employer understands and agrees that such work will be performed by another professional competent to perform the work and acceptable to the client or employer.

16. We shall not accept work for a fee, or pro bono, that we know cannot be performed with the promptness required by the prospective client, or that is required by the circumstances of the assignment.

17. We shall not use the product of others' efforts to seek professional recognition or acclaim intended for producers of original work.

18. We shall not direct or coerce other professionals to make analyses or reach findings not supported by available evidence.

19. We shall not fail to disclose the interests of our client or employer when participating in the planning process. Nor shall we participate in an effort to conceal the true interests of our client or employer.

20. We shall not unlawfully discriminate against another person.

21. We shall not withhold cooperation or information from the AICP Ethics Officer or the AICP Ethics Committee if a charge of ethical misconduct has been filed against us.

22. We shall not retaliate or threaten retaliation against a person who has filed a charge of ethical misconduct against us or another planner, or who is cooperating in the Ethics Officer's investigation of an ethics charge.

23. We shall not use the threat of filing an ethics charge in order to gain, or attempt to gain, an advantage in dealings with another planner.

24. We shall not file a frivolous charge of ethical misconduct against another planner.

25. We shall neither deliberately, nor with reckless indifference, commit any wrongful act, whether or not specified in the Rules of Conduct, that reflects adversely on our professional fitness.

Adopted March 19, 2005; Effective June 1, 2005

Source: www.planning.org/ethics/conduct.html (accessed June 16, 2006). Copyright 2006 APA. All rights reserved. Used with permission of the American Planning Association.

Organizational Ethical Climate Survey

For each item, indicate whether you agree completely [1], agree more than you disagree [2], disagree more than you agree [3], or disagree completely [4].

1. Ordinarily, we don't deviate from standard policies and procedures in my department.

2. My supervisor encourages employees to act in an ethical manner.

3. I do not have to ask my supervisor before I do almost anything.

4. Around here, there is encouragement to improve individual and group performance continually.

5. The employees in my department demonstrate high standards of personal integrity.

6. My department has a defined standard of integrity.

7. Individuals in my department accept responsibility for decisions they make.

8. It is wrong to accept gifts from persons who do business with my jurisdiction, even if those gifts do not influence how I do my job.

9. It is not usual for members of my department to accept small gifts for performing their duties.

10. Members of my department do not use their positions for private gain.

11. Members of my department have not misused their positions to influence the hiring of their friends and relatives in the government.

12. I would blow the whistle if someone in my department accepted a large gift ($____ or more in value; this amount varies by local government) from a person who does business with the government.

13. Promotions in my department are based on what you know or how you perform on the job, rather than on whom you know.

14. I trust my supervisor.

15. The jurisdiction has implemented a code of ethics.

16. There are no serious ethical problems in my department.

17. Coworkers in my department trust each other.

18. My superiors set a good example of ethical behavior.

19. I feel that I am a member of a well-functioning team.

20. All employees have equal opportunities for advancement.

21. Performance evaluations accurately reflect how employees have done their jobs.

22. Performance evaluations address ethical requirements as well as other measures.

23. Employees share negative information with supervisors without the worry of receiving a negative reaction from them.

24. Supervisors are concerned with *how* employees achieve successful results, rather than just with the results themselves.

25. When there is a disagreement between employees and supervisors on how best to solve a problem, the employees' ideas are listened to and considered.

26. When employees feel that they are being asked to do something that is ethically wrong, supervisors work with them on alternative ways to do the task.

27. In this organization, it is much better to report a problem or error than it is to cover it up.

28. When something goes wrong, the primary goal is to fix the problem and prevent it from happening again, rather than to find someone to blame.

29. The organization's decisions on how people are treated are clear and consistent.

30. The organization's expectations concerning productivity, quality, and ethics are consistent.

31. The same set of ethical standards is used in dealing with citizens, employees, and others.

32. You can rely on the accuracy of the organization's information about what will or won't happen.

33. The organization publicly recognizes and rewards ethical behavior by employees when it occurs.

34. Doing what is right around here is more important than following the rules.

35. Ethical standards and practices are routinely discussed in employee meetings.

36. If there is suspicion that some employees may be violating ethical standards, the situation is dealt with openly and directly.

37. Employees are aware of where to obtain assistance when they need to resolve an ethical dilemma.

38. If one employee is doing something unethical, the other employees in the group will usually try to correct the situation before management gets involved.

39. Employees are encouraged to report their work results accurately even when the results are less than satisfactory.

40. Employees maintain the same ethical standards even when no one is observing their actions.

Use the scale below each statement to respond to the following items; circle the number that most closely represents your response

41. My ethical standards are
    Very low   1   2   3   4   5   6   7   Very high

42. The ethical standards in my department are
    Very low   1   2   3   4   5   6   7   Very high

Circle the answer that best represents your response to this statement:

43. My behavior as a public employee is regulated by state law.
    Yes   No   Don't know

Source: "Take the Ethical Climate Survey," *PM* May 1999: 23–25. Used with permission of Stephen J. Bonczek.

Notes

Chapter 1: Introduction—and a Pop Quiz

1. For example, a nonprofit organization that provides training in a welfare-to-work program will determine whether a client meets prescribed criteria that permits the person to continue receiving benefits.
2. The scope of nonprofit organizations is large and they vary considerably in their degree of formality. This book is written for administrators in nonprofits as opposed to board members, and I assume that they work for tax exempt 501(c)(3) organizations.

Chapter 2: Administrative Ethics: Ideas, Sources, and Development

3. Definition adapted from Andre and Velasquez (1987).
4. For further explanation of approaches, see Cooper (2004).
5. Definitions are from the *New Shorter Oxford English Dictionary*.
6. Students write their answer to these questions before we talk about the course content (except to review the overall purpose and required readings). Students have 15–20 minutes to complete the assignment, but virtually all have stopped writing before the end of the time period. At the end of the time period, I take a break to permit any who have not finished additional time. Students do not put their name on the paper. I analyzed the codes written by 123 students from my nine classes since 1999. Commentary about a tenet (for example, an explanation of why it is important) is not counted

as a separate tenet nor are statements without ethical content (for example, "public officials face many challenges"). The responses are categorized in terms of the nature of ethical reasoning used: Analysis of whether the statement is based on duty/public service, virtue, principle, consequences, or some other source.

7. Rest et al. (1999), who developed the D.I.T. or Defining Issues Test inventory to measure moral judgment, classify the three major divisions or "schemas" as personal interest or preconventional, maintaining norms or conventional, and postconventional. They disagree that the stages are "hard" like in a staircase with one stage replacing the preceding one. Their "soft-stage" approach is based on a shifting distribution that draws on more than one stage. Still, there is a progression from conventionality to postconventionality. The two are "developmentally ordered—the Postconventional schema is more advanced . . . than the Maintaining Norms schema" (Navaez 2002).

8. Rest et al. (1999, 48) also refer to the P score, based on Stages 5 and 6.

Chapter 3: Refining the Sense of Duty: Responsibilities of Public Administrators and the Issue of Agency

9. Some of these cases appeared in professional training material and are in general circulation. For local government cases (including 3.1 and 3.3), see Richter, Burke, and Doig 1990, 275–277.

10. This familiar quotation was never the official motto of the U.S. Postal Service. It is adapted from Herodotus and inscribed on the post office building in New York City (Quotations Page 2005).

11. See discussion by Debra Stewart (1985) and Dennis Thompson (1985) of the impact of role theory and neutrality on moral agency.

12. The presumed lack of moral agency also ignores the obligation to resist improper commands. Officials even in military or quasimilitary organizations should not obey illegal or improper orders. For discussion of this issue, see Toner (2005, 49–51).

13. Size is not always the issue. Charles Goodsell (2003) provides evidence to support the point that most government offices are small.

14. By civil service rules, administrators are prohibited from engaging in partisan activity on behalf of political superiors (Barker and Wilson 1997, 228–229).

15. The Nuremburg Code is available at www.yale.edu/lawweb/avalon/imt/proc/imtconst.htm (accessed June 13, 2006).

16. See Gordon Tullock (1965), William Niskanen (1971), and Patrick Dunleavy (1991).

17. The values combine the contrasting perspectives of Herman Finer (1941) and Carl J. Friedrich (1940).

Chapter 4: Reinforcing and Enlarging Duty: Philosophical Bases of Ethical Behavior

17a. This chapter is adapted from James Svara (1997). It is used with permission of the Council of State Governments.

18. For a similar presentation of philosophical approaches, see also Terry Cooper (2004).

19. Garofalo and Geuras (1999, 57–59) argue that intuition is based simply on a "moral sense" of what is right and wrong without any reasons or reflection. See also Geuras and Garofalo (2002).

20. Cooper (1987) stresses virtue when he examines PA as "practice." A *practice* is an activity organized to achieve certain standards of excellence. *Internal goods* are produced in pursuit of excellence.

21. An alternative is to consider *integrity* to be the ideal of this approach. According to Dobel (1999, xii), who uses integrity to construct a comprehensive ethical framework, "integrity involves the capacity of people to make sense of their life and link belief and practice."

22. "For example, honesty is a value that governs behavior in the form of principles such as: tell the truth, don't deceive, be candid, don't cheat. In this way, values give rise to principles in the form of specific 'dos' and 'don'ts.'" (Josephson Institute of Ethics 2002).

23. In contrast, act-deontologists argue that "basic judgments of obligation are all purely particular ones like 'In this situation I should do so and so'" (Frankena 1963, 15).

24. Deontology is defined in *New Shorter Oxford English Dictionary* as "the science of duty or moral obligation."

25. According to Henry David Thoreau (1849), even private citizens who commit acts of civil disobedience to protest laws believed to be unjust must be willing to pay the consequences.

26. Garofalo and Geuras (1999, 104–05) point out that all principles do not apply to all actions in any situation. For example, the injunction against lying applies to situations when one would advance selfish personal reasons for telling a lie, but not when one is being polite or compassionate, or possibly even defending national security. These are not exceptions to the rule but rather cases in which the rule is not applicable. Bok (1989) takes a much more restrictive approach and does see these as exceptions that must be carefully justified, as discussed later in this chapter.

27. Chandler offers an example of how a constitutional protection can be reframed as a principle. Due process is an important value. For it to be an "organizing value, however, we would need a deontological principle which could show us what pattern of action would comply with this value. A common form of the due process principle, for example, is that 'law must be just, fair, and equal,' and it should not be 'oppressive, fanciful, or biased.' Under this principle, therefore, all accused persons have the protections of the Bill of Rights and the guarantees of the Fourteenth Amendment" (Chandler 1994, 149).

28. The tests that follow are derived from variations in consequentialism outlined by Walter Sinnott-Armstrong (2006).

29. Lewis broadens the range of perspectives in her three circle approach (1991, 41), which assesses decisions in terms of ethical, legal, and effectiveness considerations.

30. The Josephson Institute takes the same position: "Honesty is a value that governs behavior in the form of principles such as: tell the truth, don't deceive, be candid, don't cheat. In this way, values give rise to principles in the form of specific 'dos' and 'don'ts'" (Josephson Institute 2002, www.josephsoninstitute.org/MED/MED-1makingsense.htm, accessed June 18, 2006).

31. Toner argues for the primacy of character, but he views the dispositions based on habitus as a moral arrangement based on contemplation, not simply intuition, and an "ethical constitution, which . . . is founded in fundamental principles" (Toner 2005, 121). To expand his definition of character given earlier, "character is about habitus, settled dispositions toward the good that are open to truth and grace" (144).

32. See: www.independentsector.org/members/code_main.html (accessed June 18, 2006).

Chapter 5: Codifying Duty and Ethical Perspectives: Codes of Ethics

33. The Athenian Oath is available at www.nlc.org/about_cities/cities_101/146.cfm (accessed June 18, 2006).

34. Two of these issues have been partially addressed in a companion document, the "ICMA Declaration of Ideals." It states the value of equity in delivering services and encourages citizen participation. It is available at www.ci.novi.mi.us/Services/CityManager/DeclarationOfIdeals.pdf (accessed June 18, 2006).

35. See Article 1, Section 5 of ASPA Bylaws (ASPA 2005).

36. The ICMA process is available at http://www1.icma.org/upload/library/2005-10/{FE9AABDA-9C88-4581-8BB8-60B4965543EA}.rtf (accessed June 18, 2006). The AICP process is at www.planning.org/ethics/conduct.html (accessed June 18, 2006) in Part C: Our Code Procedures. The National Association of Social Workers has a 60-page publication on procedures for professional review. It can be downloaded at www.socialworkers.org/nasw/ethics/procedures.pdf (accessed June 18, 2006).

37. If the complainant is not a member of ICMA, he or she shall be notified that the case was considered and resolved, and that no public action was taken. When there is a public censure, in addition to informing the parties directly involved, information about a public censure is sent to local governing bodies and news media, indicating that a violation of the code took place and that ICMA strongly disapproves of such conduct and the nature of the sanction imposed. *Expulsion* means a revocation of the respondent's membership privileges, and a *membership bar* is a prohibition against reinstatement of the respondent's membership in ICMA. A member who has been barred or expelled from membership under these rules may apply for reinstatement to ICMA membership only after a period of at least 5 years from the date of the bar or expulsion or from the date of the last review of a request for reinstatement.

38. If the respondent requests a hearing, the CPC refers the case, including its recommended sanction, for a hearing before the executive board, which may vote to adopt the recommended decision of the CPC, to modify said decision, or to dismiss the case without imposing sanctions. The executive board may not increase the sanction recommended by the CPC unless new evidence, not previously

available to the CPC, is disclosed at the hearing, which indicates that the respondent's violation was more serious.

39. This right is covered in Section 11 of the AICP Code Procedure.

Chapter 6: Undermining Duty: Challenges to the Ethical Behavior of Public Administrators

40. For example, see the factsheet on sexual harassment prepared by Women's Rights Department of the American Federation of State, County, and Municipal Employees: www.afscme.org/wrkplace/wrfaq02.htm (accessed June 16, 2006).

41. The success and scandal surrounding former United Way of America executive William Aramony is a graphic example of executive hubris. He resigned in 1992 and was convicted in 1995 on 25 counts including conspiracy to defraud, mail fraud, wire fraud, transportation of fraudulently acquired property, engaging in monetary transactions in unlawful activity, filing false tax returns, and aiding in the filing of false tax returns (Sinclair 2002).

42. *The Malek Manual* was originally published by the White House Personnel Office in 1970 during the first term of President Richard Nixon.

43. The opposite of acting on the basis of vague expectations is refusing to act and the defense that it was never made clear what was supposed to be done. Pushing a superior to issue an explicit order may defuse the ethical dilemma or it may harden it if the subordinate has to confront the situation of following or refusing to follow an order.

44. The fear of reprisal is given by 33 percent as the reason for nonreporting, too great a risk is mentioned by 28 percent, and fear of having their identity revealed is mentioned by 20 percent. Of those who do report a problem, 37 percent experience retaliation (U.S. Merit Systems Protection Board 1993).

45. There is a third possibility. Some may willingly accept the order because they enjoy doing harm to others or because they believe in the purpose behind the order. A sadistic administrator in the former group belongs in the bad-persons category of administrators. A zealous supporter of the leader or the program would feel that he or she had good reasons to carry out the order. Daniel Goldhagen's (1996) study of Nazi Germany provides evidence that many participants in the extermination of Jews believed in the cause.

46. Milgram's experimental methods raised questions about the use of deception and informed consent of subjects in research (Shamoo and Resnik 2003).

47. See: www.usatoday.com/news/nation/2005-05-12-downwinders_x.htm (accessed June 18, 2006). Other field tests and intentional releases with radioactive material were often done in areas occupied by Hispanic and native American populations (Moreno 2001, 155).

Chapter 7: Deciding How to Meet Obligations and Act Responsibly: Ethical Analysis and Problem Solving

48. For discussion of rational models and their disadvantages, see Charles Lindblom (1968).

49. This model has been inspired by others, in particular Lewis (1991) and Cooper (1982).

50. This case was used at a session on ethics at the annual meeting of the International City and County Management Association, Vancouver, Canada, in 1997. We will not question the premise in the case that the city could not have succeeded in removing the employee even without the testimony of the victims in court if, for example, the conduct was known to others who felt that it contributed to a hostile environment in the workplace. The employer would have been required under Title VII to take prompt remedial action once being made aware of the actions of the staff member (EEOC 1990). It is possible that another option for the manager in North Carolina would indicate that he cannot share any further information without the former employee's permission or release, but whether this suggestion is permissible would depend on the specific terms of the non-disclosure agreement. For a discussion of the legal and ethical issues in writing letters of reference, see Smith (1999). I appreciate the helpful comments on this case of former MPA students Doris Leapley and Gregg Schwitzgebel.

51. This case was originally circulated through email among members of the Association for Research on Nonprofit Organizations and Voluntary Action (ARNOVA). I have not been able to find an original source or citation.

Chapter 8: Acting on Duty in the Face of Uncertainty and Risk: Responsible Whistleblowing

52. For the GAP's definition of Who is a Whistleblower, see: www.whistleblower.org/content/press_detail.cfm?press_id=60&key-word= (accessed June 17, 2006).

53. He did take inside action when he persuaded acting FBI director Gray not to accept the White House demand that the Watergate operation be linked to the CIA that would have put it off-limits to the FBI (Dobbs 2005).

54. At the same time he was providing information to Woodward, Felt was authorizing nine illegal entries at homes of persons suspected to be Weather Underground sympathizers in the New York area. In 1980, Felt was convicted on a conspiracy charge for this action. He was pardoned by President Ronald Reagan in 1981. Felt resigned from the FBI in June of 1973. He left following a dispute with new FBI Director William Ruckelshaus who accused Felt of leaking information about illegal wiretaps to the *New York Times* but not the leaks to Robert Woodward. Felt did not go public at that time. In fact, he continued to rely on inside sources and fed additional information to Woodward in November 1973, about erasures from the secret White House tapes. See Dobb (2005) and Corn and Goldberg (2005) for details about Felt's double life.

55. Originally presented by Government Accountability Project at www.whistleblower.org/www/retaliation.htm. This web page is no longer active.

56. These points are adapted from the Government Accountability Project at www.whistleblower.org/content/press_detail.cfm?press_id=59 (accessed June 18, 2006).

57. See: www.mspb.gov/fedemployeerights.htm (accessed June 18, 2006).

58. In calculating percentages, field investigations were counted as processed and closed. In 2003, there were seven stays secured to delay retaliatory treatment.

59. The following are examples of corrective actions from the 2002 annual report (OSC 2003, 9). They are offered to give a picture of the nature of reprisal and the kind of remedy provided. [A] A HUD employee alleged that she was not given a career-ladder promotion

and was reassigned out of her field office director position. . . . She claimed these actions were taken because she reported to the agency's deputy secretary that one of the agency's programs was flawed and had little value, the positions in the program were over-graded, and there were problems with the selection process for the positions. Prior to completion of the investigation, the agency and the employee agreed to settle this matter. The agency agreed to return the employee to her field office director position; retroactively promote her to the GS-15 level; and to pay a lump sum representing 2 years of back pay for the GS-15 salary (approximately $10,000). [B] An employee of the department of justice, U.S. marshal's service had been demoted from his GS-13 supervisory position and had con-tracting officer technical representative (COTR) duties removed from his position because he made disclosures of aircraft mainte-nance violations. In response to the OSC's request for corrective action, the agency agreed to promote the employee back to a non-supervisory GS-13 level position, restore his COTR duties, and pay his attorney's fees.

60. In a 1999 decision, the U.S. Federal Circuit Court appeared to require that the complainant have unrefutable evidence—irrefragable proof—of serious misconduct to receive protection from reprisal. The MSPB applied a less stringent objective reasonable-belief test to complaints: Could a disinterested observer with knowl-edge of the essential facts known to and readily ascertainable by the employee reasonably conclude that the actions of the government evidence gross mismanagement? See U.S. Congress, Senate (2005).

61. The Sullivan case was written by Harold Orlans and appeared in Richter, Burke, and Doig (1990, 278–279). Dr. Irvin Vann updated the case and assessed how it would have been handled under the WPA of 1989.

62. The prohibition of reprisal is contained in 5 U.S.C. §2302(b)(8). The 2002 and 2003 reports provide these representative cases of the dis-cipline and the actions that had been taken by the supervisor. They are offered to give a picture of the nature of the original reprisal and the kind of disciplinary actions taken. [A] OSC persuaded the U.S. Department of the Army to reprimand one supervisor and counsel another for having caused the reassignment of a quality-assurance specialist to an overseas position because of the employee's disclo-sure of regulatory violations concerning the shipment of munitions (2002). [B] The OSC permitted a park superintendent to retire from service in lieu of disciplinary action based on an OSC investigation

that demonstrated that the official had engaged in a lengthy pattern and practice of harassment and retaliation against a subordinate foreman who had disclosed to members of Congress and the media evidence of the superintendent's abuse of authority and gross mismanagement of the park's historical ships. The acts of retaliation included a demotion, the failure to promote, and significant changes in the whistleblower's duties and working conditions (Office of the Special Counsel 2003). [C] The U.S. Department of Veterans Affairs agreed to provide corrective and disciplinary action to resolve a complaint from an employee, who alleged that officials canceled his undocumented detail to a higher-graded position (chief of the police service) because he filed a complaint with the department's office of inspector general. The OSC's investigation revealed that a human resources officer had advised a manager to end the detail because of the employee's complaint. Based on this prohibited personnel practice (reprisal for cooperation with or disclosure of information to an inspector general), the department agreed to suspend both the human resources officer and the manager who canceled the detail for 14 days without pay. The department also agreed to document the employee's detail and to make a lump sum payment to him for damages and attorney fees (Office of the Special Counsel, 2004).

63. There was one unsuccessful complaint by the OSC in 2002. In 2003, there were two complaints filed, one of which resulted in disciplinary action.

64. It appears that relatively few disciplinary actions are pursued. There were 75 and 83 favorable corrective actions taken regarding reprisal, in 2002 and 2003 respectively, but only 13 instances of disciplinary action for managers who were responsible for the actions that needed to be corrected.

Chapter 9: Elevating Ethical Behavior in the Organization

65. Steinberg and Austern (1990, ch. 7) suggest four essentials for fostering an organizational and management culture that is positive: training, audit of management, investigation, and management control.

66. Since the passage of the Public Sector Management Act 1994, the Commissioner has been responsible for monitoring annually how the

ethics framework in the state of Western Australia is working. The latest report indicates that there is an improvement in positive perceptions about managers with 62% of staff members responding to climate surveys agreeing that management leads by example in ethical behavior and 52% agreeing that management monitors ethical conduct (Commissioner for Public Sector Standards 2005, 48).

67. For a review of organizational culture, see Edgar H. Schein (1992).

68. There is evidence that administrators saw the need for this development and supported it. In his 1989 survey, Bowman (1999, 348) found that almost two thirds of the respondents felt that an agency-specific code would be needed to supplement the ASPA code and make it more effective.

69. See: http://ethics.od.nih.gov/cbt.htm (accessed June 17, 2006). Staff members were instructed to log on to the online program. The employee's supervisor and the NIH ethics office were notified when the training was completed.

70. West and Berman (2004) offer reasons why government might not engage in training, and Geuras and Garofalo (2002, 43–46) describe what they call the ethics aversion syndrome. In my own teaching experiences in MPA classes, virtually all the students who are practitioners report that their organizations do not conduct ethics training and devote little time to talking about ethics.

71. West and Berman stress the importance of following an adult learning model of training. Targeted elements in training stressed application of knowledge and "emphasized the warning signs of unethical behavior, the importance of getting facts, dealing with inadvertent ethical missteps, addressing ethical complaints, consequences of ethical violation, and ethical issues in specific areas (e.g., law enforcement)" (West and Berman 2004, 198).

72. West, Berman, Bonczek, and Kellar (1998) report a different kind of shortcoming. Training consultants often avoid offering a "lecture-based compliance course" for fear of receiving poor evaluations and because knowledge retention may be low (6). Trainers need to find creative ways to make this important material engaging.

73. For background information on the New Orleans Police Department, see Ross (2000).

74. Evans and Berman use a statistical method called simultaneous equations modeling, which clarifies the sequential and causal relationships among a group of variables. The model is summarized in Figure 1.

75. For commentary on measures and recommendations for use of social equity in teaching, see Svara and Brunet (2004).

76. *Equal distribution* means that all receive the same level and quality of service or all that request a service receive it. *Compensatory distribution* provides services to those who meet a need or criteria (for example, the poor) or are directed to geographical areas with greater need. Distribution to achieve equal results is rare because of high costs and the inability of the government to control all the social, economic, and behavioral factors that affect outcomes. Still, the No Child Left Behind program requires extra efforts if equal results are not being achieved. Some public health programs are permitted to use any resources required and extraordinary means to stop the spread of a deadly epidemic (NAPA, 2005).

77. Sylvester Murray (in Gooden and Myers 2004) offered this example. In the seemingly straightforward case of solid-waste collection, there are income differences in the ability of a household to compact and secure store debris. Once-a-week garbage pickup may work adequately in higher income areas but lead to unacceptable outcomes in poor communities in densely populated areas.

78. There has been a lively discussion of whether citizen-oriented approaches associated with new public management and reinventing government have the effect of reducing the importance of citizens by seeing their role as simply the consumer of public services rather than being citizens who shape and direct governmental institutions. See, for example, Richard Box (1999).

Chapter 10: Mandating Duty: External Measures to Promote Ethics

79. Organizations with annual incomes of $25,000 or less, most faith-based organizations regardless of size, and nonprofits that have not applied to the IRS for exemption from federal income tax to not file the 990 form. All private foundations and most other nonprofits that (a) have incomes of more than $25,000 and (b) are tax exempt under tax code provisions including Section 501(c) must file a 990 or 990-EZ. See: www.guidestar.org/news/features/990_myths.jsp (accessed June 18, 2006).

80. U.S. Code, Title 5, Part I, Chapter 5, Subchapter II, § 552. Public information; agency rules, opinions, orders, records, and proceedings. See: http://straylight.law.cornell.edu/uscode/html/uscode05/usc_sec_05_0 0000552----000-.html (accessed June 18, 2006).

81. This incident and the report on North Carolina state government is from Rob Christensen and Matthew Eisley (2005).

82. IGnet—Celebrating 25 Years of the Federal Inspector General Act of 1978. See: www.ignet.gov/pande/igact25years.pdf (accessed June 18, 2006).

83. See: www.ignet.gov/igs/faq1.html (accessed June 18, 2006).

84. See: http://national.unitedway.org/outcomes/ (accessed June 18, 2006).

85. Information about the New York State Ethics Commission and the ethics act are available at www.dos.state.ny.us/ethc/eisg.html (accessed June 18, 2006).

86. The bill was introduced in the 1993 session of the North Carolina General Assembly. It was discussed in committee but never reported out for a vote and has not passed subsequently. I use it for illustration because the approaches proposed in the drafted bill offer useful contrasts to the New York ethics act. In 2006, the North Carolina General Assembly approved ethics reforms, including restrictions on gifts to legislators and lobbying by former members of the General Assembly.

References

Aberbach, Joel D., and Bert A. Rockman. 1993. "Civil Servants and Policy Makers: Neutral or Responsive Competence," presented at the annual meeting of the American Political Science Association.

Adams, Guy B., and Danny L. Balfour. 1998. *Unmasking Administrative Evil*. Thousand Oaks, CA: Sage Publications.

Andre, Claire, and Manuel Velasquez. 1987. "What is Ethics?" *Issues in Ethics* 1 (Fall). www.scu.edu/ethics/publications/iie/v1n1/whatis.html (accessed June 18, 2006).

Anechiarico, Frank, and James B. Jacobs. 1996. *The Pursuit of Absolute Integrity: How Corruption Control Makes Government Ineffective*. Chicago: University of Chicago Press.

ASPA 2005. Bylaws. Washington, DC: American Society for Public Administration.

Bailey, Stephen K. 1962. "The Public Interest: Some Operational Dilemmas." In *Nomos V: The Public Interest*, ed. C. J. Friedrich. New York: Atherton Press.

Barker, Anthony, and Graham K. Wilson. 1997. "Whitehall's Disobedient Servants? Senior Officials' Potential Resistance to Ministers in British Government Department." *British Journal of Political Science* 27: 223–46.

Bok, Sissela. 1989. *Lying: Moral Choice in Public and Private Life*. New York: Vintage Books.

Borins, Sandford. 2000. "Loose Cannons and Rule Breakers, or Enterprising Leaders? Some Evidence About Innovative Public Managers." *Public Administration Review* 60: 498–507.

Bowman, James S. 1990. "Ethics in Government: A National Survey of Public Administrators." *Public Administration Review* 50: 345–353.

Bowman, James S., and Russell L. Williams. 1997. "Ethics in Government: From a Winter of Despair to a Spring of Hope." *Public Administration Review* 57: 517–28.

Box, Richard. 1999. "Running Government like Business: Implications for Public Administration Theory and Practice." *American Review of Public Administration* 29: 19–43.

Brewer, Gene A., and Sally Coleman Seldon. 1998. "Whistle Blowers in the Federal Civil Service: New Evidence of the Public Service Ethic." *Journal of Public Administration Research and Theory* 8: 413–39.

Branscome, Curtis. 2005. "Reflections on ICMA's Code." *Public Management* 87 (March): 2–6.

Brown, Lesley, Ed., 1993. *The New Shorter Oxford English Dictionary on Historical Principles*, Revised edition, Vol. 1. Oxford: Oxford University Press.

Burke, John. 1986. *Bureaucratic Responsibility*. Baltimore, MD: Johns Hopkins Press.

Caiden, Gerald E., and Naomi J. Caiden. 1977. "Administrative Corruption." *Public Administration Review* 37: 301–09.

Chandler, Ralph Clark. 1994. "Deontological Dimensions of Administrative Ethics." In *Handbook of Administrative Ethics*, ed. Terry L. Cooper. New York: Marcel Dekker.

Christensen, Rob, and Matthew Eisley. 2005. "Under the Dome: No Sunshine at State Agencies." *News & Observer*, August 15.

Colby, Anne, and Lawrence Kohlberg. 1987. *The Measurement of Moral Judgment*, Vol. 1. New York: Cambridge University Press.

Commissioner for Public Sector Standards, 2005. *Annual Compliance Report for 2004–05*. Perth, Western Australia: Office of the Public Sector Standards Commissioner. www.opssc.wa.gov.au/compliancereport/documents/final.pdf (accessed June 17, 2006).

Cooper, Phillip J. 1998. "Law Against Ethics." In *Public Administration for the Twenty-First Century*, ed. Phillip J. Cooper. Fort Worth, TX: Harcourt Brace College Publishers.

Cooper, Terry L. 1982. *The Responsible Administrator*. Port Washington, NY: Kennikat Press.

Cooper, Terry L. 1987. "Hierarchy, Virtue, and the Practice of Public Administration: A Perspective for Normative Ethics." *Public Administration Review* 47: 320–28.

Cooper, Terry L. 1991. *An Ethic of Citizenship for Public Administration*. Englewood Cliffs, NJ: Prentice Hall.

Cooper, Terry L. 2004. "Big Questions in Administrative Ethics: A Need for Focused, Collaborative Effort." *Public Administration Review* 64: 395–407.

Cooper, Terry L., and Dale Wright, eds. 1992. *Moral Exemplars in Public Service*. San Francisco: Jossey-Bass Publishers.

Corn, David, and Jeff Goldberg. 2005. "How Deep Throat Fooled the FBI." *The Nation*. July 4. www.thenation.com/doc.mhtml?i=20050704&s=goldberg (accessed March 20, 2006).

DeLattre, Edwin J. 1994. *Character and Cops: Ethics in Policing*. 2nd ed. Washington, DC: AEI Press.

deLeon, Linda, and Robert B. Denhardt. 2000. "The Political Theory of Reinvention." *Public Administration Review* 60: 89–97.

Denhardt, Kathryn G. 1988. *The Ethics of Public Administration: Resolving Moral Dilemmas in Public Organizations*. New York: Greenwood.

Dilulio, John D., Jr. 1994. "Principled Agents: The Cultural Bases of Behavior in a Federal Government Bureaucracy." *Journal of Public Administration Research and Theory* 4: 277–318.

Dobbs, Michael. 2005. "Revenge Was Felt's Motive, Former Acting FBI Chief Says." *Washington Post*, June 27.

Dobel, Patrick J. 1999. *Public Integrity*. Baltimore, MD: Johns Hopkins University Press.

Dunleavy, Patrick. 1991. *Democracy, Bureaucracy, and Public Choice. Economic Explanations in Political Science*. London: Harvester Wheatsheafs.

EEOC, 1990. Policy Guidance on Employer Liability under Title VII for Sexual Favoritism. N-915.048 (January 12). Washington, DC: The U.S. Equal Employment Opportunity Commission. www.eeoc.gov/policy/docs/sexualfavor.html (accessed June 21, 2006).

Finer, Herman. 1941. "Administrative Responsibility in Democratic Government." *Public Administration Review* 1: 335–50.

Fox, Charles J. 1994. "The Use of Philosophy in Administrative Ethics." In *Handbook of Administrative Ethics*, ed. Terry L. Cooper. New York: Marcel Dekker.

Frankena, William. 1963. *Ethics*. Englewood Cliffs, NJ: Prentice Hall.

Frederickson, H. George, ed. 1993. *Ethics and Public Administration*. New York: M. E. Sharpe.

Frederickson, H. George. 1997. *The Spirit of Public Administration*. San Francisco: Jossey-Bass.

Friedrich, Carl J. 1940. "Public Policy and the Nature of Administrative Responsibility." *Public Policy* 1: 1–24.

GAO, 1998. *Information on Police-Related Corruption* (GAO/GDD-98-111). Washington, DC: U.S. General Accounting Office.

Gardiner, Lion F. 1998. "Why We Must Change: The Research Evidence." *The NEA Higher Education Journal* 16 (Spring): 71–88.

Garofalo, Charles, and Dean Geuras. 1999. *Ethics in the Public Service: The Moral Mind at Work*. Washington, DC: Georgetown University Press.

Gaus, John M. 1950. "Trends in the Theory of Public Administration." *Public Administration Review* 10: 161–68.

General Assembly of North Carolina, 2005. Session Law 2005-429, Senate Bill 393, Session 2005. www.ncleg.net/Sessions/2005/Bills/Senate/HTML/S393v5.html (accessed June 18, 2006).

Geuras, Dean, and Charles Garofalo. 2002. *Practical Ethics in Public Administration*. Vienna, VA: Management Concepts.

Goldhagen, Daniel J. 1996. *Hitler's Willing Executioners*. New York: Alfred A. Knopf.

Gooden, Susan, and Samuel L. Myers, Jr. 2004. "Social Equity in Public Affairs Education." *Journal of Public Affairs Education* 10: 91–8.

Goodsell, Charles T. 2003. *The Case for Bureaucracy*. 4th ed. Chatham, NJ: Chatham.

Gordon, Paula D. 2003. *The Ethics Map: A Map of the Range of Concerns Encompassed by "Ethics and the Public Service."* http://users.rcn.com/pgordon/homeland/ethicsmap.pdf (accessed June 22, 2006).

Hart, David K. 1974. "Social Equity, Justice, and the Equitable Administrator." *Public Administration Review* 34: 3–11.

Hart, David K. 1994. "Administration and the Ethics of Virtue: In All Things, Choose First for Good Character and Then for Technical Expertise." In *Handbook of Administrative Ethics*, ed. Terry L. Cooper. New York: Marcel Dekker.

Heady, Ferrel. 1984. *Public Administration: A Comparative Perspective*. New York: Marcel Dekker.

Hitchens, Christopher. 2005. " 'The Secret Man': The Insider." *New York Times Book Review* (July 24): 8.

Independent Sector. 2002. *Obedience to the Unenforceable*. www.independentsector.org/PDFs/obedience.pdf (accessed March 21, 2006).

Jones, Bryan D. 1995. "Bureaucrats and Urban Politics: Who Controls? Who Benefits?" In *Theories of Urban Politics*, eds. David Judge, Gerry Stoker, and Harold Wolman. Thousand Oaks, CA: Sage Publications.

Jones, James H. 1981. *Bad Blood: The Tuskegee Syphilis Experiment*. New York: The Free Press.

Jos, Philip, Mark E. Tompkins, and Steven W. Hays. 1989. "In Praise of Difficult People: A Portrait of the Committed Whistleblower." *Public Administration Review* 49: 552–61.

Josephson Institute. 1988. "Ethical Values and Principles," *Easier Said Than Done* (Winter): 69.

Josephson Institute of Ethics. 2002. *Making Ethical Decisions*. www.josephsoninstitute.org/MED/MED-intro+toc.htm (accessed June 16, 2006).

Kaufman, Herbert. 1977. *Red Tape: Its Origins, Uses and Abuses*. Washington, DC: The Brookings Institution.

Kohlberg, Lawrence. 1981. *The Philosophy of Moral Development*. San Francisco: Harper and Row.

Ladd, John. 1980. "The Quest for a Code of Professional Ethics: An Intellectual and Moral Confusion." In *Professional Ethics Activities in the Scientific and Engineering Societies,* eds. Rosemary Chalk, Mark S. Frankel, and Sallie B. Chafer. Washington, DC: American Association for the Advancement of Science.

Lewis, Carol W. 1991. *The Ethics Challenge in Public Service*. San Francisco: Jossey-Bass.

Lindblom, Charles E. 1968. *The Policy Making Process*. Englewood Cliffs, NJ: Prentice Hall.

March, James G., and Johan Olsen. 1995. *Democratic Governance*. New York: Free Press.

Mayo, Bernard. 1958. *Ethics and Moral Life*. London: Macmillan, excerpted in Sommers (1985): 171–76.

McIntyre, Alasdair. 1981. *After Virtue*. Notre Dame: University of Norte Dame Press, excerpted in Sommers (1985): 164–70.

Menzel, Donald C. 2005. "Research on Ethics and Integrity in Governance: A Review and Assessment." *Public Integrity* 7: 147–68.

Menzel, Donald C. 2006. "Ethics Management in Cities and Counties." *Public Management* 88 (January/February): 20–5.

Milgram, Stanley. 1974. *Obedience to Authority*. New York: Harper & Row.

Moore, Mark H. 1981. "Realms of Obligation and Virtue." In *Public Duties: The Moral Obligations of Government Officials*, eds. Joel L. Fleishman, Lance Liebman, and Mark H. Moore. Cambridge, MA: Harvard University Press.

Moreno, Jonathan D. 2001. *Undue Risk: Secret State Experiments on Humans*. New York: Routledge.

Mouritzen, Poul Erik, and James H. Svara. 2002. *Leadership at the Apex: Politicians and Administrators in Western Local Governments*. Pittsburgh, PA: University of Pittsburgh Press.

NAPA, 2000. *Issue Paper and Work Plan* (amended November 16). Washington, DC: National Academy of Public Administration, Standing Panel on Social Equality.

NAPA, 2005. "Sounding the Call to the Public Administration Community: The Social Equity Challenges in the U.S." Washington, DC: National Academy of Public Administration, Panel on Social Equity, Research Committee.

National Association of Local Government Auditors. 2005. "Mark Funkhouser on Auditing." December. www.nalga.org/qrtly/funk1205.htm (accessed June 22, 2006).

National Association of Social Workers. 1999. *Code of Ethics of the National Association of Social Workers.* www.socialworkers.org/pubs/code/code.asp (accessed June 22, 2006).

National Institutes of Health Ethics Program. 2006. Web-Based Ethics Training Modules. http://ethics.od.nih.gov/cbt.htm (updated January 12, 2006; accessed June 17, 2006).

Navaez, Darcia. 2002. "Moral Judgment and Theory." Delivered in the Seminar on Moral Education: Trends and Directions. University of Malaya, Kuala Lumpur.

New York State Ethics Commission, no date. *Ethics in State Government: A Guide for New York State Employees.* Albany, NY: Department of State, New York State Ethics Commission. www.dos.state.ny.us/ethc/eisg.html (accessed June 18, 2006).

Niskanen, William. 1971. *Bureaucracy and Representative Government.* Chicago: Aldine.

Office of the Special Counsel. 2003. *A Report to Congress From The U.S. Office of Special Counsel For Fiscal Year 2002.* Washington, DC: U.S. Office of Special Counsel.

Office of the Special Counsel. 2004. *A Report to Congress From The U.S. Office of Special Counsel For Fiscal Year 2003.* Washington, DC: U.S. Office of Special Counsel.

Perry, James L., and Lois R. Wise. 1990. "The Motivational Bases of Public Service." *Public Administration Review* 45: 367–73.

Peters, B. Guy. 1999. *Institutional Theory in Political Science. The "New Institutionalism."* London: Pinter.

Peters, Thomas J., and Robert H. Waterman. 1982. *In Search of Excellence.* New York: Warner Books.

Pops, Gerald M. 1994. "A Teleological Approach to Administrative Ethics." In *Handbook of Administrative Ethics,* ed. Terry L. Cooper. New York: Marcel Dekker.

Project on Government Oversight/Government Accountability Project/Public Employees for Environmental Responsibility. 2002. *The Art of Anonymous Whistleblowing.* Washington, DC: POGO/GAP/PEER.

Quotations Page, 2005. Quotation #24166 from Classic Quotes. http://www.quotationspage.com/quote/24166.html (accessed June 18, 2006).

Purdy, Matthew. 2003. "Family and System Failed Boys in Newark." *New York Times.* January 12.

Radin, Beryl J. 2002. *The Accountable Juggler: The Art of Leadership in a Federal Agency.* Washington, DC: CQ Press.

Rest, James, Darcia Narvaes, Muriel J. Bebeau, and Stephen J. Thoma. 1999. *Postconventional Moral Thinking: A Neo-Kohlbergian Approach.* Mahwah, NJ: L. Erlbaum Associates.

Richter, William L., Frances Burke, and Jameson W. Doig, eds. 1990. *Combating Corruption/Encouraging Ethics: Sourcebook for PA Ethics.* Washington, DC: American Society for Public Administration.

Riordan, William L. 1962. *Plunkett of Tammany Hall.* New York: Dutton.

Rohr, John A. 1989. *Ethics for Bureaucrats.* 2nd ed. New York: Marcel Dekker.

Rosenbloom, David H. 1992. "The Constitution as a Basis for Public Administrative Ethics." In *Essentials of Government Ethics,* eds. Peter Madsen and Jay M. Shafritz. New York: Meridian Book.

Rosenbloom, David H., and Robert S. Kravchuk. 2004. *Public Administration,* 6th edition. New York: McGraw-Hill.

Ross, Peter, 2000. "Fighting Crime and Corruption in New Orleans," *Blueprint Magazine* 8 (Fall): www.dlc.org/ndol_ci.cfm?contentid=2155&kaid=119&subid=213 (accessed June 18, 2006).

Rothman, Robert. 2001/02. "Closing the Achievement Gap: How Schools Are Making It Happen." *Challenge Journal* 5 (2): 1–12.

Sayre, Wallace S. 1958. "Premises of Public Administration: Past and Emerging." *Public Administration Review* 18: 102–5.

Schein, Edgar H. 1992. *Organizational Culture and Leadership*. 2nd ed. San Francisco: Jossey-Bass.

Shamoo, Adil, and David Resnik. 2003. *Responsible Conduct of Research*. New York: Oxford University Press.

Sinnott-Armstrong, Walter. 2006. "Consequentialism." In *The Stanford Encyclopedia of Philosophy*. Spring 2006. ed. Edward N. Zalta. http://plato.stanford.edu/archives/spr2006/entries/consequentialism/ (accessed June 22, 2006).

Smith, Joanna Carey. 1999. "Giving Lawful and Helpful Job References—Without Fear." *Popular Government* 65 (Summer): 19–26.

Sommers, Christina Hoff. 1985. *Vice and Virtue in Everyday Life*. New York: Harcourt Brace Jovanovich.

Stein, Lana. 1991. *Holding Bureaucrats Accountable: Politicians and Professionals in St. Louis*. Tuscaloosa: University of Alabama Press.

Steinberg, Sheldon S., and David T. Austern. 1990. *Government, Ethics, and Managers*. New York: Praeger.

Stewart, Debra. 1985. "Ethics and the Profession of Public Administration: The Moral Responsibility of Individuals in Public Sector Organizations." *Public Administration Quarterly* 8: 487–95.

Stewart, Debra W., and Norman A. Sprinthall. 1994. "Moral Development in Public Administration." In *Handbook of Administrative Ethics*, ed. Terry L. Cooper. New York: Marcel Dekker.

Stewart, Debra W., Norman A. Sprinthall, and Jackie D. Kem. 2002. "Moral Reasoning in the Context of Reform: A Study of Russian Officials." *Public Administration Review* 62: 282–97.

Svara, James H. 1987. "The Responsible Manager: Building on the Code and the Declaration." *Public Management* 69: 14–8.

Svara, James H. 1997. "The Ethical Triangle: Synthesizing the Bases of Administrative Ethics." *Public Integrity Annual 1997*: 33–41.

Svara, James H. 1998. "The Politics-Administration Dichotomy Model as Aberration." *Public Administration Review* 58: 51–8.

Svara, James H. 1999. "Complementarity of Politics and Administration as a Legitimate Alternative to the Dichotomy Model." *Administration & Society* 30: 676–705.

Svara, James H. 2001. "The Myth of the Dichotomy: Complementarity of Politics and Administration in the Past and Future of Public Administration." *Public Administration Review* 61: 176–83.

Svara, James H. 2006. "Politicians and Administrators in the Political Process: A Review of Themes and Issues in the Literature." *International Journal of Public Administration* 29: 953–76.

Svara, James H., and James R. Brunet. 2003. "Finding and Refining Complementarity in Recent Conceptual Models of Politics and Administration." In *Retracing Public Administration, Research in Public Administration,* Vol. 7, ed. Mark R. Rutgers. Amsterdam: Elsevier Science.

Svara, James H., and James R. Brunet. 2004. "Filling in the Skeletal Pillar: Addressing Social Equity in Introductory Courses in Public Administration." *Journal of Public Administration Education* 10: 99–109.

Terry, Larry D. 1998. "Administrative Leadership, Neo-Managerialism, and the Public Management Movement." *Public Administration Review* 58: 194–200.

Thomas, John Clayton. 1995. *Public Participation in Public Decisions: New Skills and Strategies for Public Managers.* San Francisco: Jossey-Bass.

Thompson, Dennis. 1985. "The Possibility of Administrative Ethics." *Public Administration Review* 45: 555–61.

Thoreau, Henry David. 1849. "Civil Disobedience." http://eserver.org/thoreau/civil.html (accessed June 22, 2006).

Toner, James H. 2005. *Morals Under the Gun.* Lexington: University of Kentucky Press.

Tong, Rosemary. 1986. *Ethics in Policy Analysis.* Englewood Cliffs, NJ: Prentice Hall.

Truelson, Judith A. 1987. "Blowing the Whistle on Systematic Corruption: On Maximizing Reform and Minimizing Retaliation." *Corruption and Reform* 2: 55–74 (reprinted in Richter et al. 1990, 203–212).

Tullock, Gordon. 1965. *The Politics of Bureaucracy.* Washington, DC: Public Affairs Press.

U.S. Congress. Senate. Committee on Governmental Affairs. 2003. "Statement of Elaine Kaplan on S. 1358, the Federal Employee Protection of Disclosures Act: Amendments to the Whistleblower Protection Act." Hearing November 12. http://www.senate.gov/~govt-aff/index.cfm?Fuseaction=Hearings.Testimony&HearingID=129&WitnessID=460 (accessed June 17, 2006).

U.S. Congress. Senate. Committee on Homeland Security and Governmental Affairs. 2005. *Federal Employee Protection of Disclosures Act: Report of the Committee on Homeland Security and Governmental Affairs, United States Senate, to accompany S. 494.* Washington, DC: U.S. Government Printing Office.

U.S. Merit Systems Protection Board. 1993. *Whistle-Blowing in the Federal Government: An Update.* Washington, DC: U.S. Merit Systems Protection Board.

U.S. Newswire. 2005. "Hamline Professor and Ethics Expert Calls 'Deep Throat' Qualified Patriot." June 2. http://releases.usnewswire.com/GetRelease.asp?id=48315 (accessed June 22, 2006).

United Way of Delaware, 2004, Common Questions and Concerns from Contributors: Who is William Aramony and What Did He Do? www.uwde.org/faq.asp#williamaramony (accessed June 22, 2006).

Walker, Lawrence J., Russell C. Pitts, Karl H. Hennig and M. Kyle Matsuba. 1995. "Reasoning about Morality and Real-life Moral Problems." In *Morality in Everyday Life: Developmental Perspectives,* eds. Melanie Killen and Daniel Hart. New York: Cambridge University Press.

Walker, Samuel, Geoffrey P. Alpert, and Dennis J. Kenney. 2001. "Early Warning Systems: Responding to the Problem Police Officer." *Research in Brief.* Washington, DC: U.S. Department of Justice, National Institute of Justice, Office of Justice Programs.

Wamsley, Gary L., Robert N. Bacher, Charles T. Goodsell, Philip S. Kronenberg, John A. Rohr, Camilla M. Stivers, Orion White, and James F. Wolf. 1990. *Refounding Public Administration*. Newbury Park, CA: Sage Publications.

West, Jonathan P., Evan M. Berman, Stephen Bonczek, and Elizabeth Kellar. 1998. "Frontiers in Ethics Training." *Public Management* 80 (June): 4–9

West, Jonathan P. and Evan M. Berman. 2004. "Ethics Training in U.S. Cities." *Public Integrity* 6: 189–206.

Willbern, York. 1984. "Types and Levels of Public Morality." *Public Administration Review* 44: 102–08.

Wilson, James Q. 1991. *On Character*. Washington, DC: AEI Press.

Wood, Dan B., and Richard W. Waterman. 1994. *Bureaucratic Dynamics: The Role of Bureaucracy in a Democracy*. Boulder, CO: Westview Press.

Zernike, Kate. 2005. "Newly Released Reports Show Early Concern on Prison Abuse." *New York Times*, January 6.

Index

---

page numbers followed by t or f denote tables or figures respectively